ARAB
VOICES

PETER PARTNER
ARAB VOICES
The BBC Arabic Service
1938-1988

BRITISH BROADCASTING CORPORATION

To the memory of Gordon Waterfield

Published by BBC External Services
Bush House
London WC2B 4PH

Distributed by BBC Books
A division of BBC Enterprises Ltd
Woodlands, 80 Wood Lane
London W12 0TT

First published 1988

ISBN 0 563 20669 1

Photoset 10/12 Bembo, printed and bound
in Great Britain by Redwood Burn Limited,
Trowbridge, Wiltshire

CONTENTS

FOREWORD

Peter Partner's book is a tribute to a remarkable achievement. In the fifty years since it began, the Arabic Service of the BBC has grown from a small operation, with a handful of officials, broadcasting for an hour or so a day on one or two frequencies from short-wave transmitters, to become one of the most important of the BBC's external services. It now broadcasts for almost half the day (and much more than that during the 1967 war) on powerful transmitters which enable it to reach all the Arab countries. Apart from news and talks on current affairs, it has a varied programme of music, plays and features, of which a large proportion are planned and executed by Arab members of the staff: it has a listening public all over the Arab world, and receives between sixty and seventy thousand letters a year from those who listen.

The book is more than a tribute, however. It is also an analysis of the basic problems of such an operation. The Service was conceived as an exercise in what Sir Stephen Tallents called 'the art of national projection' and Sir John Reith 'the projection of British culture in other languages'. But what exactly was to be projected? Sir Ian Jacob, Director-General of the BBC, said in 1949 that the BBC should be 'the voice of the British people and not the voice of the British government'. It was the government, however, which paid for the external services, and it could not be unaware that listeners might think that opinions expressed in the talks or implied in the presentation of news were in fact those of the government. An understanding was reached that, in the foreign-language services of the BBC, 'more intimate relations with the appropriate government departments should and could be established without any infringement of their independent status'. This understanding was never embodied in formal documents, and seems to have worked with reasonable smoothness. The BBC defended its independence skilfully and persistently. Even at the moment of greatest tension, during the Suez crisis of 1956, the BBC insisted on its right to report the whole spectrum of British public opinion, and it would have been politically impossible for the government to impose direct control, had it tried to do so.

There was another range of problems, implied in the title of the book, *Arab Voices*. Even if the first aim of the Service was to be 'the voice of the

British people', it soon moved beyond that, and tried – in full awareness of what it was doing – to project also 'a new Arab cultural identity'. This was done partly because of the beliefs and interests of those who worked for the Service, whether British or Arabs, and partly in response to listeners' requests; the Service could only succeed in attracting and keeping listeners if it appealed to their concern for their own societies and culture, and if its voice was, in some significant sense, an Arab voice.

At what level should it speak in Arabic, and to whom? At first, with its limited resources, the Service made a conscious decision to speak to the elite, both those who had a modern education and those formed by their own cultural tradition; talks by Taha Hussein and other distinguished writers were commissioned, and the day began with a reading from the Qur'an. In the last twenty years, however, the emphasis has changed. The Service is now broadcasting to an Arab world in which the number of listeners has been enormously increased by the coming of the transistor radio, and the proliferation of stations, both Arab and foreign, has widened their range of choice. The nature of the programmes has changed; in addition to news and talks, there is now a larger proportion of 'light' entertainment.

Dr Partner has brought back to life some of those who worked for the Service and gave it a distinctive character: successive directors, in particular the erudite and detached S. Hillelson and the urbane, resourceful Gordon Waterfield; the scholars Nevill Barbour and Emile Marmorstein; the war commentator M. Gom'aa and the first announcer, the 'golden-voiced' A. K. Sourour.

For me it has been a pleasure to come upon my father in these pages. His work for the Arabic Service enriched his life. Throughout most of the war years he helped to maintain the friendly spirit of the Service. He gave talks on a wide range of subjects, informed by both the culture of the Lebanon of his youth (which coincided with the *Nahda*, an age of literary revival in the Arab world), and his deep affection and loyalty to the values of late-Victorian England.

Albert Hourani

AUTHOR'S NOTE

Although this book has been written with the support of the BBC External Services, for which I am very grateful, it in no way records an official view, and both the account of events and the opinions expressed in it are my own.

Faced with a tight timetable, I decided that people's memories were less reliable about the events of forty years ago than the written record, and I therefore consulted fewer people than I could have done. I explain this not to disparage people's impartiality or truthfulness, but to make clear my choice of historical method.

The transliteration of Arabic words and names in this book is entirely unscientific.

ACKNOWLEDGEMENTS

I am grateful to Mrs Mary Barrow, to Mrs Leila Dawton, and to Mr Isa Sabbagh for having kindly shared their recollections about the Service. Mr Ronnie Icke has been generous in helping me with his unrivalled knowledge of Service matters.

Mr E. C. Hodgkin kindly gave permission to publish some extracts from a 1956 talk. Crown-copyright material is reproduced by permission of the Controller of Her Majesty's Stationery Office.

Mrs Jacqueline Cavanagh and Mrs Guinevere Jones at the BBC Written Archives, Caversham, did everything in their power to assist me; I have also had valuable help from Mr David Evans and his staff at the Radio Reference Library in Langham Place.

I am, finally, grateful to Mr Mark Dodd, Controller, Overseas Services, and to Mr Jim Norris, Head of the Arabic Service, who have between them made this book possible.

Peter Partner,
16 November 1987

CHAPTER 1

THE BIRTH OF
FOREIGN-LANGUAGE
BROADCASTING IN BRITAIN

I

Propaganda is a word which has never sounded well in British ears, and the period immediately preceding the Second World War was no exception. Its derivation from 'De propaganda fide', the title of the central office of the Catholic Counter-Reformation missions, had a popish and authoritarian flavour in the Protestant country which Britain still was in the 1930s. At that time the setting up of great propaganda machines by the right-wing dictatorships in continental·Europe aroused revulsion and fear on the British Left, and distaste among many on the Right. British experience with their own propaganda in the First World War – subsequently given a favourable mention for its technical skill by Hitler in *Mein Kampf* – had convinced many people that this was a dirty business, and Fascist and National Socialist propaganda only reinforced their conviction.

Yet at the same time the feeling was widespread that the techniques of mass persuasion, which were so obviously an integral and inescapable part of industrial society, ought to be used by British governments to influence people outside this country. These ideas had been most effectively articulated by Sir Stephen Tallents, a civil servant who is probably best remembered now for his patronage of British documentary films, and who was one of the founding fathers of the public relations industry. In *The Projection of England* (1932), a short book in which he generalised his experience at the Empire Marketing Board, Tallents set out a view which – though unacceptable to many, and at the time anathema to the British Treasury – was very influential in its day, and which continues even now to affect policy:

We must master the art of national projection and must set ourselves to throw a fitting presentation of England upon the world's screen [the film metaphor is typical of Tallents]. The English people must be seen for what it is – a great nation still anxious to serve the world and to secure the world's peace. English industry must be seen for what it is and for what it is determined to be. We must spread throughout the world a sense of English industrial quality and ambition, an impression of English adaptability and modernity no less than of English craftsmanship and thoroughness and finish. English science must be known for what it is and for what it might be – an instrument of profound importance to the health and happiness of remote millions of people. England herself must be seen for what she is – still one of the most beautiful, historic and friendly of the world's countrysides.[1]

Many people would still subscribe to this doctrine, whose aims are cultural and commercial rather than political. Perhaps the key element in it is the idea that the traditionalism of British society is quite compatible with invention and modernity in British science and technology, so that we can extol the Houses of Parliament, the British bobby, and buttered toast alongside the agricultural research stations. There is an innocuous innocence about this which seems very different from foreign-sounding 'propaganda'.

Of all the new techniques of mass persuasion, the most obvious was radio. Though in the pre-war period it enjoyed a government monopoly, and though its funds were raised through a government department, British radio was not state controlled. The Charter and Licence of the British Broadcasting Corporation gave the Corporation an independence in the day-to-day management of its programmes which has lasted through successive Charters until the present day. Like the Church of England at that time (or perhaps, with Lord Reith's loyalties in mind, the Church of Scotland), the Corporation was subject to ultimate Parliamentary control, but in many ways acknowledged in the conduct of its business a responsibility to the community and not to the government.

The BBC was clearly in a key position to take part in 'the projection of Britain' abroad. But there were difficulties in using the Corporation to set up a new broadcasting agency to disseminate the British point of view to foreign countries. The BBC Empire Service had from 1932 run a major short-wave service addressed to the English-speaking peoples of the British Commonwealth of Nations. The ideas of the British Empire Service were unashamedly imperial: this not only meant that the Service refrained from addressing itself to the non-English-speaking peoples of the Empire, but also that it refrained from addressing English-speaking peoples under other flags, such as United States citizens. The British Empire Service could be considered an instrument of imperial policy, but not of foreign policy. Some of those who ran it were hostile to the idea of broadcasting in foreign languages. A BBC paper dated March 1937 objected that:

At the present time this country stands in a unique position among the broadcasting nations. Every other broadcasting country of moment uses languages other than its own in its short-wave transmissions. England alone [it is noticeable that, like Tallents, the authors of this report speak of England and not of Britain] confines herself to her own language. She is addressing her own countrymen in the British Empire, as she has every right to do, and as the British Empire is world-wide, so are the Empire broadcasts world-wide. Their position is completely unassailable on moral grounds.

To introduce foreign languages into the Empire broadcasts would . . . inevitably prejudice the integrity of the Service . . . it would *pro tanto* be indulging in propaganda.[2]

The linguistic nationalism of this document, which reflected the opinions and doubts of the powerful Controller of Programmes, Cecil Graves, was unremarkable at the time. It showed a typical moral repugnance for 'propaganda', and a fear that the reputation of the Empire Service would be sullied by being mixed up in such matters. In British culture of the pre-war period there were (as in the document just cited) elements of quasi-mystical nationalism, but there was also an immensely powerful liberal tradition – perhaps in the end a religious tradition – of veracity. War was dreaded by many people not only for its own horrors but because 'total war' would celebrate the funeral of truth. The learned and virtuous historian, Arnold Toynbee, wrote in the first few weeks of the war when the Royal Institute of International Affairs which he directed was starting to work for the government:

It is an enormous relief to all of us here that our job will still be, as in peacetime, to try and tell the truth, and that we are not having to do propaganda . . . we try and state the truth to government departments who want it strictly for private use – truth in wartime being, like petrol, a luxury which is a government monopoly.[3]

Over the propaganda issue, as over so many other issues of the 1930s, lay the shadow of the First World War. As Harold Nicolson (who was to become a prominent figure in the wartime Ministry of Information) observed in a parliamentary debate in February 1938:

In a national emergency we can be as untruthful as, or more untruthful than, anybody else. During the war we lied damnably. Let us be clear about that. In time of peace, the ordinary Englishman does not like telling lies, and that is one reason why the whole thing [the dissemination of propaganda] is uncongenial.

The BBC's very reputation for truthfulness made it an unsuitable instrument for political propaganda; Nicolson was repeating what was already a cliché when he added: 'We all know that the news bulletin of the BBC is the most impartial statement of fact that has ever been produced in any country and that being so gives it an enormous advantage.'[4]

In government offices the discussion of the political use of propaganda was less vague and mealy-mouthed. In 1935 the British Council, which corresponded in many ways to the kind of instrument of 'national projection' proposed by Sir Stephen Tallents, was set up with the help of a very modest Foreign Office grant. Reginald (Rex) Leeper, the head of the Foreign Office News Department, saw cultural, commercial and political propaganda as essential parts of his work, and was a main influence in the setting up of the Council. Leeper, one of two talented Australian brothers who had joined the Foreign Office at the end of the First War, was a man of austere personality, and of strong political passions. He was described during the war by Sefton Delmer as 'tall and spare, with the thoughtful concentrated face of some old-time papal secretary', and he was to be of critical importance in the process by which the BBC became involved in foreign-language broadcasting. In the Foreign Office he followed the star of Sir Robert Vansittart, and was deeply convinced of the need to meet German and Italian policies with appropriate arms and measures. In 1936 he was said to 'admire Churchill greatly' and to think that he was 'the man we need': in the following year he was the closest to Anthony Eden after Vansittart, and was said to write the Minister's speeches. His personality was controversial: during the war he attracted the strong hostility of the Economic Warfare Minister, Dalton; he was criticised by others for a nervous temperament, and a tendency to crumble under pressure. He was to remain important in government information policy until 1943.[5]

One of Leeper's greatest strengths was his ability to articulate the political philosophy which lay behind his policies. In July 1937, when the Foreign Office was drawing up its submission to the Cabinet on radio broadcasts in foreign languages, he wrote a memorandum which asked:

how a democracy such as our own which desires to maintain the freedom of the press and to give as much room as possible to individual initiative can compete successfully with other countries which control not only their press but all other means of propaganda and publicity. It cannot be stated quite so simply as competition between a democracy and a totalitarian state, for other democracies such as France admit far more government control and initiative than we have so far accepted here . . . I doubt whether there is any country in Europe where government intervention is so jealously watched and criticised as it is here. One cannot therefore overlook the difficulties which may beset His Majesty's Government in attempting to organise the publicity of this country on lines which can hope to compete effectively with publicity in totalitarian states . . . Let me say at the outset that I am strongly opposed to the establishment of a Ministry of Information in peacetime [though in time of war he anticipated that the BBC would be 'completely under government control'].[6]

It seems that from early in the 1930s John Reith, the Director-General of the BBC, was interested in the 'projection of Britain' by means of broadcasting in foreign languages. Though he emphasised German propagandist competition, he certainly did not see foreign-language broadcasting in the context of what has been called 'psychological rearmament' or of speaking out against the dictators, since he was a passionate appeaser who was sticking out for German friendship far into 1938. It is more likely that Reith wanted a Stephen Tallents approach to the problem, which he defined as 'the projection of British culture in other languages, as so many countries are now doing'. Tallents himself moved to the BBC in 1936 as Controller of Public Relations, harbouring hopes, which were later to be dashed, of succeeding Reith as Director-General. At Reith's strong prompting, the Report of the 1935 Ullswater Committee on the BBC (published in February 1936) recommended that 'the appropriate use of languages other than English' should be encouraged in BBC broadcasting. As a result, the BBC made internal enquiries as to the technical means of doing this, and the principles on which it might be done.

II

By 1936 the interests of the Foreign Office and the BBC in foreign-language broadcasting were converging, but the marriage proved quite difficult to arrange. British diplomatic posts abroad were consulted in that year, and very positive interest in the idea of foreign-language broadcasts was expressed in some areas, especially the Arab countries. However, the Dominions Office enquiries at the same time produced rather negative results. The Colonial Office, which with BBC help had just set up the Palestine Broadcasting Service operating on the medium wave from Jerusalem, was rather sceptical about further broadcasts in Arabic. But the catalyst which convinced the Foreign Office and, eventually, the Cabinet, that a means of broadcasting British views into the Arab world must be found quickly, was the Italian Arabic-language medium-wave broadcasts from Bari, which were re-transmitted on the short wave from Rome.

This service had been set up in 1934 as a general means of expanding Italian influence and cultural prestige in the Arab world outside Libya, and it had no anti-British bias at first. But the acute tensions between the two countries that came with the Abyssinian war of 1935 switched the Bari service into a violently anti-British line. At the same time the deterioration of the British position in Palestine, and the outbreak of the Arab revolt there against British Mandatory rule at the beginning of 1936, made Britain vulnerable to propagandist attack in the Arab world generally, and to subversive attacks in Palestine specifically. The firmness, or in Muslim eyes, the ferocity, of British tactics in suppressing the revolt in Palestine had consequences all over the Muslim world: not only the Foreign Office but the India Office were interested in some kind of shield against the exploitation of these events by Bari radio. Jamming was suggested, but for technical and political reasons the idea was abandoned. Protests to the Italian government were, naturally enough, fruitless. The Jerusalem transmitter was low-powered, and politically not very effective as a means of affecting opinion outside Palestine.[7]

By the beginning of 1937 the question of a British reply to the Bari transmitter had been publicly aired and began to stimulate some parliamentary interest. Things advanced slowly, to the frustration of Eden and his subordinate, Leeper, in the Foreign Office. Leeper and Vansittart saw the urgency of the matter in the context of the general struggle with the totalitarian powers: they understood the urgency of rearmament and of public 'education' to avert the attitude of defeatism vis-à-vis Germany. Such a line would certainly have been unpalatable to Reith, and it is not at all surprising that, after conferences with the BBC in April of 1937, Leeper wrote despairingly about the Corporation foolishly (as he thought) dragging its feet: 'one would think from the BBC attitude that there was no international crisis at all.' On the other hand, Reith cannot be blamed for his caution. The cherished BBC independence of government control over the matter of its broadcasts was a much frailer plant than could be publicly admitted. At the moment when talks were going on about the projected new foreign-language service, the BBC was approaching the government through different channels and asking for guarantees – which were never obtained – of independence in arranging talks and discussions 'on all questions regarding foreign affairs which are freely discussed in the press.'[8] Although substantially independent in its treatment of news, the BBC was in effect government-controlled in respect of talks on international affairs. When he was on the one hand representing that 'the public – there is some evidence to show – suspect the existence of an official censorship', Reith was not going to offer the Foreign Office a Trojan horse in which to enter the BBC. In other words, he was not going to do a deal over the foreign-language broadcasts which did not include proper guarantees of editorial independence.

Such guarantees were certainly not in Leeper's mind. Internal resistance in the BBC to the idea of foreign-language broadcasts, and distrust of Foreign Office motives in pressing for them, continued to obstruct negotiations. In the early summer of 1937 the Foreign Office decided to drop the BBC from their plans altogether, and to recommend the construction of a medium-wave transmitter in Cyprus which would operate a programme under direct government control. On the BBC side, Cecil Graves positively welcomed the idea, although it was quite unacceptable to Reith. The location of the transmitter in Cyprus was also recommended, not only for its geographical position but because Cyprus was a Crown Colony, as opposed to Mandated Palestine.

On the face of it, there were good reasons for this decision. The BBC had been thinking of using either the short-wave transmitters in England which carried the Empire Service, or of constructing others like them, to carry the new service in foreign languages. But the Italian Bari transmitter operated on the medium wave. Although the medium wave reached a shorter radius in the littoral Mediterranean area, it was believed to be picked up by a much greater number of receivers than were available to receive the short-wave broadcasts. These receivers were to be found especially in cafés and public places.

It was the beginning of a debate which has lasted since foreign-language broadcasting began. Should the programme be targeted at a popular audience, or should it aim at an elite? At that time there were far fewer people who possessed access to short-wave receivers. Although an enquiry in Palestine appeared to reveal that the number of short-wave receivers in that country was much greater than had been supposed, most of these were in Jewish and not in Arab hands. By opting for their own medium-wave transmitter in Cyprus, the Foreign Office abandoned the possibility of reaching more distant audiences in the Arabian Peninsula and in Iraq. Although these geographically more remote targets included the tiny groups which ruled these countries, the café radio sets of Egypt and Syria tuned to the medium wave perhaps offered the best chance of influencing a mass audience.

III

On 21 July 1937 a Cabinet Committee was set up with these original terms of reference: to enquire into the proposed medium-wave station in Cyprus, and to examine its adequacy from the point of view of technical efficiency and of the programmes to be broadcast. The Committee was headed by the Minister of Health, Kingsley Wood, who had been responsible for the BBC in earlier governments as Postmaster-General. To Reith's chagrin, the BBC was not mentioned in the terms of reference, nor were its views even invited. BBC thinking had all been about short-wave transmission from Daventry, and restricting the enquiry to a medium-wave station in Cyprus had the effect of excluding the Corporation from the argument.[9]

At the time when the idea of Arabic broadcasts was first mooted, a demand had come from the Foreign Office posts for broadcasts in Spanish and Portuguese in order to give more support to British policy in South America. Leeper encouraged this idea, probably because his eventual aim was to broadcast in several languages, but also because the parallel pursuit of a Latin American radio service softened the public impression that the Arabic broadcasts were to be essentially anti-Italian. Several other countries, Germany among them, now broadcast propaganda in several languages, and the question was whether Britain should acquire such a capacity. It was not an entirely welcome idea to the government, which at this stage would have regarded a German-language radio service, for example, as nothing but an embarrassment. The Cabinet restricted the Committee which it set up in July 1937, both by its terms of reference and by its title, which was the Committee on Arabic Broadcasting. The restriction may have been intended to reassure those members of the government who feared a general British entry into the propaganda lists.

The Kingsley Wood Committee was quite a strong one. Though far from seeing eye to eye with Sir John Reith, Wood had a good knowledge of broadcasting from his experience with the BBC and the Post Office. Sir Alex Cadogan was shortly to become Permanent Undersecretary at the Foreign Office; F. W. Phillips was Director of Telecommunications at the GPO; Sir Cecil Bottomley represented the Colonial Office; and there were senior officials from the Treasury (an essential department because of the projected costs of setting up the station) and the India Office. The two Foreign Office advisers were Christopher Warner, who was to be an important figure in official broadcasting policy for many years, and A. S. Calvert, who went to Palestine in the autumn to arrange Arabic propagandist broadcasts from the new Jerusalem station, and who was to become, a few months later, the first Arabic Editor of the new BBC Arabic Service.

The initial exclusion of the BBC from the Arabic Broadcasting Committee proved to be a mistake. The Committee considered a number of alternative arrangements both for Arabic and for South American broadcasting, but in an atmosphere of increasing puzzlement. The main problem was that although the Foreign Office had itself asked for the Cyprus medium-wave solution, it changed its mind when it realised that the transmissions from such a station could not reach large areas of the Middle East. On 27 July, Birley, the BBC's Chief Engineer, and Cliffe, his Assistant, went to advise the Foreign Office about the proposed government transmitter in Cyprus. Foreign Office thinking on the transmitter was still at a very early stage, since they wanted to know how the programme might be organised, what sort of staff might be necessary, and who would be responsible for finding a site and handling the contract for the transmitter. They also wanted to decide who should run the transmitter, and how much it should cost – though Cliffe thought that 'money was very little object'. It seemed to be generally assumed in the Foreign Office that a medium-wave transmitter was required, and that its range was supposed to be the whole of Arabia down as far as Aden. This was a tall order, and both the BBC engineers formed an impression that the Foreign Office was trying to take decisions on the basis of some as yet very sketchy reports.[10] Birley told Leeper that, while realising the advantages of medium wave for the receiving end, the Foreign Office ought to keep an open mind as to what sort of transmitter and what power was necessary until the matter had been looked into more deeply.

On 29 July, Leeper produced a document on the proposed Cyprus station. He intended the station to be, like the Palestine station, under local government control. Its technical running would have to be entrusted to Cable and Wireless. Its programme would be intended for the whole Near Eastern and Levant area: it would consist of news bulletins and talks in English, Arabic, Greek and Turkish, and musical entertainment, both European and oriental. News would be taken from the BBC and Reuter, besides news supplied by the diplomatic posts. The entertainment programme:

would present greater difficulty owing to the lack of local talent. Much, however, could be done on the European side by re-broadcasting the Daventry programme, and on the oriental side, translated talks and readings from Arabic and Turkish literature could be given, together with records of oriental music.

Noted speakers and musicians could also be invited, on occasion, to broadcast.[11]

Leeper's remarks on the political implications of the station are also interesting. He denied that the new station would amount to engaging in a wireless war with Italy:

It is the considered view of HM Government that British material rearmament is the best guarantee of European peace during the next few years. Our weakness is a temptation to the aggressor not only to attack us, but to attack others. In the same way any failure on our part to present our case properly in the Near East is not only a temptation to Italy to exploit our difficulties . . . but also tends to undo the effect of our rearmament in a part of the world where our interests are very vitally concerned . . . Our object is solely to maintain a reliable service of British news and to see to it that false or malicious reports are not left unchallenged.

The Foreign Office consulted the Palestine government and sought through them advice from the Palestine Broadcasting Service. This, when it arrived, was disconcerting, and rather discouraged the idea of a medium-wave transmitter. A. S. Calvert wrote from the Foreign Office on 4 September that 'the information in the Palestine reply is rather disquieting and I feel that the question of whether a short-wave or long-wave transmitter should be used in the Cyprus station should receive very careful consideration by our technical advisers as soon as possible.' The answers from Palestine emphasised the good reception there of the Bari programme on the short wave (broadcast from Rome). They also asserted that 90 per cent of Arab licence-holders in Palestine had short-wave sets.[12]

The alternatives were discussed in the Cabinet Committee. The idea of substituting a short-wave for a medium-wave transmitter in Cyprus, and thus reaching Arabia and Iraq, was also rejected in the end, because the short-wave transmissions from Cyprus would only be received outside the Mediterranean area which was also a main target for the proposed British radio service. By reaching one zone, you failed to reach the other. The India Office did not want a station in India. Two transmitters in Cyprus, one short-wave and one medium-wave, were thought to be too expensive. Few of His Majesty's servants on the Committee (apart from the GPO professional) were much at home in the ionosphere, and the whole business seemed rather baffling.

About the nature of the programme to be broadcast from the new station, the Foreign Office was at first clear, but later somewhat uncertain. At the opening meeting Cadogan said that they were 'primarily concerned with securing effective action without delay to counter the stream of Italian propaganda'. Leeper also attended the Committee. In a statement which was later to be incorporated into the Committee's report, he said that the Foreign Office intended that the broadcasts:

would consist, for the most part, of restrained corrective statements and of the more subtle forms of counter-propaganda, and would not contain anything blatant or offensive. At the same time the Foreign Office consider it inevitable, in view of the unfriendly Italian wireless attacks, that the Arabic broadcasts might, from time to time, have a controversial aspect.

For this reason, the Foreign Office were 'at first averse to entrusting Arabic broadcasts to the BBC'.

The technicalities of transmitting the messages were not the only stumbling blocks for the Committee. They also found themselves obliged to consider what a programme designed for Arabic listeners might actually contain, besides news bulletins, and here the invincible decorum of senior civil servants got in their way. To provide such a programme would be difficult for professionals, and yet more so for a government department lacking experience. It seems to have been J. A. N. Barlow, the Treasury representative, who at the second meeting of the committee found the idea of a decent civil servant hiring Arab cabaret singers too much to stomach: he 'did not see how a government department could organise and provide an entertainment programme.' It seems to have been the last straw in deciding the Committee to telephone the BBC on 30 September to ask them to attend its next sitting; though technical questions of transmission were, of course, more important.

It seems that in some respects the Committee had come up against, and been beaten by, what we would call media professionalism. This was 'the new and difficult art' to which Tallents had so often referred in *The Projection of England*. Perhaps the problems were not as insoluble as they supposed. Within ten years of the Committee, the Foreign Office was exercising some kind of control over a British-owned transmitter in Cyprus which broadcast a programme of great popular appeal in Arabic. But a world war had to intervene in order to make this lapse from decorum possible.

As far as the Post Office was concerned, the decisive moment had come in the second meeting of the Committee, when it was decided that the only practical way to proceed was by short-wave broadcasts emanating from the UK. The PMG's representative (Phillips) 'could not conceive of anybody except the BBC undertaking broadcasting from this country.' He thought that the Corporation would be 'sufficiently amenable to the views of the Foreign Office to incorporate Departmental requirements in their own news bulletins, particularly if they were directed to straight-forward correction of inaccurate statements broadcast by other countries.'

Reith had been kept informed about the transactions of the Cabinet Committee, even if he had not been asked to attend either of its first two meetings. When he and his Chairman, R. C. Norman (with the Engineering Controller, Ashbridge, and the Programmes Controller, Graves), appeared before the Committee on 4 October, things went with a speed which argues a prior agreement on the part of the Committee, though it also testifies to Reith's drive and political sense. Playing the unwilling virgin, Reith pleaded the scruples which Graves had previously expressed about the integrity of the Empire Service being compromised by the BBC's broadcasting in foreign tongues.

Reith stated these objections only to brush them aside. He and Norman were willing to undertake the Spanish, Portuguese and Arabic broadcasts, and Norman laid down a number of conditions for BBC co-operation.

The foreign-language broadcasts must not impair or impede the Empire Service. Short-wave transmissions from this country must be the responsibility of the BBC (as Phillips for the PMG had already stated): this meant that the Foreign Office could not transmit an Arabic service from the UK, which they had suggested as a possibility. 'Although a start might be made on quite a small scale, e.g. by a fifteen-minute news bulletin in Spanish or Portuguese, the [new] Service must grow until it becomes quite a big thing.' There must be a supporting programme besides the provision of bare news bulletins. The Treasury must meet the cost, which could not come out of domestic licence fees. And finally if the BBC provided a Foreign Service, 'it must remain as independent in respect of it as it now is of the Home Service.' This did not mean that the BBC would not maintain contact with the Foreign Office: 'They already kept in touch with that Department on all matters in which it was interested. In the course of the establishment of a Foreign Service the points of contact with the Foreign Office would be greatly increased.'

At the meeting Reith reiterated Norman's insistence that the BBC should have the same freedom *vis-à-vis* government departments as with the Home Service. Developing this, he said:

the BBC was already amenable to representations in respect of Home and Empire bulletins, and would appreciate the Foreign Office point of view with regard to bulletins in foreign languages. There were desirable and undesirable, effective and ineffective methods of conducting propaganda. If this new Service were undertaken, the Corporation could be relied upon to give full weight to Foreign Office views.

Again, taking up Norman's point that the new Service must be 'a big thing', Reith thought that the BBC would organise an Overseas Service which would include both the Foreign and Empire Services. He considered that the foreign-language news bulletins should be kept as close as possible to those of the Empire Services (a doctrine which was to have quite an explosive future). In reply to Kingsley Wood's doubts as to whether the BBC foreign broadcasts would deal with matters of national interest as 'vigorously' as a government station would, Reith replied that he was sure that they would be criticised by the Right for not doing enough and by the Left for doing too much. He did not think there would be any difficulty in dealing with matters of fact:

In any event, if the Foreign Office were not satisfied, and the BBC did not see its way to take full responsibility for broadcasting in the particular terms which the Department desired to have used, the message could always be sent out with the foreword: 'We are asked by the Foreign Office to . . .' though this practice was not to be commended.

As Reith well knew, the practice did not commend itself to the Foreign Office either, since it took away the main advantage of using an intermediary of high prestige and credibility like the BBC.

In this discussion Reith certainly cannot be described as mealy-mouthed. He had approached the issue of propaganda frankly, and his claim for factual presentation of the news and editorial independence was free from cant, and based on the existing Licence and Charter. Both he and Norman had also made it clear that they were not discussing the possibility of short bulletins in two or three foreign languages which might be inserted in the interstices of the existing services, but a new and major Foreign Service.

To some extent Leeper's doubts about BBC participation were, he said, satisfied. He remained, however, reluctant to give up direct control of Arabic broadcasting. Using a hoary (and, some people would think, erroneous) Foreign Office distinction, he separated the 'sophisticated and westernised' peoples of South America, with whom the BBC could easily deal, from the different mentality and outlook of the Arabs, who needed 'special treatment by selection and omission'. The proposed wireless programme would offer 'an innocent form of propaganda, but it was propaganda, and as such it was hardly suitable for the BBC.' Such propaganda the BBC might 'quite properly from their own standpoint view with considerable reluctance as inconsistent with the standards of impartiality and objectivity they have hitherto so consistently maintained.'

Though Norman was willing to concede the Cyprus station to the Foreign Office (which shows that the 'big affair' he had in view was to be something like the eventual Overseas Service, if it could so easily renounce Arabic without thinning to nothing), Reith was not. He promised to meet Leeper's objections:

The BBC might have to show more elasticity and perhaps be more amenable to Foreign Office views [in the case of Arabic] than in the case of other languages. The effect obtained by a BBC news service would be based on telling the truth. Prestige depended on truthful and comprehensive broadcasts . . .

He was reluctant to regard Arabic 'sui generis': the problem created for the British government by Arabic broadcasts from Italy might arise in other parts of the world. Reith clearly felt that he was negotiating something which would provide the basis and precedent for an eventual major broadcasting service.

After the BBC representatives had left the meeting, Leeper voiced his doubts again. He was aware of the problems which the Corporation was having with the government over current affairs talks, and he cited these troubles in evidence:

[Reith] had indicated that relations with the Foreign Office were unruffled. They might be so in regard to news, but in the case of talks on foreign affairs the position was quite different. There was considerable difference of opinion on this, and he still thought it would be better for Arabic broadcasts from Cyprus to go out under sole control of His Majesty's Government.

The decisive talks show how able, far-sighted and forceful Reith was, even at a time when he had become disillusioned with the BBC. Only the financial arrangements failed in some respects to favour the Corporation. Leeper did not persist in his preference for the Cyprus solution, and within a short time decisions were made which led to the setting up of the BBC Arabic and Spanish–Portuguese Services. The Report was presented to the Cabinet on 22 October. It recounted the frustration the Committee had experienced with the Cyprus proposals, and gave the objections to the Cyprus station, besides another, very significant one:

Further, listeners would not be impressed by the claim of Cyprus to be regarded as an authoritative centre for the distribution of world news, unless the station were admitted from the outset to be what in fact it would be, namely a propagandist centre for the British Government.

In other words, the Committee had come back to what has been called 'the Foreign Office's traditional preference for conducting official propaganda through intermediary organisations in order to protect the credibility of the material put out.'[13]

The Committee's Report turned to the alternative of a short-wave foreign-language service to be broadcast from this country, and recorded the BBC's appearance before them and the conditions they had laid down for BBC participation. The Arabic broadcasts were treated by the Report, as Leeper had requested and in spite of Reith's protest, as a special case. But the way in which the Committee discussed them is of great interest, since it laid down the ground rules and also anticipated much of the debate about foreign-language broadcasting which has gone on ever since. The Committee said that even before hearing the views of the Corporation, it had always agreed:

that it was essential to preserve the principle that the Corporation should remain independent of political control and should not become, even in regard to foreign-language broadcasting, merely the mouthpiece of His Majesty's Government. Both the Corporation and the Government must be able to state publicly, in answer to criticisms, that the Service in foreign languages is provided as a normal development of the BBC's services for which the recommendation of the Ullswater Committee had prepared the way. However it became clear that the representatives of the BBC recognised that foreign-language broadcasts – and notably those in Arabic – were on a somewhat different footing to those for reception at Home and in the Empire, and that in this sphere more intimate relations with the appropriate government department should and could be established without any infringement of their independent status or derogation of their reputation for impartiality and integrity. Provided that ultimate responsibility for editing news bulletins and talks and for the method adopted for their delivery over the air rested solely with the Corporation, the Chairman and Sir John Reith were both prepared to take into account the special position of the Foreign Office in relation to foreign-language broadcasts. They undertook to work in close touch with them and consult them in regard to staff and all matters affecting the Foreign Service. In matters of Arabic broadcasting Sir John Reith said that the BBC might have to show more elasticity and perhaps be more amenable to Foreign Office views than in the case of any other language.

The financial arrangements were designed to prevent the new Service from being stigmatised as a government propaganda agency. The Committee thought it 'most inadvisable for the government to make a specific payment to cover the cost of a Foreign Service. If the Corporation expected the government to pay for such a Service "ad hoc", they could not resist the demand that it should be controlled by the government.' If this was done, and the Foreign Office was responsible to parliament for the grant and not the Post Office, 'the Corporation could not prevent a public acknowledgement that in this respect they were simply the mouthpiece of a government department. Such a position would be intolerable both for the Corporation and [a significant admission] for the government.' The cost of the new Service was therefore to be regarded as a part of the normal expenses of sound broadcasting, covered by the existing agreement between the Postmaster-General and the BBC. This was a disingenuous statement, covering up the fact that the BBC was actually going to apply to the government to be indemnified for the costs of the new Service.

The Committee therefore recommended that the idea of a government-controlled station in Cyprus be abandoned, but that the Cabinet should accept the principle of foreign-language broadcasting. This broadcasting was to be carried out by the BBC, who were to have the same independence in the matter as they possessed in regard to their other broadcasting services. The Corporation should accept responsibility for the delivery of all material sent out in connection with the broadcasts in foreign languages. The BBC undertook to maintain close touch with the Foreign Office about the broadcasts, particularly those in Arabic, and would do their best to meet the Foreign Office views. This understanding was to be incorporated in a 'gentleman's agreement' which might take the form of an exchange of letters between the Director-General and the Permanent Undersecretary. (Such an exchange of letters never in fact took place, and the obligation of the BBC to follow Foreign Office views was never extended in the way that a sharper definition would almost certainly have imposed.)

As to the financial arrangements, no special payment was to be made to the Corporation by the Exchequer for broadcasting in foreign languages, but any representations for financial assistance were to be submitted on the basis of the existing agreement, and would be considered by the Treasury and the Post Office on their merits. Of course, the Committee neglected to say that the Treasury and the Post Office would have to turn to the Foreign Office for advice on the BBC requests. It was in one respect a disadvantageous arrangement for the BBC, which failed to secure a permanent government commitment for the new Service. On the other hand, some of the ambiguities of the financial situation could be used to the advantage of the Corporation. The Foreign Office did not become directly responsible for administering the grants-in-aid to the BBC foreign broadcasting services until 1977; only after that date did some of the illogicalities of the financial arrangements become fully evident.

The Cabinet accepted the Kingsley Wood Committee's report in its entirety. Following Reith's recommendation, if there was a dispute about the transmission of government material in the foreign-language Service, the Corporation, though obliged to transmit the material, could say that it was transmitted at government request. The government could also prohibit the BBC from transmitting material.

IV

Thus the circle had been squared, and BBC independence had been clearly recognised, alongside a commitment by the BBC to pay attention to government views not only in special cases but in the everyday running of the new Service. Calculated risks had been taken on both sides. In order to acquire for Britain the capacity to keep up with other nations in the possession of a major foreign-language broadcasting service, the government conceded to its chosen instrument, the BBC, the same degree of independence for the new services as it possessed for the existing Home and Empire Services. The concession was made in order to secure credibility and status for the new services, and also so that the government should not have to answer directly in Parliament for all that was transmitted in them: if queries came, they would be dealt with in Parliament on the same basis as queries about the existing BBC Services. The government also obtained a cheaper service than it would have done if new transmitters and a new organisation had had to be created for a separate service.

On the BBC side, a delicate new relationship with the government was embarked upon, which strengthened the Corporation's monopoly position and its status as a national institution. Certainly, it opened new possibilities of government interference, but these were limited by the known reluctance of the government to compromise the credibility of the new Service, and its repeated professions of respect for existing BBC independence. Reith had rightly implied that the supposedly special position of the Arabic Service as subject to an additional degree of Foreign Office control was something transient, which would fade from view as other branches of the new Service came into being.

There remains a certain doubt about the way in which the Cabinet Committee, set up specifically to consider the Cyprus broadcasting station, ended by recommending an open-ended commitment to foreign-language broadcasting without any restriction upon the languages to be broadcast. Did the Committee realise, for example, that German would be one of the first languages to be introduced into the foreign-broadcasting programme? This was a move in the direction of 'war on the air waves', the implications of which are unlikely to have been lost upon the Cabinet.

Leeper's own memorandum about the Cyprus station, issued in early

August, makes the connection between material rearmament and a more aggressive information policy. Leeper was a man of great subtlety and some deviousness; Sir Alexander Cadogan thought he was 'too clever by half', and never plays quite straight'. It is unlikely, though the possibility cannot be totally excluded, that his influence was so persuasive that he could lead the Committee by the nose about the political implications of their final decision, and so force the decision upon a reluctant or un-comprehending government. But one wonders, nevertheless, at what stage the Committee took on board that it was being required to introduce general overseas broadcasting into government policy. It is certainly odd that a Cabinet Committee should have been persuaded so gaily to abandon its own terms of reference, and to negotiate with the BBC something completely different from what it had originally been asked to do. When the same Cabinet Committee was reconstituted in January 1938, it bore the quite different title of the 'Committee on Overseas Broadcasting', a change which registered the shift in policy that had taken place.

There is also some uncertainty about the role played by the BBC in Leeper's policies, and the extent to which Reith was aware of the full broadcasting implications of those policies. Leeper had certainly known long before the Committee was first set up in July, that Reith 'wanted to do the work', and would make BBC resources available for overseas broadcasting whether he was fully consulted at this stage or not. The BBC engineers had in any case been consulted about the Cyprus station in the course of the summer, and been supplied with some of the relevant documents, so the BBC was not entirely out of the picture. Leeper had not needed in July to tell Reith – towards whom his feelings were not good – that BBC exclusion from the original Cabinet committee and from the execution of the original Cyprus project would not prevent the Corpor-ation from subsequently assuming a major role in broadcasting in other languages. It seems fairly clear that he always contemplated calling in the BBC for the purpose of the South American broadcasts.

Be that as it may, in October the die was cast for the new Arabic Service and the new Services in Spanish and Portuguese, as well as the new Overseas Service which was bound to follow them. The announcement was made in Parliament, and the BBC hurriedly prepared to start the Arabic Service in the New Year.

CHAPTER 2

THE EARLY DAYS
OF THE SERVICE

I

The Arabic Service of the BBC made its inaugural broadcast on 3 January 1938. There was a flurry of congratulatory messages from Arab dignitaries, and a cordial welcome in the House of Commons when the event was debated, but the pattern of the programme during its first eighteen months was modest. The duration of the broadcast was just over an hour daily, from 1715 to 1820 GMT which, as Middle Eastern local time was two hours in advance of GMT, was a good listening time. The transmission was on one or two frequencies from the short-wave transmitters at Daventry which carried the Empire Service. New transmitters for the new Overseas Service had been ordered, but they were not to be ready for use until the summer of 1939. The Arabic Service was beamed to an area which included Egypt, Syria, Palestine, Saudi Arabia, Yemen, Aden, Iraq, the Gulf, and northern Sudan. Reception could not be assured in the western part of North Africa from Morocco to Tunis (the Maghreb).

British political influence in the Arab world was reflected in the inaugural first programme of 3 January. An introductory announcement in Arabic was followed by a brief recital by a group of Cairo musicians led by a zither player. There were messages from one of the sons of the Imam of the Yemen, and from the Egyptian Chargé d'Affaires and from the Saudi and Iraqi Legations. At six o'clock Big Ben sounded, and Sir John Reith spoke in English. Later there was a message from the Governor of Aden, Sir Bernard Reilly.

The first news bulletin (of fifteen minutes) followed, and proved to be the most famous and perhaps the most controversial in the history of the Service. The first and longest item concerned Egypt. The third concerned Palestine and began: 'Another Arab from Palestine was executed by hanging at Acre this morning by order of a military court. He was arrested during recent riots in the Hebron mountains and was found to possess a rifle and some ammunition.'[1] The bulletin was describing incidents in a daily state of emergency, as can be gathered from the other Palestinian items:

A small battle took place yesterday between a police force and an armed band at Safad . . . A train travelling in the hills near Jerusalem was fired at, but there were no casualties. The IPC pipeline was damaged, holes being made in two places. A section of railway track was removed today near Jerusalem, but was discovered before any trains passed over.

Sir Reader Bullard, the British Minister to Ibn Saud, described the reception of this bulletin in the King's tent in Muhditha in Arabia, where he was listening with his secretary and a Minister, and with the British Envoy. At the news of the execution:

there was silence in the tent and our party broke up without any talk. When I saw Ibn Saud the next day he spoke of the broadcast. For months, he said, he had refused to listen to the Arabic broadcasts from Jerusalem, because he found them so painful, but he had looked forward to the inaugural Arabic broadcast from London, and had filled his tent with his followers so that they might listen too. 'When the announcer spoke of the execution of that Arab in Palestine,' he said, 'they wept and I wept,' and as he spoke a tear rolled down his cheek and he scrubbed it off with his kerchief. 'Now,' he said, 'as a ruler I know that the first business of a government is to maintain order. I also know that no man has been punished in Palestine by the British for his political opinions, but only for some offence against a law. Nevertheless, if it had not been for the Zionist policy of the British government that Arab would be alive today.'[2]

The disorientation produced in pro-British Arab circles by that bulletin came as no shock to British diplomats. Reader Bullard had himself written a week before the broadcast:

I have always been in favour of trying the effect of broadcasting accurate and interesting news from England, but never prepared to believe that the effect in the Near East will be very great, so long as the Palestine question existed to poison the atmosphere.

Sir Miles Lampson, the Ambassador in Cairo, wrote in almost exactly similar terms after the disputed bulletin had been broadcast:

As long . . . as our policy in Palestine remains unacceptable to the Arab world, the Italians must continue to have a very great advantage over us in propaganda, Palestine will remain a thorn in the flesh until our line is changed: it is in fact a veritable mill stone round our neck.[3]

The ambassadorial mixed metaphors marked the extent of his concern.

Reader Bullard was a mild and judicious man, and his cable to the Foreign Office reporting the incident was much less dramatic than the way in which he later described it in his memoirs. At the time, he cabled only that it 'spread a painful tenseness in the atmosphere', and added (repeating his earlier opinion) that while he did not question the wisdom and integrity of our attitude in broadcasting such items, he had to report the effect, which was that Palestine news would overshadow everything else.

George Rendel, the head of the Eastern Department, who was known for his opposition to the 'firm' policy in Palestine, minuted Bullard's telegram rather in the spirit in which it was written. Though 'much disturbed' by the reference to the Palestine execution, and thinking the reaction in Arabia to the news announcement to be 'most unfortunate',

Rendel accepted the factors in favour of the BBC which had been pointed out to him: first, that the reference had already appeared in the BBC English-language news bulletins (in fact in the Empire Service), and second, that 'the fact that we had not concealed this item of news was a guarantee of our statement that our news would be straight news, and not carefully selected for the audience'. However, we were 'now faced with the great difficulty that practically all news from Palestine must be intensely painful to the Arabs, and can only send our stock down still further in the Middle East.'[4]

Rex Leeper was less charitable. He was appalled by the news bulletin, and by the favourable reference in the Foreign Office to 'straight news', which he described as 'a BBC expression'. Nor did the fact that news of the execution had already been broadcast in the English-language Empire Service in any way excuse the BBC in his eyes (although reference to the minutes of the Kingsley Wood Committee would have told him that Reith had specified that the foreign-language news bulletins should be kept as close as possible to those of the Empire Service). The song and dance the BBC had made about their moral purity (implying that the Foreign Office were immoral and impure) had persuaded the Foreign Office to lay down the conditions for Arabic broadcasting which he thought the Corporation had immediately broken: 'Is the BBC to broadcast to the Empire the execution of every Arab [to be condemned] in Palestine? It seems to me unnecessary, though I suspect that it gives their conscience a warm glow.'

A week later Leeper carpeted Graves and J. B. Clark, the Director of the Empire Service. 'I reminded them of their undertaking to work in the closest touch (daily touch) with the Foreign Office in connection with the Arabic broadcasts which had to be regarded as something quite separate from Home and Empire news. I also emphasised the need for selection and omission of news . . . In general I think,' he concluded, 'the BBC are ready to fall in with our wishes, but it may take time to get things working smoothly.' Practical measures were in fact agreed at that meeting. Translations of the Arabic news bulletins would be sent daily to the Foreign Office, and there would be fortnightly liaison meetings in the future. The fact that the Arabic Editor of the new Arabic Service, A. S. Calvert, was a Consular Service officer seconded to the post, cannot have improved Leeper's temper; Calvert was the first of a number of civil servants seconded to the BBC to find themselves falling in with their second master's ways.[5]

Leeper's report of his interview with Graves and Clark exaggerated the extent of BBC penitence. The meeting was one of a series between the BBC and the Foreign Office on the topic of the Arabic broadcasts. A couple of days after it had taken place Clark and the Empire News Editor, Troughton, met Barker of the Foreign Office, who complained that the whole attitude of BBC officials was entirely contrary to Foreign Office ideas as to how the Arabic broadcasts should be run. Clark was more recalcitrant than he had been with the formidable Leeper. He emphasised that in Arabic broadcasts as in their other news bulletins, the BBC must be entirely independent. Broadly speaking, anything put out in the Empire bulletins must appear in the Arabic broadcasts. As an example, Clark instanced that Calvert had edited out of the Arabic broadcast the communiqué issued at the end of the Budapest Conference (which had registered a British diplomatic defeat). Clark had insisted on its inclusion in the next Arabic news bulletin.[6]

Within the BBC, the worried Calvert was seeking BBC authorisation to satisfy the Foreign Office about the selection and omission of items in the Arabic news bulletins. This Clark refused to give him. In a strangled, bureaucratic cry which has acted as a call to arms for BBC officials of later generations, Clark objected that:

The omission of unwelcome facts of news and the consequent suppression of truth runs counter to the Corporation's policy laid down by appropriate authority. If external bodies wish the Corporation to modify an established policy, under which I have been directed to guide our new Services, suitable representations should be made in the appropriate quarter.[7]

In the external body all was not running smoothly. Leeper's patron, Anthony Eden, was on the edge of resignation from the government. His more immediate patron, Vansittart, had already been shunted to the edges of power, and had just been appointed to head a co-ordinating committee for publicity and propaganda for which Leeper had himself acted as the Baptist, but which the new Foreign Secretary was going to use as a means of keeping Vansittart where he could do least damage. At this juncture Leeper attempted to 'bring things to a head' with a letter to Graves (18 January 1938), in which he tried to get the elusive BBC to agree to his conditions for the new Overseas Services. Leeper:

understood you [Graves] to agree, first, that the foreign-language broadcasts should be regarded as a special service distinct in character from the Home and Empire Services, and that while the news and talks should be straight [here Leeper used the abhorred word] in the sense of being strictly truthful and accurate, the idea of giving a favourable impression of ourselves in the countries to which they are addressed should be the guiding motive of the whole Service.

It should be regarded as permissible to omit items of news which might have a harmful effect, and when it was found necessary to include such an item, care should be taken to add an explanatory comment. There should be daily consultation with the Foreign Office, to whom any item should be referred when the editor was in doubt as to the effect it might produce abroad.[8]

Had Leeper's letter been accepted by the BBC, the effect would have been to consecrate in a sacred text that 'gentleman's agreement' which the

Cabinet Committee had wanted the BBC to seal with the Foreign Office. But, not surprisingly, no reply by Graves (still less by the Director-General) to Leeper's letter of 18 January is to be found on the files. The issues of principle were gradually pushed behind the everyday administrative chores. There was a great deal to discuss between the BBC and the Foreign Office, because at this stage the diplomatic posts in Arab countries were themselves being encouraged to supply news for the newly formed Arabic Service. This news had to be cabled, collected, sifted, and somehow handed on to the BBC. The covenanted 'liaison' meetings were not eagerly anticipated by the Corporation, although there was nothing especially sinister about them. Clark wrote to Leeper to confirm that the text of the Arabic bulletins had been despatched to the Foreign Office, though only on the day following their radio transmission. On 1 February Clark was 'looking forward' (though without urgency) to the meetings, the first of which seems to have taken place on 1 March.[9]

Other parties to the row over the first news bulletin were the Colonial Office and the Palestine government. The Colonial Office had from the first taken a dim view of the BBC Arabic Service, which they regarded as a piece of poaching on the part of the Foreign Office in respect of Palestine. On 18 January, Stephen Fry of the Palestine Broadcasting Service wrote to Tallents in the BBC that the 'unequivocal opinion' there was that the Arab world in Palestine, Syria, Iraq and to some extent Egypt was just laughing at the Arabic broadcasts. News from Daventry was no more comprehensive or interesting than that from Jerusalem, and lacking in the up-to-date local news to be obtained from the Jerusalem station. Adapting anti-British sentiments to his own argument, Fry maintained that the average Arab feeling was: 'Let England settle the Palestine problem satisfactorily if they want Arab friendship, and until they do that, England can go to hell!'[10]

This defeatist attitude to British information policy was not surprising, coming from an official in a Palestine which was still virtually under a state of siege. The Colonial Office wearily tried, in an unconsciously macabre way, to ensure that future executions would not be announced by the BBC in too harmful a manner. Distinctions were made between the findings of the military courts (which occasioned the only locally broadcast announcement), the decision of GOC Palestine as to sentence, and the execution of sentence. A weekly summary of Palestine justice by the BBC was considered and, wisely, abandoned. In the Foreign Office Rendel cynically noted that Colonial Office policy had hitherto been 'to make the most of these executions, on the principle of what may perhaps be called "counter-terrorism"'.[11]

The first Arabic Service bulletin had indeed created a little ripple of disquiet in the Arab world, rather than a wave of approval. The Iraqi press was especially critical, and one Bagdad paper began its comment with:

'Oh God help us against Satan: accursed of God be the radio!' and ended it with the proverb: 'Between the hammer [of the British] and the anvil [of Palestine] our beards have gone to the devil!' Others were less picturesque but equally critical. [12]

II

Whether the BBC had committed a gaffe or not, the first news bulletin was soon forgotten, and buried under the growing mounds of cables as the Foreign Office sought to nourish its young protégé with copious supplies of news from the Arab diplomatic posts. The Cairo Embassy set up a special news desk for this purpose. In Jedda, Reader Bullard lamented that the current gossip about the Saudi ruling family was quite unusable by the BBC and that picturesque details about the pilgrimage were too trite for an Arab audience ('owls to Athens', said Sir Reader). In Bagdad the Oriental Secretary, Vyvyan Holt, percipiently queried whether diplomats were good newsgatherers:

I confess that I have missed one or two news items recently which could have been of use to Daventry, and I will try to do better in future. The difficulty is that training as an official produces the wrong habits of mind: the official has to be like an oyster and the news-monger ready to trumpet everything to the world through the microphone. It takes time to think of events simultaneously in the different manner of the official and the reporter. [13]

Even the critical Leeper was happier with the BBC after a time. He had in any case to protect the new Service against Treasury assault: Sir Percival Waterfield complained that the expenditure on the Service would be in 'very large figures'. Critics at the Colonial Office had supplied Sir Percival with ammunition against the Arabic Service, and in February Leeper was compelled to defend it. A few months later Leeper was benign in conceding that the BBC should be allowed to start talks on current affairs in the Arabic Service:

Having had to deal with news myself for many years, and knowing how open to criticism anybody must be who handles that dangerous commodity, I have a fellow-feeling for the BBC. I think [he continued with an unction which would have infuriated those he was talking about, had they seen the minute] they have developed their sense of responsibility very greatly since I first had to deal with them. [14]

Perhaps political adversity under Lord Halifax had already begun to mellow Leeper!

The row about the first Arabic Service news bulletin may appear to have been a storm in a teacup. [15] Politically, it was. The displeasure it aroused in the Arab world was momentary and expressed feelings which were largely conventional. Politicians all over the Arab world had wrung their hands over British repression in Palestine, but knew that they were powerless to do anything about it. Ibn Saud is a conspicuous example: it has been observed that the tears he shed over the Palestinians never made him do anything which might diminish his oil revenues. On the other hand, propaganda is concerned with just that no-man's-land in men's hearts where the difference between convention and moral conviction is very vague. The task of the BBC bulletins was not to inflame or exploit, but to appeal to the still, small voice of reason, and also, on occasion, to the slightly louder voice of regional self-interest. It was not an easy job, particularly as listeners knew that the not-entirely-disinterested British government stood in the background. Moreover, in spite of the conscious elitism of most British propaganda in the 1930s, its target was not only politicians and 'statesmen': the audience which listened to the radio in the coffee-shops was not unimportant.

For the BBC the most important thing about this tiff with the Foreign Office was that it raised the issue of principle about freedom of news policy, which in the end was relegated to the limbo of unfinished business. Its significance was to pinpoint the issue, not to settle it. But if we look at the incident from the standpoint of our own times, it does have a political meaning. It was to be demonstrated many times over during the subsequent war that propaganda cannot supply muscle to policies that lack it. From the rebellion of 1936 onwards the Palestine issue was an incubus which encumbered the British until it dragged their whole policy down in ruins, twelve years later.

But in 1938 British policy in the Middle East cannot be said to have lacked muscle: it was indeed the central period of the time later described by one of its former wartime propagandists as 'Britain's Moment in the Middle East'.[16] In Egypt and Palestine, Britain had a strong military presence, as well as a minor one in Iraq and (by proxy) Transjordan. In two of these countries its position was guaranteed by treaty with the independent government; two were governed under a mandate from the League of Nations. Saudi Arabia, although distrustful of the British-sponsored Hashemites in Iraq and Transjordan, was led by a ruler well-disposed to the British, who was during the war to accept a British subsidy. The Gulf Emirates were firmly subjected to British advice: Aden was a Crown Colony, and the Hadhramaut a British Protectorate. British petroleum interests were dominant in Iraq and Persia, and the Iraqi fields were linked by pipeline to Haifa in Palestine. The pivot of the whole system was the Suez Canal, which linked the British-dominated Levant with India. In the whole area it was Britain which had come closest to inheriting the mantle of the defunct Ottoman Turkish Empire. Russia was absent; the American future was scarcely suggested yet by the Aramco oil concession in Arabia. Britain's only serious competitor for influence in the Levant was France: the Italian Empire of Mussolini had made no appreciable dent on the eastern Arab world.

The British diplomats and administrators who ran this imposing system were well aware that it was a lot more precarious than it looked. Its weaknesses had been exposed several times since the First War, notably in the Egyptian nationalist disorders of 1919–22 and by the Iraqi coup of 1936. Persia, moreover, had offered a resentful and on the whole successful resistance to British tutelage, whether political or through the oil companies. Occasionally, as sometimes happened with Lampson in Cairo, their sense of pro-consular dignity got the better of the British representatives in the area, but they were realists on the whole.

British power was long on diplomatic pressure, short on military resources. In Iraq, particularly, the treaty which sustained British influence and permitted the presence of British armed forces had been negotiated with an insecure government which commanded only limited support. The Wafd government in Egypt which supported the 1936 Treaty was broader-based, but the secession of Ahmed Maher from the party and the majority of King Farouk, which both occurred in 1938, weakened the arrangement. In Iraq, after the 1936 coup, King Ghazi used to broadcast anti-British propaganda from his private radio station, reading the material over the microphone himself. Of the modest army Britain could afford to defend its interests in the area, a good many troops were occupied in containing the Palestine rebellion. Educated Arab opinion was therefore an imponderable but important factor in maintaining the British position in the Middle East. It is small wonder that the new BBC Arabic Service was welcomed by most of the men responsible for keeping the fragile structure of British political influence intact.

Britain's cultural presence in the Middle East was, like its army, small in proportion to its political pretensions. In spite of the long British domination in Egypt, British influence on Egyptian education had been notoriously small. The knowledge of this had partly inspired Lord Lloyd (Egypt's former High Commissioner) to play a leading part in the setting up of the British Council to further British cultural resources abroad, in the early thirties. British educational activity in Egypt was restricted to two or three secondary private schools in Alexandria and Cairo, which received some British government support channelled through the British Council. By 1938 the British Council had set up Institutes in Cairo and Jaffa, but these were only just establishing themselves. In the Sudan there was a rather stronger British educational influence, especially through Gordon College in Khartoum.

The British learned societies in Egypt and Palestine, the Egyptian Exploration Society and the Society for Biblical Archaeology, were both long-established institutions with traditions of sound learning. In Mandate Palestine there were a couple of British schools in Jerusalem, though there was strong British inspiration and leadership in the Mandate's Arabic educational system. In Lebanon and Syria, both French Mandates, British presence was naturally weak, and amounted to no more than one or two small missionary schools: there was nothing to compare with the influential American University in Beirut, nor with the French Jesuit University there, the St Joseph. There was, indeed, no British-inspired University anywhere in the Arab world. There was everything to be said, not only for a British broadcast Arabic news service, but for an Arabic radio service with a strong educational element.

III

The to-do over the first Arabic Service news bulletin went no further than a small group of officials. British public opinion welcomed the new Service unreservedly. A Commons debate on the supply of British news abroad, held on 16 February 1938, was mainly concerned with the Vansittart Committee to co-ordinate British publicity abroad. But it also threw a few bouquets in the direction of the Arabic broadcasts, and showed both government and opposition support for the continued independence of the BBC. Winterton, for the government, thought the new Service had been very successful: he made a suggestion about catering for the 'broad' Arab sense of humour, apparently unaware of the hideous traps which a sense of humour can set for propagandists. For his rejection of the criticisms made of the Service, he had to admit in a parliamentary debate a year later that the severe Foreign Office – 'the powers-that-be' – had made him stand 'in a white sheet'. But on this occasion, as a year later in the similar debate of 15 February 1939, the matter of British publicity was non-controversial between the parties: Herbert Morrison said in 1938 for the opposition that this had been 'one of the most peaceful debates we have had in the House of Commons', and an 'enjoyable change from the more turbulent discussions that usually take place here'.[17] Such was the innocence of the British attitude to propaganda in 1938.

The British and American press welcomed the BBC Arabic Service. The *New York Times* (6 January 1938) referred with some exaggeration to 'The democratic countries' propagandistic counter-offensive'. German and Italian propaganda was feared as a sinister new mystery worked by hostile forces: the idea of new voices for democracy was welcomed on both sides of the Atlantic, and this was not only the period of the genesis of the BBC Overseas Services but also of the 'Voice of America'. There was a sudden spate of books and lectures purporting to explain 'propaganda' to the British public, and when these writers took notice of the new BBC foreign-language services, they approved them. On the whole the decision of the BBC to broadcast 'straight news' in foreign languages was welcomed on the grounds that 'Truth will out, and a lie once revealed will reduce the effectiveness of subsequent propaganda.' Conscience was however a little elastic, and although one writer talked about 'corrective broadcasts [of the Axis-biassed transmissions] of unimpeachable trustworthiness and accuracy', he also mentioned British preference for the 'indirect and subtle forms of propaganda' over the overt and direct forms.

The differences between BBC views on 'straight news' and 'projection' and the more cold-blooded Foreign Office outlook corresponded to differences of approach in the country. One writer, A. J. Mackenzie, was radical, and called for a propaganda policy whose methods would not be too far removed from the German ones.[18] In fact by 1938 all the different views on propaganda which two or three years later revealed themselves in the factional struggles of the Ministry of Information and the Ministry of Economic Warfare were already apparent.

IV

The BBC hurriedly assembled a small team to run the Arabic Service, between November and December of 1937. To some extent, the way things were done set a pattern for the organisation of other BBC foreign-language broadcasting services. The Arabic Service came under the Programme Division's Empire and Foreign-Language Broadcasts Service, whose Director was J.B. (later Sir Beresford) Clark. Four years earlier he had helped set up the Egyptian State Broadcasting Corporation in Cairo. There was initially an Arabic Editor (the seconded Consular Service official, A. S. Calvert), an Arabic Translator (M. A. Rifaat), and an Arabic Announcer (A. K. Sourour), with an auxiliary Announcer-Translator. Additions were made to the Overseas Intelligence Department (in later terms an audience research department), which studied the audience who listened to the programme, and reported about it to the programme and news departments. S. Hillelson was Assistant Director in Intelligence, and there were two new Public Relations Officers, the junior one an Egyptian. The pattern of using British administrative staff assisted by native speakers of the language was a very natural one for the Britain of 1938.

Save perhaps for Calvert, who was qualified enough, but whose heart was not in the job, it was not an unimpressive team. The Arabophone staff were more experienced in publicity work than the British. Rifaat had formerly been Director of Talks and Drama in the Egyptian State Broadcasting Corporation, and Sourour had been one of their star announcers. M. Naguib was an experienced Cairo journalist. On the Intelligence side, Hillelson was a rather distinguished Arabic scholar. He was a pupil of the British teacher D. S. Margoliouth, had studied in the Sudan and passed into government service there as Assistant Director of Intelligence. Engaged by the Foreign Office to monitor the Bari broadcasts, he passed thence to the BBC. Of Scandinavian Jewish extraction, Hillelson ('Hilly') failed to fit easily into any ordinary category of British bureaucrat: in this he resembled many other British 'Arabists'.

In the spring of 1938 Calvert acquired a useful assistant, Donald Stephenson. Stephenson was an able organiser who was later to prove his worth in a BBC career outside the Arabic Service. He had learned some

Arabic during RAF service in Aden and elsewhere, and first came to the BBC in 1938 on secondment from the Royal Air Force. By the summer of that year Stewart Perowne had also joined the Arabic Service as Programme Organiser. Perowne was an imaginative man with literary ability who had become enthusiastic about the Arab world while in government service in Palestine. Some years later, as Oriental Counsellor in Bagdad, he was to perplex the Foreign Office with despatches heavy with historical allusions. He was a close friend of the writer and orientalist, Freya Stark, whom he was later to marry. Perowne was perhaps more like the literary intellectuals of the Home Services BBC intake than the rest of the Arabic Service recruits, and it is interesting that he remained in the Arabic Service for no more than a year, leaving it for government information service in Aden in 1939.

The complicated system of BBC administration did not make life easier for the new service. As Stephenson complained, early in 1939, the separation of 'the only three Englishmen in Broadcasting House who speak Arabic' by placing two (Stephenson and Calvert) in the News Divgaision and one (Perowne) in the Programme Division, made life hard for such a small service. Once the Arabic Service was seriously involved in producing world affairs talks, and other talks involving Anglo-Arab cultural relations and travel (which he thought was probably the largest general class of talks broadcast), the hard-and-fast distinction between news and talks could not easily be maintained. The crux of the matter was that Calvert was classified as a News Editor and not as the head of a language service. One result was an unequal distribution of work: Perowne as Programme Organiser was over-loaded, whereas 'on a normal non-crisis day, when Calvert and I are both on duty, I (as sub-editor) have frequently to kick my heels for a large part of the afternoon.' Stephenson recommended that the Arabic Editor should become head of an Arabic Section, with the programme assistant as a subordinate, but this recommendation was not acted upon at the time.[19]

V

The same suggestion that the Arabic Service be placed under a single administration had been made a few months earlier, in September 1938, by Perowne, in an interesting paper which is our best written source of information on the early months of the Service.[20] About news, he complained that the service organised through the diplomatic and consular posts was too amateurish, and worked well only from the Cairo Embassy:

The ordinary consular, air force or administrative officer is an overworked individual, and it is too much to expect of him that he should undertake an additional burden on behalf of a body with whose needs and aims he is only vaguely familiar. It is also a fact that not every officer has a flair for communicating information. Many of them indeed are more adept at suppressing it.

The point was not unreasonable, and was indeed the same one that had been made within the Foreign Office by Vyvyan Holt in Bagdad. The question of the supply of local Arab news remained difficult, and was not really solved until the setting up of the Arab News Agency after the war.

Perowne's paper looked to the future, and tried to decide to what class of listener the Service was broadcasting, and what should be broadcast to them. The basic question was whether to seek a mass audience or an elite. Perowne was definite:

Our listening body is drawn almost entirely from the Effendi class. That is to say, government officials, school teachers, students, and men and women of leisure and means. This is only natural, and in my opinion is far from regrettable. It is in the hands of this class that the destinies of their countries must lie for some time to come.

One is reminded of the dedication of Freya Stark's *East is West* (1945), 'To my friends the Young Effendis'.

Perowne's clear verdict that the purpose of the Service was not to appeal to 'the man under the palm tree' may seem to be merely typical of the elitist views of his time, but when the Service was broadcasting for only an hour a day, it was nothing but common sense. There was at the time an awareness that propagandist broadcasting could and perhaps should direct itself at a mass audience, and that awareness was nowhere stronger, curiously, than in the elitist inner fastnesses of the Foreign Office.

But the essential element of a programme with mass appeal was entertainment, and entertainment meant a long period on the air. Only if the project of a medium-wave programme broadcast from Cyprus had come to fruition could the idea of a mass-appeal programme have become a practical one. Such a British-sponsored programme in Arabic was, in fact, to come into being three or four years later as a casual result of the exigencies of war, but it was to have nothing to do with the BBC. And it is also arguable whether the BBC of 1938 was a particularly suitable medium for such a programme. Responsible news broadcasting, responsible current affairs talks, and cultural programmes of a formidably 'highbrow' kind were the staple diet of the early Arabic Service, and they were not untypical of the BBC as a whole at that time. It was not a very appropriate format for anyone thinking of entering into direct competition with Goebbels. The debate was to continue for a long time in the Arabic Service, as it was within the BBC generally. In 1958 it was still being urged on one side that the Arabic Service broadcasts should be directed at the 'youthful, earnest intelligentsia', and that we should aim at providing a 'well-advertised Third Programme for the Middle East'.[21]

Perowne's division of the audience into an illiterate one of the men under the palm trees and a semi-westernised one of 'Effendis' was in any case over-simplified in an important respect. A later paper submitted to the General Advisory Council of the BBC, and probably drafted in this section by Hillelson, distinguished between three different social groups among the audience: first a more or less westernised group who could be called the 'intelligentsia' (i.e. Perowne's Effendis), second 'Arabs educated in the traditional forms of Moslem culture, but ignorant of European languages and therefore only in indirect touch with the Western world', and thirdly the illiterate masses. The insistence on a traditionally educated Arab audience was essential to a programme like that of the BBC.

Nevertheless, Perowne's paper raised many important issues. His attitude to the 'projection of England' is especially interesting. Our aim, he thought, should be to:

present to the Arab those aspects of English life which are of most immediate and practical interest to him: not necessarily, in every case, those which, to our thinking, would exhibit England in its most favourable light; and secondly, to stimulate in him pride in his own traditions and institutions. Taking the latter point first, I suggest that no opportunity be missed to display the Arabs, their country and their religion both prominently and favourably.

Perowne's view shows the enthusiasm which had been awakened in many gifted young Englishmen and Englishwomen in the circle of George and Katy Antonius in Jerusalem for a rather idealised Arab national culture. George Antonius's *Arab Awakening*, published two months after Perowne wrote, was for that generation the manifesto not only of the wrong thought to have been done to the Arabs in Palestine, but of an Arab national consciousness put forward as not irreconcilable with British ideas. 'Arab unity is the most abiding and sustaining hope of every Arab,' Perowne continued. 'We must do everything we can to realise it within our sphere of broadcasting . . . We must link not only Arab and Englishman, but Arab and Arab. No other country can do that. We can.' Somehow in Perowne's mind the projection of England had been subordinated to the projection of Arabdom: the Foreign Office would have found this distinctly worrying.

Yet, from a practical, propagandist point of view, Perowne's Arabophile ideas were not a bad way for the new service to proceed. Politically Pan-Arabism was too hot a potato for the BBC to hold: it led, for example, straight to the ideas of Haj Amin al-Husseini, the exiled 'Mufti of Jerusalem', and the Iraqi opposition. But a programme which displayed genuine enthusiasm for Arab tradition and achievement, and honoured contemporary Arab literature and learning, could and did find a real welcome in the Arab world. It is true that at this point the programme still had a very Egyptian flavour, and a survey made for the General Advisory Council in December 1938 said flatly that 'The majority of the talks are written and delivered by Egyptian graduate students or visitors to this country.' The religious talks of the Egyptian theologian al-Maraghi, talks by the Egyptian men-of-letters Tawfiq al-Hakim and Taha Hussein, all reflected the Egyptian provenance of the Arabic-speaking staff.

Another way in which Perowne seems to have intuitively glimpsed the way forward was in his appreciation of the Arab enthusiasm for education. Enthusiasm for self-improvement was to be, and still remains, one of the most powerful engines for the creation of an audience for the Arabic Service. Perowne's ideas on the students who ought to be influenced as 'the rulers of the next generation' were probably, like those of many of his generation, not so much too elitist as too naive. What did exist in the Arab world was a huge audience of autodidacts which could respond to Englishmen who had not entirely forgotten Samuel Smiles's *Self-Help*, and the concepts of the Society for the Diffusion of Useful Knowledge. This was in its way a mass movement and a mass audience, and one which proved immensely important to the Arabic Service. Perowne also mentioned the possibilities which awaited an English language-teaching programme: this was not to be long in coming.

A concept bound to be present in the mind of the friend of Freya Stark was that of the aspirations of Arab women:

We should, I think, have a regular series of talks addressed specially to women. It must be remembered that many Moslem women still live a life of almost complete seclusion, and that, in consequence, the entertainment afforded by the radio is all the more welcome to them; but they would seek not only entertainment, but also instruction, and our talks should, I think, deal with quite simple matters such as the care of the home and the family.

Woman's Page did not come to the Service until after the war.

Of the entertainment side of the programme, principally of music, Perowne had relatively little to say. This was what had particularly daunted the Foreign Office planners, and even with the help of Egyptian programme assistants the new Service found progress in this field slow. The Arab music of the early programme came entirely from gramophone records. Some co-operation could be had from Egyptian State Broadcasting in Cairo (whose Anglophilia went so far that their studios were tastefully decorated in mock-Tudor style), but, as Perowne observed, the ESB could hardly be expected to record programmes for the BBC which Cairo would not eventually broadcast. Whatever was planned for the Arabic Service, so long as its programme was limited to an hour a day its achievement was bound to be modest, and the news element was bound to dominate.

VI

A critical element in the new programme was the kind of Arabic in which it was to be broadcast. Three varieties of Arabic were then distinguished. There was classical Arabic, which was a virtually dead language like Latin or Greek, though still sometimes revived for literary use as Latin had been in Europe. There was modern literary or 'standard' Arabic, the language of much modern literature and of the Arabic press. Finally there were the various colloquial forms of Arabic which were used in ordinary everyday life. In these colloquial Arabics the enormous regional divergences of the Arab world were revealed: pronunciation, vocabulary and even syntax varied enormously from one region to another, so much so that (as one BBC analysis observed) the dialect of Morocco is almost unintelligible in Egypt. For the broadcaster this was a world full of traps. It was, for example, practically impossible to produce a humorous domestic pro-gramme that was not performed in one colloquial Arabic or another, but the producer then had to resign himself to the programme being hardly intelligible to a large part of the audience. There is nothing particularly oriental about this problem (it could present itself to the producer of an Italian regional programme or indeed to the producer of a Scottish one), but it still inhibited broadcasting in a very evident way.

It was not very difficult for the BBC to decide to broadcast in 'standard' Arabic, as was done. But this was not the simple matter it may sound. To begin with, the number of qualified broadcasters whose Arabic was up to the required level was very small. To term a variety of Arabic 'standard' did not make its form and quality non-controversial. The quality of the Arabic used by any writer or speaker aroused (and arouses) ferocious debate. The Egyptian literary world certainly enjoyed high prestige for its use of the language in a modern form, and the Egyptian press was probably the most developed of the Arab world: the Egyptian State Broadcasting Corporation was at that time virtually the only Arabic broadcasting agency of any scope and prestige. The BBC had, therefore, been sensible in taking on Egyptian staff. But that did not mean that their Arabic was not criticised, nor that their provenance was not deplored by Arabs from other countries.

Equally important were the outlook and training of the British staff. All four had made their earlier careers in government service, Calvert in the Consular Service to which he was to return, Hillelson in the Sudan Political Service, Stephenson in the Air Force, and Perowne in the Col-onial Service (he was later to serve in the Foreign Service and again in the Colonial Service). That did not mean that they were faceless civil servants: on the contrary, Stephenson was an independent-minded man, and Pe-rowne and Hillelson were eccentric individualists of a kind not uncom-mon among British Arabists. To Hillelson the pursuit of scholarship was more important than politics; Perowne was a learned romantic to whom travel, discovery and the re-living of historical knowledge mattered more than administrative detail. In 1938 he and Freya Stark were planning a joint trip (which never materialised) to Arabia. He and Hillelson understood the official point of view, but were not smothered by it.

By the spring of 1939 the Arabic Service was properly and wisely organised, and the main lines of its policy laid down. Calvert was replaced by Stephenson, and the umbilical cord with the Foreign Office was thus cut. In the autumn of 1938 the European foreign-language broadcasts of the new Overseas Service had begun, and the Arabic Service found itself no longer an isolated experiment, but part of a growing and potentially important organisation for the defence of the British point of view in an increasingly hostile world.

CHAPTER 3

THE ARABIC SERVICE AT WAR

I

The enthusiasm of the government for what was beginning to be called 'the fourth arm' or 'the propaganda weapon' was tepid. Nor was the BBC anxious to have its activities described in these terms. It was generally acknowledged that war would mean the creation of a 'Ministry of Information', and that broadcasting would in one way or another come under the control of that ministry. But planning for the Ministry of Information advanced in 1938–9 on leaden feet.[1] Sir Stephen Tallents, originally designated Director-General of the proposed new ministry, was dismissed in December 1938, after two years of inconclusive preparatory work, and returned to the BBC. His dismissal was probably due to Sir Samuel Hoare, the Home Secretary, who shortly afterwards assumed responsibility for the nascent MOI, and was later stigmatised in the waspish judgement of Duff Cooper, made after a frustrating year as minister:

I have long known that the MOI is a misbegotten freak bred from the unnatural union of Sir Horace Wilson [the Head of the Civil Service and the *éminence grise* of Whitehall] and Sir Samuel Hoare (considering the progenitors I wonder the offspring is not even more revolting) but I have tried to strengthen the freak's limbs and make it serve some useful purpose, as the only alternative was to scrap it and begin again from the beginning, which was hardly practicable.[2]

The wartime problems of the MOI all stemmed from the confusion and the infirm political purpose of its setting up. Sir Samuel Hoare, who was largely responsible, told Parliament in October 1939: 'There is no question of propaganda. It will be publicity and by that I mean straight news.'[3] The troubles also derived from the way in which, before the war, the secret agencies were allowed to organise departments to plan covert propaganda independently of the proposed ministry. Part of the problem, however, was Leeper's own reluctance to relinquish any Foreign Office control over information policy in peacetime. Leeper was denied any major role in the propagandist policy he had done so much to prepare. After the dismissal of Tallents, men of straw were chosen to head the embryo ministry, and in the civil service back-up the most influential people were Treasury officials like Sir Warren Fisher, at the top level, and below him Sir Percival Waterfield, men wedded to the sluggish policies of the *ancien régime*.

The first wartime Minister of Information was the lawlord, Lord Macmillan, who proved entirely ineffectual. His stated intentions must have been very acceptable to the BBC; his opening speech at the MOI advisory council on 7 September 1939 stated that 'all broadcast information should be truthful and objective', and he heavily emphasised the ethical justification of the war, which was a crusade undertaken with no selfish aims for ourselves.[4] It was all very edifying, but like much else that was said in those early days, it had little to do with the terrible struggle that was to come. In January 1940 Sir John Reith himself became Minister of Information, but this did not significantly change either the stature or the effectiveness of the ministry: nor was the BBC's own position modified very much under Reith, who deliberately refrained from using his inside knowledge to influence Corporation policy.

II

Within this insecure framework the Arabic Service of the BBC expanded its personnel and capacities. By the summer of 1940 the Arabic-speaking staff actually engaged in broadcasting had risen to seven. It still included Sourour, its best announcer, who had spent some time with the Expeditionary Force in France, and it had added Sheikh M. Gom'aa, an academic who now became an effective war commentator, as well as another good announcer, the Palestinian I. K. Sabbagh.

On the Intelligence side Nevill Barbour was taken on from the Ministry of Information, to become one of the formative influences of the Service. Barbour was a freelance enthusiast who had gone to the Arab world in the late 1920s. He had the unusual qualification of having lived in Arab North Africa (the 'Maghreb'), before going to Egypt and Palestine. In Palestine he acquired a knowledge of Hebrew and threw himself into a passionate study of the Palestine question; he also had some small influence before the war as the local *Times* correspondent in Palestine. Barbour had great energy and some administrative ability.

Two other Englishmen were recruited who were perhaps of a more academic turn of mind than Barbour, but were also of importance to the development of the Service, E. H. Paxton and L. P. Elwell-Sutton. Paxton was a sensitive Arabist, the translator of Taha Hussein's *Egyptian Childhood*, which represented an introduction to modern Arabic literature for a whole generation. Elwell-Sutton was also a competent scholar, with a knowledge of the Persian as well as of the Arab world: he was to be of importance as the first editor of the *Arabic Listener*. It is notable that none of the three had spent more than a few months in government service before joining the BBC: this was to be of some importance in giving a more independent and less official character to the Arabic Service staff. It was a typical development of the time: in the BBC, as in other organisations, the day of the patriotic amateur had come.

As happened elsewhere, the amateurs immediately found themselves getting to grips with problems more grave than the professionals had previously had to face. Before the war the BBC Arabic Service had assumed an attitude of gentlemanly riposte. Its appearance had naturally been unwelcome to the German and Italian governments, and for a time the Italians had tried jamming the station, until in March 1938, British recognition of the Italian conquest of Abyssinia procured a truce in the radio war. The German government were principally concerned by the British German-language broadcasts, which began in September 1938, but they also took a critical interest in the Arabic broadcasts. Unsurprisingly, a German researcher was told by the BBC in 1939 that the Arabic broadcasts did not go in for explicit denials of claims by others, and that the policy was one of stating the truth.[5]

With war the BBC at once found themselves in direct competition with the feared German propaganda machine. The Arabic broadcasts from Zeesen were most successful. The German star announcer on their Arabic programme, the Iraqi Yunis al-Bahri, dominated the German programme from early in the war until the beginning of 1942. He was reputed to have been refused a post by the BBC, though no record could be found of this. He was an able performer, later described in the BBC as a thorn in their flesh, and a broadcaster of genius, albeit a genius of scurrility and misstatement. The Germans gave al-Bahri a free hand in presenting his programme, which had an authentically Arab feel to it. It was a long way from his vulgar chit-chat to the gentle and carefully planned confines of Broadcasting House. In the early spring of 1939 an internal description of the activities of the Arabic Service begins with a quotation from Aristotle, and says that many of the talks are 'too highbrow for any except the "intelligentsia", for whom, of course, the programmes are chiefly designed'.[6]

By April 1940 little had changed. The transmitter and aerial facilities at Daventry were being expanded rapidly, and the two senders originally designed to carry the Arabic and Latin American Services were commissioned in February 1939; two further senders were in service from June 1940. But at the same time the wartime explosion of the Overseas Services was taking place, and the demands on transmitting and studio equipment were intense. It was also hard to find suitable announcers in Britain, and the institution of a dawn news bulletin and Koranic reading (0530–0545 GMT) did not take place until June 1940; even then the total programme was five minutes short of an hour and a half a day.[7]

III

Until the spring of 1940 some fairly gentle criticism of the Arabic Service had come in from the diplomatic posts. It was mostly constructive: in Bahrein, for example, several members of the ruling family formed themselves into a little BBC listening club which sent suggestions to the British representative every now and then. Occasionally their comments were sharper.[8] With the Narvik campaign of April 1940 everything changed, and cold arctic winds began to blow round the BBC organisation, as they did round the whole government apparatus. From the time of the first British defeats the BBC began to find itself in the unenviable position of all purveyors of bad news.

Foreign Office discontent began as soon as the parliamentary crisis broke, on 7 May. The next day the Arabic broadcast quoted the *Times* leader on the attacks made on the government in Parliament: 'Authoritative circles in Egypt are agreed that the British government is too tolerant and slow in running the war, and that if new blood were injected into the Cabinet's veins, the British would become active and go forward.'

That the realities of British parliamentary democracy at its moment of crisis should be exposed to the vulgar gaze of the Egyptians was far too much for Lampson in Cairo. On 19 May he wrote with his usual Olympian verbosity to Reith at the Ministry of Information: 'Those in close touch with that [Arabic] public realise that it is composed, as to the vast majority, of imperfectly literate, volatile people who by and large prefer to sympathise with us in adversity rather than rejoice with us in victory.' The BBC, he thought, addressed itself to an Arabic public which was assumed to be, if not positively friendly, at least competent and willing to give dispassionate consideration to the statements broadcast to it. If they wanted to improve the broadcasts, they would adapt them to the mentality of the majority rather than the well-disposed elite.[9] Reporting what was still a free press was one of the major hazards of the BBC, and was to remain so until the Suez crisis of 1956 and after.

Reith had ceased to be Minister of Information a week before Lampson wrote. Churchill replaced him in the coalition government by Duff Cooper. He also wrote to Cooper on 17 May: 'I should be glad to receive some proposals from you for establishing a more effective control of the BBC. Now that we have a government representing the Opposition as well as the Majority, we should have a much freer hand in this respect.' On the same day Duff Cooper saw the Director-General of the BBC, Ogilvie, and Powell (the Chairman of the BBC governors), and reported: 'I found them perfectly willing to accept any suggestions put forward by me, and to place themselves entirely under the control of this ministry.' The Prime Minister minuted the note: 'Proceed as proposed'.[10] For the BBC, which entered the national crisis under a policy of government interference and suspicion, the outlook was gloomy. However, it is probable that the humble submission of Ogilvie and Powell before the government contained as many mental reservations as Reith's had before them.

As the military disasters increased, so did the dissatisfaction of the Ministry of Information and other government departments with the

BBC, though in the summer of 1940 the friction showed itself only in minor complaints. It is likely that these symptoms of discontent formed part of a larger disquiet whose object was not only the BBC but many other branches of government and administration, which it was felt were sticking too closely to old procedures and precedents at this time of supreme emergency. From its inception the Ministry of Information had been a collection of clever, disorganised men who had been given little guidance as to their task, because there was no firm, single concept of what a propaganda ministry ought to do – nor, indeed, even a clear decision that it was a propaganda ministry.

The MOI was unable to regulate its relations satisfactorily either with the Service departments or with the mushrooming covert propaganda organisations. What was especially objectionable to the BBC was the way in which the MOI interposed itself not only between the Corporation and the Service departments, but also between it and bodies such as the Foreign Office posts with which it had previously enjoyed direct contact. Instead of supplying the BBC with a good stock of fresh news and information, particularly the secret information which it was so difficult to give a news medium in wartime, the MOI sat on the information it got, and subjected the BBC departments to a stream of irritating criticism and 'advice'. Duff Cooper chose Frank Pick as Director-General and Sir Maurice Peterson as Controller of Foreign Publicity. Both were forceful, prickly men who would take no nonsense from broadcasting officials, though Pick's views on propaganda were so virtuous that he attracted a comparison with Jesus Christ from the Prime Minister. The mild but able Deputy Director-General, Sir Walter Monckton, was more to BBC taste.[11]

In the summer of 1940 the two most sensitive areas for the BBC were their reporting of the enemy bombing raids on Britain and the style in which the Arabic Service and the Overseas Service broadcast to the Middle East. Middle East broadcasting was particularly vulnerable to official criticism largely because of the feeling of isolation and exposure which affected Middle East Command and British officialdom in the Middle East generally, at the time of the fall of France. The momentous and terrible things happening in Europe, including the entry of Italy into the war, could be known to them only in a bitty way. They were behind in appreciating political changes; Lampson from Cairo still addressed Reith as Minister of Information a week after he had been sacked, in the most critical change of government in modern British history.

The effect of the French armistice on the French Levant and French North Africa, and the outbreak of the war with Italy, meant that immediate solutions had to be found for immense military and political problems in the new Eastern and Southern war zones. There was pressing concern about the morale of the troops in the Middle East and also about the state of neutral opinion in the area, especially in Egypt and Iraq. There was a perfectly natural conviction that the men living on the spot, among the Arab peoples concerned, and responsible for many of the policies which affected them, were far better qualified to decide what should be said to these peoples on the radio than unknown bureaucrats in London.

There was also great frustration with the way in which the military and civil authorities in the Middle East could not get answers to the most simple bureaucratic problems without reference to London. As late as April 1941 the Commander-in-Chief Middle East cabled to the War Office:

There is little doubt that events in Iraq and Syria, plans to revive rebellion in Palestine, and fifth-column activities in Egypt are part of a co-ordinated German plan to cause us maximum trouble in Arabic-speaking countries and, probably, to prepare the ground for German intervention. Germans have the great advantage of unified direction and execution of this policy. . . We on the other hand have no authority nearer than London who in major matters can decide on political policy in relation to strategy, authorise expenditure, or initiate important measures to counter enemy activities or propaganda when required on a Middle East basis. In almost every major Middle East problem local representatives of up to six departments of HMG have to be consulted and their views cabled home . . . You know our views on the need for centralised local control and execution of propaganda in the Middle East . . .

The Colonial Office also said that 'In the Middle East the effective military authority is in Cairo. But the effective diplomatic and propaganda authority is in London.'[12] This correspondence was the immediate prelude to the setting up of a War Cabinet representative in Cairo. But the same arguments had been used, both about politics and propaganda, from the spring of a year earlier.

At the beginning of July 1940, the MOI began a sharp attack on BBC transmissions to the Middle East. The attack was originally inspired by R. A. Butler, the Under-secretary of State at the Foreign Office. The grounds for his discontent were the grouses expressed by the Foreign Office representatives in Egypt (Lampson's complaint has already been quoted) and the Gulf about the BBC. Harold Nicolson of the Ministry of Information referred to 'the criticisms which pour in from our representatives in the Middle East' (though 'trickle' might have been a better verb than 'pour').

The appointed MOI executioner was Professor L. F. Rushbrook Williams, a former ICS official, prolific in publications, who had passed thence to the Colonial and Foreign Offices in the 1930s, and was skilled at keeping several Whitehall desks warm at the same time. In 1940 he was working simultaneously for the Colonial Office, the Foreign Office, and the Ministry of Information.[13] From his ministry desk he began a campaign against the BBC Arabic Service which was eventually to have very serious results for the BBC as a whole, though it would not have done so without the preceding worries of the Middle East authorities about propaganda control.

To the diplomatic and military complaints, Rushbrook Williams added a vague comparison between the BBC and the Palestine Broadcasting Service. This comparison was unfavourable to the former, and took no account of the very different interests of the latter from those of the BBC. He spiced the mixture with copious unacknowledged citations from a memo drawn up by Glubb Pasha about the kind of broadcasting he thought suitable for the Bedouin of Transjordan. Particularly damaging to the BBC was the frequently repeated statement that the BBC broadcasts were far inferior to those of Zeesen and that German programme management was more efficient – though Rushbrook Williams clearly had not read the transcripts, as he was under the false impression that the German-Arabic broadcasts included an entertainment programme. This did not stop him referring to their 'devastating political weight'.[14]

There was a more sober assessment of the Arabic broadcasts from the BBC Intelligence Section, which thought that far more care and thought went into the British broadcasts than the German:

As befits an old-established power, the presentation is dignified and sober as compared with the impertinent and aggressive tone of the would-be empires. In fact the position of the BBC is comparable to that of the conservative statesman addressing the electorate as compared with that of the reformer or agitator.

This was a reasoned judgement under the circumstances. But at that time it was impossible to get the perspective which enabled Richard Crossman to say after the war that the British in the second half of 1940 had had very little to say to the outer world except that they were not going to give in.[15] The highly charged atmosphere of July 1940 did not allow such a thing to be said.

Innuendo and hearsay evidence were not absent from the Rushbrook Williams charges. Nevill Barbour (who had already clashed with Rushbrook Williams at the MOI in 1939), Stephenson and Hillelson struggled to counter the accusations without making much impression on their tormentors. The MOI's suggested remedies were not very practical: Williams called on the BBC to make its announcers deliver an 'extempore harangue' from notes. It may be imagined what the finicky political analysts in the Foreign Office would have made of that, when the texts of the extempore broadcasts reached them! The core of the whole matter was a judgement borrowed from one of the intelligence agencies, MI7, that 'BBC programmes in Arabic have not succeeded in building up pro-Allied feeling to the extent to which the German programmes from Berlin have succeeded in building up anti-Allied feeling.' There was no mention of the crushing Allied defeats which might have contributed to the difficulty in influencing Arab sentiment. Rushbrook Williams also quoted General

Wavell, the General Officer Commanding-in-Chief Middle East: 'Arabic broadcasts still lose force by being too academic to reach masses, and lack "punch" of Yunis al-Bahri. Locally we are doing a lot but matter direct from London could carry greater weight.'[16] The Arabic Service was both technically and ideologically unequipped to deal with this injunction to address propaganda to 'the masses'.

The main defence was mounted by Donald Stephenson. In his view, the occasion of the MOI attack was the unfavourable course of the war, which 'began to lead our harassed diplomats abroad to look more and more to the BBC to turn "planned withdrawals" (i.e. defeats) into victories.' Only then did Rushbrook Williams try 'first to criticise and then to dictate'. Defeat hangs over the whole correspondence like a marshy smell; Rushbrook Williams himself wrote gloomily that 'it is not by any accident that German methods of coordination are so superior to our own. In almost every sphere, diplomatic as well as military, the Germans have unfortunately retained the initiative.' In actual fact German propaganda suffered just the same sort of restraints as the British, but Williams was not to know that.[17]

On theory of propaganda the BBC was a little uncertain. Stephenson, defending himself against propagandists, said that it had never been the past policy of the Arabic Service 'to provide the Arabs with an entertaining or uplifting broadcast from purely altruistic motives. The service is, as it has always been, first and foremost a propaganda medium. At the same time it was always realised that good entertainment would provide a ground bait for our propaganda . . .' But Hillelson's 'Note on planning for the Arabic Service', written at the same time, takes a rather different line: 'The BBC had built up its Arabic Service in accordance with its traditional standards of good broadcasting, but it did not immediately on the outbreak of war become propaganda-conscious in the fullest sense of the term.' In effect, the last line of defence for traditional BBC policies in wartime was the newspaper distinction between news and comment:

The BBC news bulletin has built up its reputation by a policy of dignity and restraint in the presentation of straight news. Is there any reason why this policy should not continue and need it conflict with a vigorous campaign of propaganda presented in the form of news talks? The indirect propaganda value of straight news items will of course be constantly in the news editor's mind, but direct propaganda would be excluded from the bulletin and presented in the form of talks and feature programmes.[18]

The skirmishing with the MOI continued through August 1940. The BBC defence of the Arabic Service had not been very strong: Beresford Clark, the Assistant Controller (Overseas), had implicitly admitted deficiencies in organisation by starting to look for a 'Director' of the Service, a post which had often been called for since 1938, but never approved. In spite of consultation with the doyen of Arabic Studies, Professor H. A. R.

Gibb, the desired paragon could not be found. On 20 August Harold Nicolson came to see Tallents and said that Lord Lloyd (the Colonial Secretary), General Wavell and others were much concerned about the Arabic Service, although Rushbrook Williams had reported it as 'very recently improved'. Tallents talked to Lloyd and found the latter 'friendly and uncomplaining', but this was no guarantee of future peace for the BBC.

Counter-complaints by the BBC about their lack of access to secret government information were treated by the MOI with ill-disguised contempt. In spite of his own BBC provenance Lindsay Wellington replied loftily to Clark from the Ministry of Information on 22 August:

I cannot say that I expect other departments to see eye to eye with us on the relative importance of security and publicity. The problem does, as you know, very often reduce itself to this particular point. It is a matter which has to be fought out, I fancy, at Cabinet level rather than at the level of the Middle Eastern Section.[19]

IV

The projected BBC reorganisation went ahead. No new Director was appointed to the Arabic Service, but Hillelson was made Assistant Director of a new Near Eastern Department to comprise the Turkish, Persian and Arabic Services. His appointment was a vote of confidence in the way he had run the Arabic Service: Tallents had earlier said that he was 'externally unsuitable as a Jew', but to the credit of the BBC this doubt did not prevail.[20]

At the same time the blitz on London drove the BBC departments into the country: in September 1940, the News and Programme Departments of the Arabic Service moved to Wood Norton, near Evesham, where the Monitoring Service had been since the beginning of the war, while the Intelligence Division went to Park Hall at South Newington, near Banbury. Large parts of the rest of the Overseas Services (including the European Services) remained in London, first at Broadcasting House, and then at 200 Oxford Street and at Bush House. At a time of petrol rationing and poor transport this splitting up of the BBC offices made them in some respects more vulnerable to ministerial interference; however, in the end the whole Service transferred to Aldenham.

The simmering government disquiet about the BBC went on. Sir Maurice Peterson, trying to crack a walnut with a sledgehammer, wanted to appoint Sir Kinahan Cornwallis from the Political Intelligence Department to supervise the Arabic Broadcasts and to help dispel 'the smoke-screen which the BBC, consciously or unconsciously, has thrown round the activities of its overseas services.' The illustrious diplomat was furious to have been 'brought back to London merely to provide cover for a bunch of second-rate journalists and amateurs who know nothing about their job,' and the projected appointment came to nothing.[21] In October the Ministry received information from the Middle East that Turkey was broadcasting in Arabic in a manner 'far more virile and pro-British than our own [broadcasting], and I think better informed.' Lindsay Wellington (who knew not a word of the languages concerned) kindly suggested that the BBC Arabic Service was so far inferior to the Turkish that the BBC might do better simply 'to translate [sic] and relay the Turkish broadcasts'.[22]

In early November things came to a head. The Secretary of State for War, Anthony Eden, cabled from his Middle East tour:

Wherever I go I hear complaints of BBC announcements both in English and Arabic. They are continually putting out rumours obviously emanating from enemy sources . . . In general BBC announcements show lack of virility and incisiveness and compare most unfavourably with Turkish broadcasts which are excellent. In fact it has been suggested to me that it would be a great improvement if the BBC were to discontinue their own broadcasts and merely repeat those of Turkey.

On 7 November, in forwarding this telegram to the Director-General, Ogilvie, and remarking that no improvement appeared to have taken place in the Arabic broadcasts, Duff Cooper said: 'I am beginning to wonder whether the time has not come for putting the whole foreign broadcasting [sic] directly under the control of this Ministry . . . Do you see any objection to your Controller of Foreign Broadcasting becoming a servant of the Ministry?' To this brutal question Ogilvie vouchsafed no reply, hoping to pursue the Reithian policy of side-stepping the government's threats. A meeting with the Foreign Office and Ministry of Information representatives produced mildly reassuring noises from both, and Stephenson hastily started to draw up an explanation for the profane government world of what the Arabic Service was about, and how it was organised.[23] But on this occasion the propitiatory bureaucratic moves were in vain: the BBC would be made to walk the plank.

As Reith later remarked, 'The BBC was in a bad way: dissatisfaction within and without through 1940 and 1941. The complaints were mostly on lack of leadership and decision.' Ogilvie spoke to Eden and Duff Cooper, but without placating either. Eden, interestingly enough, became rather vague when asked for his personal view on what was wrong, and said he thought that most complaints were directed against BBC Overseas English-language broadcasts, not against those in Arabic.

Pick, the MOI Director-General, held a meeting on 19 November at which, according to Tallents, he treated the Eden complaint as 'a mere peg on which to hang a prolonged rehash of all the complaints which had ever reached his Ministry about our Arabic Service.' The minutes of the meeting do not entirely confirm this judgement: the BBC were clearly allowed to present a reasoned defence of their case. Tallents expressed the optimistic opinion that 'so far as the Ministry is concerned I should think that we need do no more about this particular trouble.'[24] He was mistaken.

The bickering over the BBC Overseas Services was only part of the government's much more general discontent with the press and broadcasting generally. Churchill, in spite of the mythical photograph with a BBC microphone he left behind, was no friend either to broadcasting or its authors. Reith, who loathed Churchill, recorded how at this time the Prime Minister spoke of the BBC 'with great bitterness: an enemy within the gates: continually causing trouble: doing more harm than good: something drastic must be done about them . . . Cooper accepted it all without protest.'

Pick's observation to Tallents that 'our masters, the politicians in the Cabinet, will not stop to reflect upon the situation' was rendered obsolete on the very day he wrote it. 'Something drastic' was done on 18 November, when the Cabinet's irritation with the BBC's reporting of the air raid on Coventry on 14 and 15 November led it (spurred on by Eden) to appoint a Committee under Kingsley Wood, with Morrison (the Home Secretary) and Duff Cooper, to 'examine and report what changes, if any, were necessary in the constitution and management of the BBC, in order to ensure its effective control by HMG.'[25]

On 20 November Eden drew the War Cabinet's attention to 'the great differences between this country and the Middle East for propaganda purposes, and the need to adapt our propaganda accordingly.' He doubted whether this was done sufficiently. Repeating the criticisms made in his earlier telegram, he wondered whether the machinery for co-ordinating propaganda policy was adequate. Ten days later he sent his complaints about the BBC to Duff Cooper, proposing a much stricter control over BBC broadcasting.

Duff Cooper was worried about the BBC for very different reasons. From the summer of 1940 onwards Hugh Dalton at the Ministry of Economic Warfare had been uniting the two main secret organisations for 'covert' propaganda under his own ministry, and was creating a new organisation which threatened to make the MOI a secondary affair. The BBC German broadcasts were in touch with one of these organisations (SO1, or from September 'the country' under Leeper at Woburn), and Ministry of Economic Warfare imperialism was bound to spread further in the BBC. Duff Cooper realised too late the threat that Dalton posed to a rational, centralised propaganda policy. The MEW, through Gladwyn Jebb, were claiming that the MOI did not really control the BBC foreign broadcasts, and this had to be denied: 'All the foreign broadcasts are controlled from here [MOI],' wrote Oliver Harvey, 'the execution only being left to the BBC. It is not correct to say the BBC have too much say; we have had our difficulties with them, but in fact I think that we can claim that we impose ourselves on them.'[26]

On 9 December Duff Cooper had a note from Churchill about the proposed changes at the Ministry of Information and the BBC, which mentioned 'the question which Dr Dalton is anxious to raise about the "overt" broadcasts'. On 13 December he pointed out to the Prime Minister that if the probable proposals of the Cabinet Committee were accepted, the transfer to the Ministry of Economic Warfare of broadcasts to enemy countries would 'only lead to confusion'. He also pointed out that broadcasting to foreign countries was not confined to the BBC. 'There exists,' he said, with some exaggeration, 'a whole chain of stations round the Mediterranean – Cairo, Aden and others – which are controlled by the press attachés, who are the representatives of and receive their instructions from the MOI.'[27]

The Kingsley Wood Committee (perhaps it should be called the Second Kingsley Wood Committee) reported on 26 December 1940. Its conclusions were unfavourable to the BBC and, had they been strictly applied, would have entirely crippled what remained of BBC independence for the rest of the war. However, they fell short of displacing Ogilvie in favour of a ministry official, and did not recommend that the government should assume complete control of the BBC. The Committee did, however, want two new official advisers to be appointed to the Corporation, one general adviser on home news and the other to be responsible for foreign broadcasts: both were to have the appropriate BBC staff under their immediate direction. Each of these two officers was to have 'the supreme direction in his own particular sphere'; in the case of a dispute arising with the Director-General, the matter would be referred to the MOI. In order to include the Foreign Office in the control organisation, it was to make arrangements with the BBC and the MOI to ensure that its view on foreign affairs was correctly interpreted. It also proposed regular meetings between the MOI, BBC, and the Services, and recommended the early construction of new transmitters for the Overseas Services.

The Cabinet approved the Committee's proposals on 30 December: it then remained to execute them, and the main part of the action was entrusted to Duff Cooper as Minister of Information. Decisions of the War Cabinet were extremely secret, and everything depended on the way in which the responsible minister interpreted them. In the BBC's case, the Corporation benefited from a mixture of kindness and confusion. The Committee's recommendations broadly followed the conclusions reached by Lord Hood (the Private Secretary) and Frank Pick in MOI discussions earlier in December. They rejected Ogilvie's suggestion of a Broadcasting Council with the Minister of Information in the Chair and representatives of the Foreign Office and the Services, though some trace of this remained in the 'regular meetings' proposed by the Cabinet. Hood and Pick certainly did not propose a gentle compromise: Hood thought that under the new regime the BBC would have no more than a formal control over many aspects of its activities, though he offered them 'a show of independence'.[28]

Fortunately for the BBC, though perhaps unfortunately for orderly administration, Duff Cooper entrusted Sir Walter Monckton with the job of telling the BBC what was to happen, and in doing so he slightly but decisively altered the terms of the War Cabinet decision. 'I don't think,' he minuted to Monckton, 'we need give the actual wording as recorded in the minutes. The words underlined in red seem to me much too crude and likely to give offence.' 'The words underlined in red' were almost certainly the reference in the Cabinet decision to the 'supreme direction in his own particular sphere' of the two 'advisers' to the BBC. It was a critical omission, and a telling illustration of the incurable Whiggishness of British government even at the gravest points of the war. Monckton was the right man to give the BBC the kindest possible notice that it had been tried and found guilty. In Monckton's mouth a guilty verdict sounded like a mild and friendly reproof, and that was what the BBC was only too willing to hear.

Curiously Reith, who was no longer Director-General, seems to have known what the exact terms of the Cabinet decision were, whereas Ogilvie did not – or at least, he did not know them officially, which was all that mattered.[29] The result was that inconclusive negotiations, conducted on the basis that the BBC should give its prior consent to any new arrangements about 'advisers', dragged on for months. These negotiations continued into 1941, and still had not come to a proper conclusion when Duff Cooper left the MOI in July.

It would be interesting to consider how a wartime government with virtually dictatorial powers failed to secure the unquestioning obedience of a corporation which owed its existence to a state monopoly, but this would lead far outside the confines of the Arabic Service. The Arabic Service had played an important (and occasionally unhappy) part in the events which led to the BBC's crisis at the end of 1940. In the resolution of the crisis in the following year it played no part at all. As so often happens in government, factors which seemed important while political decisions were being taken retreated into the background once the decisions had been made. Most of the grievous deficiencies which were supposed to affect British propaganda in the Middle East as a result of supposed BBC incompetence were pure make-believe, as those who ran the Arabic Service well knew, and the charges against the BBC at home were perhaps not much different. Rushbrook Williams ceased troubling them, and soon turned up in the BBC itself, where he was a rather successful Director of the Eastern Service, running transmissions to India and the Far East. The real overseas issue was the isolation of the British military and civil authorities in the Middle East from government power in London, and this was tackled in 1941 by setting up a Cabinet pashalik in Cairo.

V

1941 – the year of Rashid Ali's regime in Iraq and its suppression by British forces, of the announcement of future Syrian and Lebanese independence from France, of the British invasion of Iran and the overturning of Reza Shah – was a year of crisis and decision for Britain in the Middle East. The military and political crisis came to a head with the British coup in Cairo on 4 February 1942, when Lampson, much to his own private satisfaction, surrounded the royal palace with British troops and forced King Farouk to accept the government of Mustafa Nahas Pasha.

One of the main propagandists in the MOI at that time has written that until the military tide turned in Britain's favour at Alamein in November 1942, 'impressive propaganda to the inhabitants of the Middle East was usually impossible for lack of any good news to provide raw material for it.' Moreover, Britain's apparently arbitrary violations of Arab and Iranian sovereignties, although politically inescapable in the struggle against Nazi Germany and its allies and sympathisers, aroused fierce resentment. As Elizabeth Monroe's book adds:

Set against the prospect of a victorious Hitler in Cairo or on the Persian Gulf, the contemporary cost of arbitrary acts was a small price to pay . . . Yet they were difficult to explain away even at the time, and BBC broadcasters in Arabic, speaking indiscriminately to listeners in all countries, were hard put to it to compose reassuring bulletins about British policy.[30]

That the BBC had to a considerable extent abandoned its earlier ideas about the proper use of radio for 'propaganda' was shown by Hillelson, writing in the 1942 *BBC Handbook* about the Arabic and Persian Services and their political uses in Iraq, Syria and Persia: 'In each case, the course of events provided an object lesson in the use of the radio weapon in close co-operation with diplomacy and the armed forces.' This vaunting of British radio propaganda by the Director of the Services concerned betrays the same mentality as that shown by a press correspondent who referred to the abdication of Reza Shah in 1941 as 'the first instance in history in which a ruler has been hurled from his throne by radio.' This statement was inexact. Richard Dimbleby, the BBC observer in the Middle East at the time, commented on the way the Iranians had been alerted to the events leading to the abdication of the Shah by their announcement in the BBC broadcasts in Persian. But it was British military and political action which overturned the Shah, not British radio, which merely announced what had happened and asked people to accept it. The same was true of the overthrow of the Rashid Ali regime in Iraq, which was announced to the Iraqis by the Arabic Service in a special broadcast on 2 May 1941, which adjured them to 'overthrow these mercenary intriguers and let law and order reign once more'.

The claims made by Hillelson and others for the achievements of propagandist broadcasting were exaggerated, though they were only reflecting the views current in the MOI and the BBC from the end of 1940 onwards. A paper on programme policy written in January 1941 takes the Zeesen programmes of Yunis al-Bahri as its starting-point, and lays down that 'the programme is not an end in itself, but that every broadcast should serve a purpose related to the war effort and to propaganda.'

Later in the year Stephenson said that the Arabic Service had resisted the demands for direct propaganda to the point where it might eventually have driven all news from news bulletins, but that the Service had included a large proportion of direct propaganda:

Our theory in those early days of direct war on the ether was that if one wanted to call Hitler a son of a dog, the more abusive the epithets that could be devised, the more effective the broadcast would be.

By the end of 1941 this policy had been modified in favour of excluding abusive propaganda from the news bulletins and relegating it, in a more subtle form, to appropriate places in the programme. The news bulletin had remained something in whose general veracity the listener could trust, but it was to be presented vigorously and concisely, and allied reverses were to be worked into the report so as to present the defeat as only one incident in the worldwide field of war: 'At the time of drafting these notes [31 December 1941], while things are going very badly for us in the Far East and very well in Russia and Libya, almost every day the news invites this kind of "perspective" treatment.'[31]

The main addition to the Arabic Service armoury in 1941 was a service broadcast largely in colloquial Moroccan Arabic, and beamed to North Africa from 27 July. The object of the new service was to get British information into the parts of North Africa controlled by Vichy France, and also, perhaps not in 1941 but certainly in 1942, to maintain some liaison with De Gaulle and the Free French. The Moroccan or Maghrebi Service, a large part of whose transmission was to be in colloquial dialect, went against the Arabic Service's original ideas about 'standard' Arabic. It was difficult to staff, and even when staff were found it proved hard to supervise them from a linguistic point of view. Nevill Barbour took a keen interest, but the inspiring genius of the new branch of the Service was not a member of the BBC at all: he was Albert Abulafia, a member of a family of Moroccan Jewish merchants settled in Manchester, who worked in the MOI.

In the course of tortuous and inconclusive negotiations about the way in which the 'advisers' he was supposed to appoint to the BBC were going to operate, Duff Cooper dropped away exhausted, and Peterson, one of his main advisers, resigned, though not specifically on this issue. Monckton and Radcliffe were also on the brink of withdrawal. In July 1941, Kenneth Clark, a senior MOI official, admitted that the MOI had no real control over the Corporation. Monckton told the Cabinet Office that Clark's statement did not accurately represent the situation, but the damage had been done. The burden of the MOI complaint was that the BBC frequently expressed themselves as willing to accept directives, but that they subsequently failed to carry these out. On 17 July the MOI were themselves asking Ogilvie to clarify the position of the advisers, and saying that they 'despaired of discovering what the understanding at this end may be'.[32] It was at this point, when his feebleness in this respect and others was quite exposed, that Duff Cooper gave up the MOI and was replaced by Brendan Bracken.

Ivone Kirkpatrick, an active, peppery Foreign Office official who attracted strong loyalty or antipathy from colleagues and subordinates, came to the BBC in February 1941 as Adviser on Foreign Affairs, but without a properly negotiated position. Persistent friction persuaded Churchill to send in Sir John Anderson as mediator between the warring Foreign Office, MOI and MEW in their struggle to influence or control propaganda, but his decision or 'award' given in May 1941, asking for better ministerial liaison, failed to still the conflict. In August a new department was created called the Political Warfare Executive which was to supervise propaganda to enemy, satellite and occupied countries. The PWE was to be responsible to all three ministries, through a committee which was to 'act as a General Staff for the conduct of political warfare'. This was an arrangement which satisfied no one, but remained in place for the rest of the war. At the same time, in an unconnected move, the two government advisers to the BBC, Kirkpatrick and Ryan, were made into BBC officials, Kirkpatrick becoming European Controller.

In the somewhat bizarre arrangements for the control of 'white' broadcast information services which were not under the covert propaganda services at Woburn, the Arabic Service emerged as an organisation less tightly controlled than the European Services, but by no means independent. Because Kirkpatrick's job was the European Service, and the PWE brief was restricted to satellite and occupied countries, the only part of the Arab world under the PWE aegis for broadcasting purposes was French North Africa: the rest counted as 'neutral'. The MOI continued to concern itself with the Arabic Service. In May 1941, Nevill Barbour wrote that 'the further development of the [Arabic] Department as an instrument of total war calls also for a more specific organisation and control of propaganda functions.'[33] In this atmosphere the Arabic Service neither got nor expected much independence. The way in which military operations were reported and military communiqués were treated was a bone of contention with the Services. Kirkpatrick told Stephenson to refrain from comment or expansion concerning the first announcements by GHQ, Middle East, of the Libyan advance of 19 November 1941: 'I need not reiterate their sensitivity to your broadcasts.'[34]

Government control was seen at its tightest and most irritating in the case of the North African broadcasts. Albert Abulafia, who worked for both the MOI and the PWE and had placed a brother in the Arabic Service, pursued the Arabic Service in the most pernickety manner. In spite of protestations that he had never had any intention of exercising pre-censorship or control over the BBC, he constantly reproached them for the slightest imagined failure to follow the fortnightly 'directives' issued for propaganda policy by the PWE. These were approved, it is true, by a committee on which Stephenson sat, but they were asserted to 'have the force of law' for the BBC.

The 'scatterbrained' Abulafia (as the BBC thought him) over-reached himself in the summer of 1942, when he insisted that the Maghrebi broadcasts should say that Allied post-war policy would be based on the Atlantic Charter and the Four Freedoms. Stephenson showed at once that the BBC officials could demonstrate a much firmer grasp of political issues than the ministries who were supposed to be supervising them:

> if we were in a position to assure North African 'natives' that the fundamental principles of the Atlantic Charter would be applied to their territories, then we would have a propaganda theme of the highest potential effectiveness. Are we, however, in a position to do so when not even that part of France which is nominally allied to us – i.e. the Fighting French – is incorporated in the United Nations; and so, lacking such incorporation, has not subscribed to the principles of the Atlantic Charter? We know only too well how reactionary and illiberal is France's attitude to her Arab colonies, and unless we are prepared to make a guarantee in her name any propaganda on this theme will inevitably strike a critical native audience as being so much hot air.[35]

The PWE, devoting more thought to departmental responsibility than to political theory, suggested that the BBC's recalcitrance might be due to the Arabic Service not being directly under Kirkpatrick's control. Desmond Morton wrote to Kirkpatrick:

> for some worthy reasons of administration, broadcasts in Arabic are classed as 'neutral', whereas PWE and your [Kirkpatrick's] department are scheduled to deal only with broadcasts to enemy and enemy-occupied countries. If this is so, it would seem that Arabic broadcasts to North Africa are an exception.

On this occasion, blind Whitehall departmentalism lost the day. Clark and the BBC Director-General backed up Stephenson's analysis, which had put its finger on one of the touchiest issues of Allied policy, one which involved both Allied relations with Vichy and Free French colonial policies, and the post-war future of colonies in general. The dispute went to the Cabinet, where it was decided that Stephenson's doubts about the advisability of proclaiming the Atlantic Charter to all and sundry were well-founded.[36] It was a notable example of the BBC's ability to stand up to the ministries on an issue of political judgement, and win.

VI

In 1940–41 the Commanders-in-Chief and the Ambassador in Cairo were more worried about propaganda and information than about any other non-military issue. In May 1941, Anthony Eden and Duff Cooper were corresponding about finding 'someone of high standing, able to take over the whole question of co-ordinating our propaganda, both overt and covert, in the Near East.' GHQ Cairo was itself under attack for the incompetence and over-optimism of its communiqués during the Crete campaign of May 1941. Setbacks in the war made it even more important to have a skilful and consistent propagandist policy, to cover the cracks until better times came.

The question of a Cabinet representative in the Middle East was solved at the end of June 1941 by the despatch of Oliver Lyttelton to Cairo as Minister of State. Within a few weeks Brendan Bracken, the new Information Minister, was telling him to do nothing about propaganda there yet: 'Beware of brigadiers and diplomats: propaganda is an art.' He followed this up with a taunt about Lyttelton's Curzonian proclivities, and the usual ministerial claim for his department:

Doubtless you will soon establish your own Treasury and Foreign Office in Cairo, but this ministry intends to have its fair share in the selection of the propaganda chief for the Middle East . . . We want to be treated as colleagues not fellaheens [sic].

Lyttelton replied, signing his telegram as 'Lord Curzon', and describing the bureaucratic chaos of the various propaganda organisations he had found in Cairo:

You will be as surprised as I was to learn how many of them there were. The Army, Navy, Air Force, SO1 and SO2 with many sub-divisions and offshoots are all engaged in propaganda besides your ministry . . . I require a co-ordinator to keep these heterogeneous bodies in step. I hope you will read this after a good lunch at the Carlton Grill and will help to get me a man, so that I may fulfil what I have been told to do.[37]

The man for the Cairo propaganda job was Walter Monckton, who went there in November 1941. There was at that time no BBC presence in Cairo, and there is no mention of the BBC in Monckton's first report from Cairo to the MOI. However, the scale of other broadcasting may be gauged from a description of the Cairo Propaganda Directorate dated January 1942, which records a 'Foreign Broadcasts Section' under W. Hillier with a staff of fifteen. In Palestine there was the Palestine Broadcasting Station, but there was also from some time in the first half of 1941 a covert British broadcasting station run by SOE and transmitted by RAF equipment in Jaffa, at first under the name of the Freedom Broadcasting Station. The Jaffa station was concerned with broadcasting to the Balkans, but from an early point it also broadcast in Arabic. In June 1942 Monckton was already complaining that this station, well known to be controlled by HMG, was embarrassing his Directorate of Propaganda by putting out material in Arabic which was flatly inconsistent with that coming from the official Palestine station.[38]

In November 1942 the tides of war in North Africa turned at the battle of Alamein, and the great period of wartime Cairo began. For two or three years Cairo assumed a political importance it had not known since the heyday of Muhammad Ali. It was a great military headquarters, not only the centre of most North African and all Middle Eastern operations, but the base of the Civil Affairs Administration for recovered enemy territories over a huge area. With the reopening of communications in the Mediterranean, it became the principal connecting link between the European, Russian and Far Eastern theatres of war. As the BBC official, E.G.D. Liveing, wrote in 1943, the city itself had become a world cosmopolis, and its streets and hotels teemed with soldiers and civilians from Britain, the Dominions, India, the States, Russia, Greece, Yugoslavia, Poland, France, Belgium.[39] Exiled governments like the Greek were centred there. The Minister of State's offices were an administrative centre for all the British heads of diplomatic missions in the Near East, as well as for the High Commissioners of Palestine and the Governors of Cyprus and Malta. The Middle East Supply Centre became one of the most ambitious programmes for supplying the needs of a group of countries to have been set up by the British Government, rivalling the organisation of Victorian India.

Liveing, who was a life-long BBC career man, and not an Arabic Service recruit, went out to Cairo in August 1942 to report on the possibility of establishing a BBC office there.[40] His report reflects the long-present official discontent at Cairo with BBC transmissions, especially those in English:

I have been told in many quarters in Egypt that certain commentaries and bulletins in these transmissions during the so-called 'flap' [i.e. defeat] in the Western Desert in July came near to causing consternation. While the British temperament may be able to stand up to unpalatable prophecies of serious crisis, such as a possible evacuation of the Delta, this does not apply to the native population.

Coming to the future, Liveing produced a rather dynamic picture of the possible function of a BBC office in Cairo which differs notably from the more sceptical views of the contemporary Arabic Service chiefs in London. In particular he wanted 'a projection of the Middle East, both in our relationship to Arab and associated communities and as a theatre of war, with all the opening-up of new activities, such as economic developments, communications, supply and transport, which this entailed. . .'

There is a new sort of reciprocity in Liveing's view of possible new stimulus to the BBC Arabic programme from a Cairo subsidiary. It was a point of view which had long been absent in London, cut off as it had been for three years from the Middle East, and it is interesting that it should have come from a non-Arabist:

Up to the present the bulk of our Near East Programme Service has been produced in the UK with a recent addition of a number of talks supplied at the Cairo end. As the dominant power in the Middle East, however, we have unrivalled propaganda resources denied to the Axis. Through the medium of recording material of all kinds on the spot, outside broadcasts of important events, eyewitness accounts, and also various forms of entertainment material produced in Middle East studios, we can present a picture of life in this area, and re-broadcast to the Middle East in a way which no other country is able to do. . . The flattery and general-interest value of re-broadcasting the Middle East to itself is immense.

This proved to be an over-optimistic prophecy of the capacity and variety which a Cairo office could add to the Arabic Service, but the enthusiasm of Liveing's outlook is attractive.

Liveing was made 'Middle East Director', and he and his assistant Pennethorne Hughes duly opened the Cairo Office of the BBC in February 1943. The Arabic output of the office developed much more slowly than he had hoped, due to the scarcity of suitable Arab broadcasters and officials, and the shortage of equipment. Both Stephenson and Sir Arthur Rucker (a pundit in the Cabinet Office) had approached the idea of a BBC branch office in Cairo rather cautiously: Stephenson said it would be concerned with 'listener reaction and intelligence, with the provision of programme material, and with the recruitment of staff.' Rucker was most concerned about the liaison function of the office with the representatives of the central government in Cairo; it was to be 'a focal point of contact with the Minister of State's office'. Both he and the Minister of State, R. G. Casey, saw the red light when there was any question of introducing any new 'Arabist' organisation into Cairo; there were in his view far too many Arabists there already, and 'amateur Lawrences of Arabia grow on every bush'.[41]

The Cairo Office was taken over by C. J. Pennethorne Hughes in 1943: he became 'Middle East Representative' in 1944. By then it had acquired momentum. In the second quarter of 1943 the Cairo Office sent by radio link and air to London nine Arabic talks and a dozen Arabic programmes: the musical programmes included twenty- or thirty-minute musical monologues on 'Stalingrad', 'Montgomery', 'Churchill' and 'Australia'. In early 1944 the Cairo Office was sending back about a hundred programmes a month to all divisions of the BBC. Pennethorne Hughes appointed an inventive and active Assistant, Y. M. Sharara, who by the end of the war was quite influential in programming policy, to the extent that officials in London were having to defend the 'projection of Britain' concept against his pressure for less talks on 'Tuberculosis in British cows' and a more authentically Arab programme. By that time the Arabic Service was spending about a quarter of its programming budget in Cairo.[42]

In Cairo rival intelligence and covert propaganda organisations struggled with one another with almost as much venom as they devoted to the enemy. Most of these feuds were irrelevant to the BBC, but one was not.

By the end of November 1942 the broadcasting station which had been set up by SOE in Palestine had the use of the first of two $7^1/2$ kW transmitters built by the Royal Corps of Signals and housed at Beit Jala, near Jerusalem. There were offices in Jerusalem. The first transmitter was for Balkan programmes, but the second shortly afterwards carried the overt Arabic service called the Near East Broadcasting Station, 'Sharq al-Adna', previously the 'Freedom Station': the studios for Sharq al-Adna were at Jaffa, whence there was a land line to Beit Jala.[43]

The political wrangles over the Jaffa station came to a head in the autumn of 1942. The agreement between the Foreign Office, the MOI and the MEW made in August 1941 provided for the management by the new Political Warfare Executive of propaganda to enemy and enemy-occupied territories. This was welcome news to the Cairo Propaganda Directorate, which had been especially annoyed by SOE's incursion into Persian and Turkish politics via the Jaffa transmitter. In September it was represented that the Minister of State in Cairo was 'distinctly fed up with the number and variety of organisations which have in varying degrees concerned themselves with broadcasting to the Middle East, and that he was resolved to erect Lord Moyne's office [the office of the new Minister of State in Cairo] into a position of unassailable authority.' In pursuance of this policy Lord Glenconner, the head of SOE in Cairo, agreed in December 1942 to hand over the SOE broadcasting station in Palestine to PWE. The agreement specified the existing offices in Jerusalem, and the two transmitters at Beit Jala outside Jerusalem. The station was actually handed over to PWE in March 1943.[44]

Sharq al-Adna was amply financed, and it soon had a good supporting Arabic entertainment programme as well as a news programme. Its first Director was Squadron Leader A. H. Marsack, who had served in Egypt and the Sudan before the war, and had converted to Islam. The Egyptian State Broadcasting Corporation loaned experienced staff, and Sharq al-Adna rapidly got a reputation for slick and effective programmes: broadcasting on the short wave, it could still reach a mass audience throughout the Middle East and not just in Palestine. Its broadcasting hours were longer than those of any other Arabic-language station at that time: in February 1943 the BBC reckoned that Sharq al-Adna was transmitting between ten and twelve hours daily, at a time when the BBC Arabic Service was on the air for $1^3/4$ hours, and even Egyptian State Broadcasting at Cairo only for seven and a half.[45]

Sharq was definitely a 'light' programme: it transmitted news bulletins, but the proportion of music to other material was more than three times what it was in the BBC service. By the end of the war the Sharq transmissions had come down to $8^1/2$ hours daily, but this was still a good domestic service supplied on the short wave to the whole eastern Arab world. The programmes were at a very good level of general competence, including the news, which was not just crude propaganda.

Sharq al-Adna, in spite of its odd origins, was of some importance in the development of broadcasting in Arabic. It was to be of consequence to the later history of the BBC that this station was not closed down at the end of the war. Control in Sharq was in all probability transferred to the Foreign Office in 1945 along with the rest of the PWE responsibilities. The legal structure of the station appears to have been changed into that of a commercial company some time after the war, but it is virtually certain that HMG retained some form of controlling interest.[46] The BBC had no direct contact with Sharq al-Adna, although the former Sharq Director, A. H. Marsack, after he left Sharq was in 1945 made the BBC Middle East Representative in Cairo.

Increased transmitter capacities, particularly the new senders built in 1943 at Woofferton and Skelton, and the link with Cairo, enabled the Arabic Service to get a big increase in output in the course of the war.[47] In 1942 a 'midday' news bulletin was instituted, broadcast for half an hour in mid-morning. By the end of the war there were four daily news bulletins besides headline news in the final evening transmission. Besides the dawn and mid-morning transmissions there were two evening ones. The whole daily programme occupied three hours, excluding the Moroccan transmission.

Music occupied only a modest place in the programme, and current affairs not unnaturally took pride of place. A news commentary was broadcast daily except on Sundays, and *On the Margin of the News* was broadcast five days of the week. Other news features and talks like *Round the World* (Hawl al-'Alam), *Mirror of Events, The War Week by Week* topped up a very solid diet. Iraqi and Cairo news letters, a weekly Cairo talk, and *Arab News Review* did quite a bit to give the programme a feeling that it was part of the Arab world, and not just a British propaganda exercise master-minded by British academics. There was also, towards the end of the war at least, occasional outside broadcasting which did something to transmit the immediacy of a country at war.

Pan-Arabism was always approached by the Arabic Service with the utmost caution. The lesson of Palestine was constantly in the minds of diplomats and broadcasters. Pan-Arabism in its simplest and most immediate form had been professed by the Arab rebels against Britain in Palestine, and chiefly by the Mufti, Haj Amin al-Husseini. Papers on propaganda policy during the war emphasised the freedom from political commitments in the Arab world which enabled the Germans to say more or less what they liked when broadcasting in Arabic, and the vast and immediate responsibilities which weighed upon the British. 'We know,' wrote Stephenson in a typical document, 'that every promise, every hint of a promise, must be redeemed – or we suffer a catastrophic loss of prestige. We are debarred from holding out specious hints of favourable solutions to the "Arab problems".'[47] The embarrassing consequences of the British promises to Arabs and Jews during the First World War were always present to propagandists during the Second.

Yet the Arabic Service was broadcast to all Arabic-speaking countries, and Palestinians, Syrians and Moroccans were recruited as broadcasters. During the war it lost its original Egyptian flavour and acquired a sort of Pan-Arab feeling which was not lost upon the people who ran it. A 1941 report suggests that the Service had 'gone some way towards becoming a microcosm of the Arab world, responsive to the intellectual movements of its various parts. . .'[48]

Nevill Barbour suggested in his book published in 1946 that broadcasting in the Arab world, both local and that from outside powers, had itself been a powerful contributor to ideas and ideals of Arab unity, quite apart from its spreading the knowledge of modern journalistic Arabic. The growing correspondence from all parts of the Arab world which flooded in to London in response to the Arabic broadcasts, and was analysed by the audience research specialists, contributed to this consciousness of the Arabic Service as a mirror of Arab cultural unity, and also to some small extent as a factor in its development. Hillelson wrote at the end of the war:

To become the 'national programme' of the Arabs was not our conscious aim, but it was in the nature of things that an Arabic service from London should be metropolitan rather than regional, and thus work in harmony with the Arab urge towards the strengthening of their common nationhood.[49]

These sentiments fitted in with a somewhat vague British policy, which had been expressed by Anthony Eden in a 1941 speech, that Britain should give some kind of encouragement if the Arabic-speaking countries moved in the direction of federation. No doubt the original idea had been to seize on any policy motif which might to some extent lighten the dead weight carried by British policy in Arab lands because of the Palestine factor. In the atmosphere of wartime Cairo, especially because of the illusion of a unitary Middle East policy in the Middle East Supply Centre, British propagandists regarded a future Arab federation or customs union as a possible and not undesirable development: the feeling can be seen, for example, in Liveing's 1942 Report to the BBC. Barbour's book spoke of Transjordan, Syria, Lebanon, Iraq, Saudi Arabia, the Yemen and Egypt as of a group of nations 'which are today [1946] striving to create one great cultural and economic unit'. Conversely, many Arabs saw the movement which ended in the setting up of the Arab League in Cairo in 1945 as in some sense British-influenced.

It would be misleading to suggest that these tendencies were of great importance inside the Arabic Service. They were part of the trend of the times, but they were counter-balanced by other things. Hillelson himself had always been critical of people (especially of diplomats) who talked about the 'Arab mentality'. It had been said early in the war that:

the BBC must remain conscious of the fact that the broadcasts are received by listeners of different social classes, different education, and different political and cultural outlook. They range from the highly westernised graduates of European universities to the tribesmen of Hadramaut. . . It can be asserted with confidence that the intelligentsia of Arab countries would bitterly resent any attempt on our part to approach them on the basis of an ill-considered interpretation of 'Arab mentality'.[50]

During the course of the war a small and devoted group of people, British and Arab, though much interfered with by government ministries, had succeeded in making the BBC Arabic Service into an established part of the cultural and political life of the Arab world. These intelligent but politically innocent men had been used, at times shamelessly bullied, by others who sometimes seemed to be more devoted to the exercise of power than to anything else. The attack mounted by the government against the BBC in 1940 is hard to account for, but it might be described as a kind of nervous paroxysm directed against an organisation which seemed unaccountably to escape direct control by the state.

But in spite of great pressure to do otherwise, those who ran the Service had maintained the Arabic news bulletins as a reliable and universally respected source of information, and given the Service a reputation for integrity and competence which was afterwards to serve the BBC and the national interest well. They had also developed a supporting programme which used a variety of talents, and which entertained and informed in ways which were accepted and appreciated all over North Africa and the Middle East. It is possible that in one or two places like the Sudan, the BBC Arabic Service was by the end of the war accepted as a kind of Home Service.

It would be a mistake to exaggerate what had been done. The Arabic Service had been built up to defend Britain and the values for which she stood, during the crisis of a great war. Three hours of broadcasting time a day allowed space for a respectable programme, stronger in its news presentation than any other station in the Arab world; but the restricted broadcasting time and the wartime circumstances meant that although the framework for a major cultural institution had been set up, it was still only in the first stage of its development. At the end of the war the BBC service remained, as its hardest-headed defender, Stephenson, said, primarily a news and information service from London.

CHAPTER 4

THE PROGRAMME
AND ITS PUBLIC: I

I

The daily transmission time of the Arabic Service grew only slowly. It began in 1938 with sixty-five minutes; in July 1940 it rose to an hour and twenty-five minutes; in 1942 to something short of two hours; by the end of the war the whole programme occupied three hours, excluding the North African or Maghrebi transmission which was discontinued in 1945. The core of the programme was the news bulletins. The initial 1938 programme carried only one news bulletin; then a second, dawn bulletin was added in 1940 to follow the morning Koran reading. In 1942 a so-called 'midday' bulletin was instituted, which went out at 1045 GMT (the two-hour time difference between Greenwich and local Levant time must be remembered). By 1945 an extra evening bulletin had been added so that there were in all four daily bulletins (0455: 1045: 1745: 1932), besides headline news in the final evening transmission. The Maghrebi programme contained only one news bulletin, broadcast in mid-evening in Moroccan instead of in standard Arabic.

Essentially the Arabic news bulletins depended on an organisation which was already in being when the Arabic Service started. In 1938 there was an Empire Service News Editor and a Foreign Language Service News Editor; it was an agreed condition when the Arabic Service came into existence that its news bulletins should be kept as close as possible to those of the Empire Service. By 1941 these officers had become an Overseas News Editor and, for the Arabic, Turkish and Persian Services, a Near East News Editor (Stephenson).

But it was also understood from the start that the Arabic Service would require its own specialised sources of information. The Foreign Office itself undertook to provide some of these, by requiring its diplomatic posts in the Middle East to transmit local news direct to the BBC in London. There was an additional advantage to the Arabic Service in this arrangement, in that it kept the Service in direct and independent contact with the diplomatic posts; the partial loss of this facility was one of the most regretted effects of the insertion of the Ministry of Information into the chain of information supply.

The BBC had not, however, been entirely happy with the original arrangement, and in 1939 it had obtained a modification by which there should be British agents to supply news to the Arabic Service who would not be 'official hacks', but persons known to and accepted by the Corporation. These agents were often Air Force Intelligence officers: the agent in Khartoum, for example, was Squadron Leader Marsack, whose brother later played a role in Sharq al-Adna.[1] However, after the war, in 1946, the practice of transmitting news from the diplomatic posts in Beirut, Damascus and Bagdad was revived. 'Press attachés would examine the material as a general check on authenticity, but they would not exercise any form of censorship such as would prejudice the independent and unbiased nature of the news letters.'[2]

There was no direct way for the Arabic Service to get news from the Middle East before the setting up of the Cairo Office in 1943, and even then the Middle East Director was not responsible for news transmission, though the daily despatches in English of the BBC observer in the Middle East theatre of war went through his office. Nothing was transmitted from Cairo in Arabic which could be described as news, except for the Cairo News Letter of local Arabic news (which in 1945 was beamed in Arabic direct from Cairo).

The first big change in news input from the Middle East came after the war, when in 1949 a contract was signed with the Arab News Agency in Cairo for an average of two thousand words weekly, later reduced to a thousand words weekly, and in 1954 reduced to two thousand words a month. Tom Little's Arab News Agency was a competent outfit which on the whole gave the BBC what it wanted, which initially was 'news not views'. Particularly after the Palestine War, when it became difficult to get full and unbiased news out of the Palestine area, such an agency was important. The Agency reported quite a few items which were more interesting and important to the Arab world than to the world outside it, and hence went unreported by the big European news agencies. But 'views' were also important. The Agency supplied news commentaries of a very high standard, particularly in the early 1950s when a new generation of British journalists began to assess the new post-war situation created by the appearance of Syria and Lebanon freed from French tutelage, and by the advent of the regime of the Free Officers in Egypt. Tom Little who managed the Arab News Agency in Cairo was an able and well-informed journalist. For example, the quality of the political analysis of the 'Surveys of important events and significant trends' which the Agency contributed to the Arabic Service in 1954 was high: these were subtle and thoughtful surveys of the new Middle East politics.[3]

News talks were the most important part of the output after the bulletins. In the very early pre-war programme they were much less prominent, and in any case a daily hour's broadcast left little time for them. In September 1938 Stewart Perowne was still reporting opposition to the idea of a regular talk on foreign affairs in the programme, on the grounds that any opinion expressed in such talks would be attributed to H.M. Government, and that this made the idea impractical. Perowne spurned such timidity, and recommended that political talks should be inaugurated forthwith. By 1940 there was a weekly *Talk on World Affairs*, and frequent 'news shorts' which were in the nature of brief commentaries.

The most successful wartime speaker was the Egyptian Muhammad Gom'aa, a rather able man who had been a lecturer at the School of Oriental Studies before the war, and whose propaganda talks escaped the common charge of 'lack of virility'. By 1943 news and news talks took up 37 per cent of the programme. There was a variety of talks on the progress of the war (particularly by the anonymous 'observer', al-Raqib), but one commentary which lasted through the later years of the war and after was that given every evening after the news, *On the Margin of the News* ('Ala Hamish al-Akhbar, familiarly known as 'the Hamish').

There was a limited amount of outside broadcasting. Sourour had been sent to France in the early days of the war, and Isa Sabbagh was sent to Germany in 1944, where he flew (on one occasion making a forced landing which almost made for an early end to his career) in American Liberators. Sabbagh also made an ebullient broadcast on VJ night from Trafalgar Square, in which he referred to the possibility of another war if statesmen had failed to learn their lessons: this led to his being hauled up before Sir Ian Jacob.[4]

But though the political commentary was never abandoned by the Arabic Service (nor, indeed, by the External Services in general), new ways of dealing with political matters were found all the time. As the volume of correspondence from listeners grew rapidly in the early 1950s, and the *Question and Answer* programme which is described below came to flourish, *Question and Answer* grew an offshoot in *Political Question and Answer*, which enabled the Service to reply directly to the very often awkward and indiscreet questions of the listeners. This was another way in which the Service modernised its political attitudes, and responded directly to the growing political consciousness of the Arab urban population, and the emergence of a much more articulate and sophisticated Arab nationalism.

The Service normally called upon London-based journalists to reply to these questions. The journalists were an able and distinguished lot. Brian Crozier of the *Economist*, W. N. Ewer of the *Daily Herald*, Wayland Young, Francis Watson, Robert Stephens and Colin Legum of the *Observer*, Edward Hodgkin of *The Times*, Guy Wint of the *Guardian*, Dennis Healey the Labour politician – this was an impressive list, which showed that the Eastern Service Director, Gordon Waterfield, was willing to use the most enlightened talent available. The policy was consistent with BBC pre-war practice of using independent commentators, which could be seen in the translation for the pre-war Arabic Service of occasional talks by writers on international affairs like Charles Tower. But the volume of news talks on the Arabic Service after the increase to a four-hour daily transmission in 1952 was substantial. It was important for the Service that the flow of outside contributors was so great, since this impeded the development of anything like a narrow official line within the Service.

There was also a rather specialised category of political talks, which was those delivered on the occasion of the national days or national commemorations of Arab states. These 'protocol' talks could involve the Service in awkward political decisions. For example, Stephenson on the occasion of Anglo-Egyptian Treaty Day (26 August 1942) had contemplated 'quite a big set-up' for the Arabic Broadcast, with messages from Eden, the Egyptian Ambassador, Nahas and Lampson. The Foreign Office, knowing how tricky the situation still in Egypt was after the British coup of February, vetoed the broadcasts.[5] As late as 1944 the Treaty Day broadcast was a general reference to 'the spirit of co-operation which the Treaty had produced and developed during the war.' In 1953, in a very different political climate, it was decided to have a commemorative programme for the first anniversary of the Neguib Revolution.[6]

Although they were, strictly speaking, features, the predominantly political nature of one series of discussions makes it convenient to deal with them here. These were the *Discussions Before an Invited Audience* which came into the programme after 1950. They were developments of the earlier *Brains Trusts*, but adventurous developments, since the guests were frequently prominent Arab politicians, and the discussions unscripted and controversial. The most controversial was the programme in which Habib Bourguiba, the nationalist and anti-French Tunisian political leader, appeared, transmitted on 13 September 1951. The topic for discussion (which took place on 26 July) was 'Is Communism a danger to the Arab countries, and if so what is the best means of combating it?' The programme is of interest also because Bourguiba expressed his gratitude to the BBC for giving him the opportunity to 'speak on the radio for the first time in his life'.

Bourguiba's discussion, with Edward Atiyah and Fikry Abaza, is worth looking at both for its political consequences and for what he said. The great issue of the decade was to be the choice between social justice and nationalism, and Bourguiba was fully aware of it. Atiyah said of social ills that the only answer was socialism. Bourguiba agreed, but said that 'so long as foreign rule exists, in spite of all these reforms the people may be led to Communism to rid themselves of foreign rule because the need of the people for social justice is not equalled by their need for freedom.'

The aim of the whole programme was to emphasise the nationalist rejection of Communism, which Bourguiba duly affirmed. But in the discussion A. H. Bishlawi, the staff chairman, went rather further than he should have done in agreeing that the Arabs have 'neither democracy nor freedom', and implicitly accepting Bourguiba's national thesis; he also wished Bourguiba 'success in his work'. This much provoked the French government, which protested vigorously against the broadcast. It was another chapter in the old story of French irritation with British tolerance extended to the Maghrebi nationalists. Waterfield made his peace as best he could with the Quai d'Orsay, but he does not seem to have much offended the Foreign Office.[7]

In the Arabic Service programme local news was represented by the *News Letters* which from the wartime period onwards were produced for Cairo, Bagdad, Aden, Damascus, Khartoum and (occasionally) Beirut, though not all these centres had a news letter regularly on the programme. It was recognised that it was important to give a local feel to the programme in this way: on the other hand, it was very difficult to maintain the absolutely up-to-date flow of local news which was essential for a local news letter to be taken seriously in its place of origin. Quite often there was only a Cairo News Letter as a regular weekly feature. But a better handling of the local news was to consolidate news from the Arab world into an *Arab News Letter*, the programme put out in the early 1950s.

The experiment of popularised news talks in dialect as opposed to standard Arabic really belongs to the history of wartime propaganda. In the war, apart from the Maghrebi Service, two such series were put out, one in Egyptian colloquial called Abu Haggag (the news vendor) and one in Syrian colloquial called Abu Sham. Both sought propaganda advantages from a satirical technique. They were put out by good broadcasters (Sabbagh did the Syrian colloquial), but like many uses of the colloquial, they got too much stick from listeners to give rise to permanent features. Listeners who spoke the colloquial being used tended to find the material trite or familiar: listeners who did not often found it either unintelligible or laughable.

II

Bulletins and talks depended on the personalities and speaking capacities of those who gave them. The early programme recruited some talented microphone personalities. A. K. Sourour, who had been an announcer in Cairo, and Isa Sabbagh, a Palestinian who joined early in the war, both secured great reputations. Both were 'golden-voiced': listeners wrote that 'their beautiful diction attracts Arab hearts', and Sabbagh was described by an admirer in the Hadhramaut as 'the lion cub of Arabdom'. Sabbagh left the BBC in 1949 and later worked for the Voice of America: Sourour had already left in 1946. It was not to be expected that many Arab broadcasting staff would remain for very long periods with the BBC, since, after the war at least, they were frequently young men on short-term contracts.

In the later wartime and immediately post-war periods, between a half and a third of the material broadcast by the Arabic Service was composed in Arabic and not translated. The lower point was critical if the Service was to carry conviction in the Arab world, and to avoid parading its foreign origins: it could only maintain credibility if a minimum of something approaching half the programme was thought out from the beginning in Arabic. Of the talks broadcast by the Service, rather more than half were written especially for the Service: the rest were taken from talks originating in other Overseas Services.

One thing which vouched for the credentials of the Arabic Service in the Islamic world was its religious content. Without any apology the broadcasts emanating from a Christian capital city began (as they begin still) every morning with a reading from the Koran. No doubt the influence on the Service of the programme of the Egyptian Broadcasting Service was one reason for this, but it also had a symbolic meaning. The Koranic broadcasts certainly did not seem strange to the Englishmen in the Service, with their conviction that the Service should play a part in the renaissance of Arab culture and in the affirmation of its traditional values.

They also appeared far more natural in the radio transmissions of the imperial power of pre-war Britain than they perhaps seem now: King George VI ruled over many scores of millions of Muslim subjects, and beside pre-war British rule over Muslims in the Indian sub-continent, Africa, Palestine and Aden, Malaya and elsewhere, the million or so British Muslim subjects of Queen Elizabeth II form a very modest body. But there is no doubt of the psychological importance of the Koranic broadcasts to the Muslim audience: more than one letter received by the Arabic Service from its listeners began: 'You will feel as fellow-Muslims. . .'

The religious readings of the Arabic Service were never perfunctory. In Egypt religious broadcasting was one of the main links between the urban culture of the broadcasters and the rural masses. Good Koranic readers were highly prized and well paid, and so were the shaikhs who could broadcast good religious talks. The BBC spent quite substantial sums of its programme allowance in getting the services of well-known shaikhs to read the Koran: usually these were recordings made in Cairo. Such readers were Abdul Fattah Shi'sha'i, and Muhammad Rifaat who was the most popular.

The capacity of a Muslim audience to appreciate a good, long broadcast sermon was already by 1939 not to be compared with the semi-paganised Christian west. The Arabic Service did not have the time available for long religious talks, but from the beginning it broadcast short ones; its best-known early religious broadcaster was the Egyptian theologian, Abdul Aziz Mustafa al-Maraghi. The religious programme did not go unappreciated: in 1945 7 per cent of the letters received by the Service praised the

Koranic readings. Surveys in the early 1950s found that in the Egyptian country districts the most popular aspects of broadcasting were still the religious ones. The Service was also careful to see that the main Muslim religious feasts were properly marked. Ramadan and its end, the pilgrimage, the Ascension of Muhammad (Lailat al-Miraj) and also the Shi'a feasts such as the anniversary of the Martyrdom of Hussein were marked by talks or readings.

Christian Arabs in the East did not let this Islamic preponderance in the BBC output pass without comment. An example is the protest made to the BBC and the Foreign Office in 1956 by the Patriarchs of the Catholic Copts, the Orthodox Copts, Orthodox Armenians, Maronites and Greek Catholics, against what they saw as the absence of the Christian message and of Christian instruction on the BBC Arabic Service.[8] The reply given on this as on other occasions was that the major Christian feasts were regularly marked on the Arabic transmissions by special programmes. Easter and Christmas were invariably so marked, the latter sometimes by a Nativity play. There were always, after the earliest days of the Service, enough Christian Arabs working on the programme to put out such features. But the fact remained that the basic framework of the programme was Islamic, and nothing happened to change this.

III

When the Arabic Service began transmission BBC audience research at home was only beginning to take shape. Significantly, one of the main influences on its development had been Sir Stephen Tallents, the inventor of the 'Projection of Britain'. The need for audience research was in a way more urgent for the Foreign Services than for the Home, because they needed to find out, not what listener preferences were, but whether people listened at all. 'Mass observation' or market research by visit or questionnaire was impossible in the earlier years; first because of the lack of the appropriate organisation abroad, and later because of war conditions. There was a project to investigate listener habits in Syria and Palestine, launched by Professor Dodd of the American University of Beirut in 1943, but its results never reached the BBC in a form they could use as up-to-date information. Small local initiatives like a sample of ninety-two Iraqis asked to give the times of the BBC broadcasts in 1941–2, or the questions occasionally addressed to Freya Stark's 'Friends of Freedom' in Egypt, were too amateur to help much. The 'listening committee' formed by the ruling family of Bahrein reported right through the war, but such an aristocratic gathering could not help with information about popular preferences.

When the programme started in 1938 Hillelson was Assistant Director of Overseas Intelligence, and there were two 'Public Relations' officers. From 1940 the Near and Middle East Intelligence Section was run by

Nevill Barbour. 'Intelligence' about listener reaction was very hard to gather: had it been easier the Arabic Service would never have got into such a pickle with the government in 1940. From the beginning reports from the diplomatic posts were used, Arabic press reports, and monitoring reports from foreign broadcasting stations.

Provoking listeners into writing letters to the BBC in London was not easy. This was one of the functions of the *Arabic Listener*, which was launched in 1939 to publish the cultural talks in a way calculated to arouse interest in the Arab world. From a literary point of view the *Arabic Listener* was a remarkable success. Between nine and ten thousand copies were distributed worldwide, about three-quarters of them in the Middle East. In Arab literary circles the publication was highly esteemed: but this did not give it the kind of contact with popular listener reactions which was available to the British *Listener*. Letters from listeners were few and far between (for example, most of the hundred and twenty-eight received in 1939 were requests for the English lessons pamphlet), and after the entry of Italy into the war in 1940 they virtually dried up altogether. This was, indeed, one aspect of the utter isolation of Britain in the summer of 1940. Arabic letters began to trickle in to the BBC once more in 1943, though of the two hundred and fifty received in that year more than half were from Lebanese migrants living outside the Arab world. When the great effort which was being poured into the Arabic Service is considered, the audience reaction available at this stage was pitifully small.

As the war ended the correspondence increased. It was much stimulated by programmes like *Question and Answer* and *Listeners' Forum*. There were almost seven hundred letters in 1945, of which more than a third came from Iraq, and a good number from North Africa. This was to remain the regional balance of correspondence for some years. Egypt was not a big centre of audience reaction, nor was Palestine. In 1946 there were one thousand five hundred letters, in 1947 two thousand, in 1948 three thousand. This number more than doubled in 1950, and rose to seven thousand five hundred in 1951, after the increase in programme output. In 1951 the Iraqis remained the keenest correspondents, then the Saudi Arabians and the Tunisians.

IV

When the Arabic Service came to organise its talks, it seemed quite natural to employ British officials who worked in the Arab world. It was not strange that Sir Bernard Reilly, the Governor of Aden, who had taken part in the inaugural programme of 1938, should speak on 'A hundred years of British rule in Aden', nor that Harold Ingrams, another prominent member of the Aden Secretariat whose book, *Arabia and the Isles* (1942), was a rather distinguished contribution to British literature on the peninsula, should also speak on the programme. Humphrey Bowman, the then

Director of Education in Palestine, had contributed a talk 'On the education of girls' in 1938: interviewed in 1946 he recorded a personal greeting in Arabic which included the memorable observations:

There is a very strong affinity between the average Englishman and the average Arab . . . for some reason or another God has made us very alike – there is no doubt about that. That is why, in spite of occasional disputes, we always seem to understand one another and remain friends.

These officials from Palestine, Aden, Egypt, loved the Arab world without questioning the dominant place their own country occupied in it. Another was Glubb Pasha, the commander of the Arab Legion in Transjordan, who not only broadcast on the programme but sent it a painstaking memoir on the character that it ought to have. These, and the hunting Major C. S. Jarvis, the author of *The Back Garden of Allah* and the biographer of Peake Pasha, were among the quintessential British 'Arabists'. Other officials were able to contribute technical talks which although unexciting were informative: example are the talks on irrigation in Egypt, Palestine and Transjordan, given by Major Newhouse and by M. G. Ionides.

Some Arabists were more popular with the Service than others. H. St John Philby, the great maverick Arabist of his generation, and a former British government official, although a rebellious one, broadcast on the Service only once, although it was acknowledged that he was one of the very few Englishmen who could broadcast in Arabic without attracting mockery. His name was resolutely excluded from the possible candidates to run the Service, as belonging to someone who was 'persona non grata' to the government. To Sir Ronald Storrs no such blackball was applied, and he contributed two or three talks: the Service also broadcast an interview with Lady Storrs, which gave the listeners some information denied to readers of her husband's lengthy autobiographical memoir, *Orientations*, in which the lady attracted affectionate but scanty mention.

Freya Stark, the great oriental traveller, was an obvious contributor, not only because of her close connection with Stewart Perowne, but also because she had been contributing talks to other BBC Services since the early 1930s. She spoke, for example, on 'Famous women of the East', including Zenobia, the classical Queen of Palmyra, and Lady Duff Gordon. But it may be doubted whether the Freya Stark genre was, in spite of her great experience, ideally adapted for Arab listeners: those qualities which made her an expositor of genius in the West did not help her so much for an Arab audience. Freya Stark was not, however, a government servant at the time of her first broadcasts: she entered government service only temporarily, and during the war.

The other group of British Arabists to whom the Service naturally turned for talks was that of the linguistic scholars, the 'orientalists'. D. S. Margoliouth and H. A. R. Gibb, who both spoke, were the two most distinguished British orientalists living at that time. As the teacher of Hillelson and Paxton Margoliouth, who was now old, was the grandfather of the programme. A whole series of talks by Bernard Lewis, then in the earlier stages of his academic career, gave the history of oriental scholarship in England from its medieval beginnings. Joseph Schacht, the Oxford expert on Islamic law, was also a major contributor, who on one occasion undertook the mammoth task of sifting all the entries to the Arabic Play Competition.

A. J. Arberry, the Cambridge orientalist, was also the collaborator of Rushbrook Williams at the Ministry of Information, and a good friend of the Service almost from the start. He gave many learned talks, of which one was on 'Kushajim the Poet of Cooking', the Chief Cook to the medieval ruler of Aleppo, Saif al-Dawlah. Arberry mixed medieval cooking with modern politics, allowing his propagandist and his learned bents to blend in a bizarre way:

While we are engaged in the high enterprise of ridding the world of Nazi and Fascist barbarism, we can hardly spare the time or the money to partake of such orgies of rare dishes; nevertheless, there is no reason why we should not indulge our intellectual appetites. . .

He was a little more fetching on 'Four poets' in 1941: 'As the world reels under the blows of stark aggression, and one nation after another loses its liberty to inhuman tyranny. . . I turn to browse among the pages of the loved Arabian classics on my bookshelf.' Arberry also added to the catalogue of British oriental studies – 'Professor R. A. Nicholson the British Orientalist', and 'Sufi Studies in Great Britain'. One may wonder what his less learned listeners made of it all. Or what they made of Harold Bowen's *seven* learned talks on 'The Trousers of Virtue', about an aristocratic society for the cultivation of virtue which under the medieval Caliph al-Nasir made its adherents don ceremonial trousers at their initiation.

At a distance of forty-odd years, some of the weaknesses of these academic contributors are more apparent than they were then. These talks were written by, and sometimes also concerned, men who had devoted their lives to oriental scholarship in an almost completely disinterested way. But in a few of them at least there was, as Edward Said has recently pointed out in his book, *Orientalism*, something condescending and even monopolistic in their approach to the eastern world. A weakness of British oriental studies had been that outside India they had tended to be directed to an exclusively western audience: for some orientalist scholars the delivery of their talks on the Arabic Service was the first time they had ever addressed an oriental public. The judgement of that public, when it came, was not always favourable.

For reasons which are explained below, there was very little audience reaction available to the early programme, but when that reaction came after the war it soon became clear that the place for such talks in the programme was much smaller than it had been during the first few years. Paxton remarked of the British orientalists that 'their number and radiogeneity are limited. Some refuse to play, others are dull and academic.' It also became easier after the war to get hold of Arab scholars to cover the same ground in a more authentically Arab way.

From the beginning a warm welcome was extended to Arab literary men when they could be found to broadcast on the programme. At the start they were usually Egyptian, and in the very early days of the programme they were normally Egyptian graduate students studying in England. The relations between the Service and the Egyptian educational establishment were quite close: Paxton had taught at the Fuad I University in Cairo. The connection with the Egyptian Broadcasting Service also gave entry to the Egyptian journalistic and literary establishment. Moreover, Egyptian literary men did not mind picking up an occasional broadcasting fee.

The most distinguished of these contributors was Taha Hussein, who by this point stood at the peak of the Egyptian literary scene. He contributed his first script in May 1938 ('Syria's personality in ancient poetry', an essay on the Christian Umayyad poet, al-Akhtal), and gave a series of unscripted talks on old Arabian literature as late as 1955. Possibly the most interesting were the score or more talks on 'Democratic tendencies in old Arabian literature', broadcast in 1941. There were also readings from some of his published works, notably two stories from the religious series, 'Ala Hamish al-Sira. There were murmurings towards the end of this period that Taha Hussein's influence over the Service was too close. But the prestige of such an author was valuable, particularly outside Egypt in the Maghreb, where intellectuals were pleased to hear his work.

Other Egyptians who took part in the early programme were the academic Ahmed Amin, the poet Tawfiq al-Hakim, the poet and critic, Abbas Mahmud al-'Aqqad (who was particularly appreciated), the scholarly lady, Suhair Qalamawi, and Mahdi Allam. The Syrians and Lebanese were sometimes to be found in London, and were probably located for the programme by a cultivated Manchester Lebanese merchant who worked extensively for the Service, Fadlo Hourani. So there were talks by Lebanese such as the diplomat, Nadim Dimishkiya, businessmen like Emile Bustani, scholars like Sami Haddad and Constantine Zureiq. According to an intelligence report of 1944, complaint that the programme was too highbrow had ceased, and its cultural success was acknowledged in letters which called it 'the university of modern times'.

V

During the war the 'projection of Britain' element in the programme was subordinated to war propaganda needs. The need for commercial propaganda had disappeared: the need to represent Britain as a crusading and valiant-for-truth nation overshadowed everything else. There was a 'Britain in wartime' element in the programme, but this, too, had been directed to showing national pride and pluck. The elderly Lebanese merchant-turned-broadcaster, Fadlo Hourani, gave talks in the summer of 1940 which reflected the way in which the British were counting their blessings at that moment of national danger. 'Fifty Years in England' (where he had arrived as an immigrant in 1891) praised not only the beauty of the countryside but the trim Manchester housing estates where every worker could have a garden: it referred to 'Parliament's Beautiful Influence', and to the voluntary principle in British society exemplified by the Blackheath hospital founded two hundred and fifty years ago by an Aleppo merchant. Hourani's 'Christmas Day in England' (1940) vaunted the plenty of early wartime England: of his own house he said in effect that it snowed with meat and drink (though his womenfolk may have had other views). Mary Dib, a young Palestinian girl who later worked in the programme, gave a naive and charming view of her first year in England, also in June 1940:

The English refer to their country as 'home', maybe because they love their homes so much, that the whole country is 'home' to them. . . Englishmen can control their emotions: they can laugh in cases where others would weep.

But the lyrical mood of 1940 could not endure: the painful slog of war wore down such feelings long before its end.

Paxton said in 1949 that he had always tried to

maintain the balance between talks reflecting Britain and British ideas to the Arabs, and those which dealt with things Islamic or Arabic and their influence in the west; also between translated talks written by Europeans and read by the staff, and those conceived, written and delivered by Arabophones.[9]

In 1950 it was suggested that as a means of projecting Britain there should be a series of programmes dealing with the Arab communities in various towns like Glasgow, Manchester, Leeds, Cardiff, to show how Arabs lived happily and prosperously in the United Kingdom and enjoyed the benefits of its Social Services and the National Health Service, 'though without dwelling too much on the seamy side.'[10] Arabophone talks producers were necessary, and I. H. Rizq and M. Bishuti were among the first.

But the changing mood and composition of the Arab audience in the early 1950s meant that the Service was no longer broadcasting (if it ever had been) to a complacent Arab bourgeoisie with comfortably pro-British tendencies. The audience was beginning to want answers to a lot of very awkward political and social questions. In the 1950s the Arab world was entering a period of revolutionary ferment, and it was impossible that this should fail to make itself felt in audience reaction, or not to have its effect on the programme. The impatient mood of those times in the Arab world comes out in a Libyan letter to the Service in 1950:

Most of your talks are about the English, their prosperity and way of life. We beg you to cease broadcasting such talks because they only create in the Arab listener hatred and malice towards his own nation; since with the exception of a few, we Arabs are deprived of the enjoyments and pleasures of life.

This was a mood of despair which the Englishmen running the Service may well have felt they could do little to address. But the letter is also interesting because it treats the Service as an Arab one which is not compelled to praise life in a foreign country, but may behave in a more Arab way if it pleases.

There was, therefore, a distinction between the talks in which British life was discussed and assessed by Britons, and talks which gave the reactions of Arabs to their stay, brief or long, in England. The visitors were first represented on the programme by Hussein, the fourth son of the Imam of the Yemen, who had visited London for George VI's coronation, and who spoke about his stay in England when he left in February 1938, only a few weeks after the programme began. Two pictures of English life had, he said, remained with him: one of the thousands of people whom he had seen attend an Army tattoo ('military manoeuvres'), and who had sung the hymn, 'Abide with me'. The hymn had been explained to him. 'The beautiful and glorious words rang in my ears. . .,' representing 'the beautiful moral standard of the English nation in this era of tyrannical materialism.' The second picture was that of a young boy strolling on the pavement with a book in one hand and a bar of chocolate in the other. 'This shows the benefits of English culture in encouraging the young to study.' The idyllic vision of English culture did not remain with Hussein for long: when Harold Ingrams visited the Zeidi rulers in the Yemen three years later in 1941 he found that London had made little lasting impression on the 'schoolmasterly' Hussein and his accompanying Minister. 'Neither,' Ingrams reported, 'had much opinion of British civilisation.'[11]

One inevitable topic in the earlier projection of Britain programmes was the colleges of Oxford and Cambridge. The elitist element in such talks came to the surface as early as 1946, apropos of a talk by Adib Nassur, then President of the newly formed Arab Students' Association, called 'How the British ruling classes are brought up at Oxford.' Although it was thought by some listeners to be a charming description of the environment in which the young Nassur found himself, Paxton felt that the emphasis on the aristocratic nature of Oxford education made the talk very superficial, and not a true picture even of the Oxford that he had known twenty years earlier. At a moment when the propagandist accent was to be placed on the achievements of British social democracy in the Attlee government, he felt that the talk gave 'a picture of a Britain which is half

Hollywood and half Franco Spain'.[12] But this did not stop the programme from continuing to commission such talks: in 1949 the two talented sons of the Lebanese writer and teacher, Edward Atiyah, gave successive talks (which their Arabic was apparently good enough for them to write and deliver in the language) on 'Life in an Oxford College' and 'Life in a Cambridge College'. Both were later to achieve high distinction in British academic life, as Oxford Professors of Law and Mathematics.

The list of worthy talks on British democracy, Parliament, local government, transport systems, education, social welfare, trades unions, is endless, and would be tedious to catalogue. That does not mean that the talks themselves were all tedious: some were given by lively people and all by well-qualified people. But that almost all these talks were translated meant that they came over with only a minimum of regard for the special needs and interests of the Arab audience. It was this, perhaps, which made Gordon Waterfield, at least when he first came to the Eastern Service, rather sceptical about the propagandist effects of the Arabic Service, and inclined to feel that it 'tended to reinforce the prejudices of the listeners, or to leave them to stew in their own juice' (although Waterfield continued to favour efforts for the projection of Britain). It is perhaps significant that one of the few series of talks on the British Constitution which aroused genuine listener reaction was that given by an Egyptian, the lawyer Maître Alexander (1944). The post-war series of talks, *Mirror of the West*, was successful in assembling Arabic speakers to describe developments in Britain instead of relying on translations.

The scientific and technical talks (for example, those given in *Student's Period, World of Science, Science and Life*) would again be too many to list. But it is worth noting two or three which reflect the great changes of the age. The first talk on computers seems to have been that on 'Calculating machines' by a Cambridge don, Sam Lilley, in 1945. Another talk on computers, 'The mechanical brain: how far can machines think?' was delivered at the age of twenty by Michael Atiyah, in 1949: it is not surprising that he is now Sir Michael, the Royal Society Professor of Mathematics at Oxford. John Boyd Orr, who became after the war the Director-General of the Food and Agriculture Organisation of the United Nations, gave talks in 1944 and 1949, the second on 'Doubling the World's Food Supply'. This was a topic very close to the interests of the Arab world. Another topic of the future, 'The biological hazards of atomic energy', was broached by Anthony Barnett in 1951. But these were mostly talks which came from other parts of the BBC for translation: the Atiyah talk originated in the Arabic Service.

One 'projection' of Britain which was always popular was that of its language. English lessons were broadcast from very early on in the programme: a second series was launched in 1940. After the war English by Radio continued to be one of the staples of the programme. The lessons could not be transmitted without an Arabic commentary, however, and this had to be supplied by the programme staff. Their reception could be poetic: one listener wrote in 1945: 'give us English lessons after the light dance music, when we should be feeling strong and happy, and ready to listen to the beloved English language.'

VI

Features were a very important part of the output, occupying a large proportion of the growing time in which the Service was on the air. The wide discretion allowed to the producer of a feature meant that in this important field the Arabophone staff had great freedom to make the programme in the shape that they wanted. The BBC also had in the production of features, as Paxton pointed out in 1944, vast technical skill and resources, and he felt that in this field the Service could 'claim to give the Arabs something which they cannot get from their own stations'.

As a new generation was taken on to the programme after the war, some of them very talented broadcasters, a new imprint was given to it. 'Abd al-Rahman Bushnaq, a Palestinian educated at Cambridge, and the former Vice-Principal (until 1948) of the Arab College at Jerusalem, was the senior and the most distinguished of the Palestinian recruits. Leila Tannous (Leila Dawton) was a generation younger than Bushnaq; she was a Lebanese woman who joined the programme briefly after the war in 1945 and returned to it in the early 1950s: Leila Tannous was, with Mary Dib (Mary Barrow), the organiser of the early women's programmes, and was to be important as a features producer in the later programme. In the early 1950s a capable features organiser was Hassan Karmi, the inventor of the long-lived *Saying on a Saying*.

The oldest and most influential of the features was produced by the Intelligence (or Audience Research) Unit in its earlier days, entitled *Listeners' Forum*. This was first broadcast on 24 November 1942, and was in a format which enabled the programme to use its audience research facilities to have a readers' column, 'Nadwat al-Mustami'in'. For example, an August 1945 edition begins with an account of his military service in the British Army from a Syrian Lance-Corporal, follows with a letter from Berbera, Somaliland, requesting a Muhammad Abdul Wahab song (which is played), and ends with the description received from Ismail Khalidi, the Secretary of the Institute of Arab-American Affairs in New York, describing the work of the Institute. The programme was simple, but required firm and skilful handling. Its effectiveness was such that it has continued to the present day. It also spawned numerous derivatives such as *Puzzle Corner, It Happened to Me*, and other correspondence-based features.

The second immensely influential and long-lived feature based on listener research was *Question and Answer*, which first went out on 13 January

1946. *QA* touched one of the most active popular movements in the Arab world, the hydroptic search for miscellaneous knowledge. It was – and is still – a cultural world full of autodidacts, looking for information outside the channels of formal education. It was not an unfamiliar world to the British: there were journalistic equivalents like *Everybody's* and *Enquire Within*, and its distant cousins in British sound broadcasting were the Brains Trusts. The Arabic Service did run Brains Trusts, but they were quite distinct from *QA*, whose absolutely random, ragbag nature had no Home Service equivalent. The clientele of *QA* were the Arab opposite numbers of the clientele of British travelling salesmen for popular encyclopedias, who in the 1940s and '50s had as yet no widespread Arabic version.

The format of *QA* was a brief listener's question and a brief broadcast answer. In 1947 the subjects included honeymoons, the symbolism of the olive tree, the pigeon in Arabic poetry, the age of the earth, television, the hypocrisy of women, the peculiarity of bee and scorpion stings, and 'What was the original colour of human beings?' There has never been any end to the variety of *QA*, and whoever distributes the questions must find people to reply about who invented chess and the steam engine, what is the history of the town of Aden and what is the difference between home and supermarket freezers. Medical questions, science and technology questions, and history questions were and are staple fare. There was also a big spill-over on to the problem page, and a listener was as likely to ask *QA* how to deal with his mother-in-law as how to deal with his piles, though the reader's problem letters were primly rejected, and no Arabic Service agony aunt emerged.

It was nevertheless the biggest foray into popular journalism that the Service had so far made, and its contribution to keeping the Service aware of its listeners was immense, quite apart from its programme value. It also emphasised to the listeners the absolutely catholic nature of the Service, since the questions came not only from all over the Arab world as normally understood, but from East and West Africa and all the outposts of the Arabic language. In its early stage the programme attracted most response from Iraq and North Africa, which was simply a reflection of general listener reaction at that time. An early opinion was that in Iraq there was a disproportionate interest in 'British affairs and the occult'.

The early *QA* programmes sternly discouraged their listeners from posing political questions. But the pressure to answer these stimulated the Service in the early 1950s into launching *Political Question and Answer*, a series which asked for considerable political courage on the part of the Service. Most of the questions for *Political QA* were of a kind likely to be quite unwelcome to the Foreign Office: they were, indeed, exactly the political questions which British official policy did not want to hear. It was a sign of the independence that the Arabic Service had gained from government influence since the end of the war, that *Political QA* was started, and was maintained right through the troubled period of Suez and after.

Another new feature programme to meet Arab social needs was the women's programme which was broadcast from early 1946 onwards (*Woman's Page*, from 2 January 1946; later *Woman's World*). An interesting characteristic of the earlier programmes was that they were broadcast in a slightly simplified standard Arabic, on the supposition that female vocabulary would be much smaller than male. The programme was relentlessly serious, with only an occasional breather for a word on make-up or hair treatment, though perhaps it was not much more earnest than the Home Service *Woman's Hour* which was its exact contemporary. Arab ladies were offered such solid fare as – 'Women and the Social Services: How British Prisons are Controlled Today', 'The Scientific Requirements of Children Under Seven' and 'The Hospital for Mental Diseases in the Lebanon'. Mary Dib took her listeners round the 1947 Ideal Home Exhibition and Leila Tannous and Isa Sabbagh dealt in November 1947 with 'The Royal Weddings'.

Leila Tannous, especially, exercised a healthy scepticism about the 'new Arab woman', and when Emily Bisharat turned up in London on her way to the International Conference for Women's Affairs in the States, Leila described her talks as 'old-fashioned, shallow, and even ridiculous in places' – but she used them, and similar ones like that of Maida Mahmud on 'The new woman in modern Iraq'. The women's programme was, however, dropped in the early 1950s, perhaps because of indifferent audience reaction; but the reason might equally have been the loss of both Mary Dib and Leila Tannous from the Service (though the latter returned). The suspension of the programme was to be regretted, especially because such a high proportion of its items were composed by Arabic speakers.

In the same post-war period the children's programmes found some first-rate serials, of which the best were probably the *Exploits of Brigadier Gerard* and *Treasure Island*. There were also some successful children's competitions. A weekly children's hour had, in imitation of the Home Service children's hour, been broadcast from 1944 under various titles, including *Family Period* and later as the *Programme for Young Listeners*.

The strongly academic element in the early programme had included a lively appreciation of Arabic poetry. In 1940 the Mandaean scholar, Lady Drower, who was then living in Bagdad, suggested that the Arabic Service hold a poetry competition for its listeners. This proved a very successful idea, and a great many entries were received, so many that later poetry competitions were held on a regional basis. The first winner was a Palestinian from Safad with a poem on Shakespeare: Sudanese and Egyptian entries were the runners up with poems on the war in the air. The poetry competitions continued right through the war.

The situation with short stories was a part of the relations between the Service and the Arab literary world. In the post-war period the main contact between the Service and the Egyptian and Syrian literary scenes was the BBC Cairo office assistant, Sharara. When his taste was challenged, as it was, for example, over a story by Bint al-Shati, he replied that he sent the best manuscripts available: 'We cannot bake the pie, but once the baker has prepared it we do our best to give you the best slice.'

Some distinguished writers like Mahmud Taimur contributed stories: his best was the satirical 'How I missed Oxford', which put down this academic disaster to a weakness for the bottle. Darwish al-Gamal was another able writer, who contributed 'Two tickets to Lebanon'. In 1946 an invitation through the Arab press to contribute short stories brought some fifty entries. Muhammad Fathi Abu l'Fadil (who came by way of this competition), Husain Muhammad al-Qabbani, and Ahmad Shukry were other competent writers whom the Service used; Tawfiq al-Hakim's work was used, but only material which had already been published, since his delivery of manuscripts was so notoriously unreliable. Virtually all these writers were Egyptian, though some work was bought from Syrian writers.

Against the modest number of stories which the Service managed to commission or to have read from published work in Arabic must be set the much larger number of stories broadcast in translation. Many of these translations were much appreciated, as audience reaction showed. Inevitably the Arabic Service drew on the huge literary patrimony available to it in English, in other BBC services, and in print. That it did not become a more important literary patron in the Arab world is probably due mainly to its restricted access to that world. It was not due to ignorance: Nevill Barbour and Paxton had both translated well-known Egyptian literary works.

VII

How far, with its limited transmission time and its limited financial resources, the Arabic Service could entertain its listeners, was debatable from the moment the Service was conceived. An Arabic entertainment programme supposes Arabic entertainers. It was impractical to find Arab artistes in London, and during much of the wartime period it was impossible to find and record them in Cairo either. Even when they could be found, and recorded work commissioned from them, the best singers, such as Muhammad Abdul Wahab and Umm Kulthum, were almost prohibitively expensive. Some work could be bought from them, but only occasionally. Nor could Arab actors be hired as a matter of course to record drama in Cairo. Compromises had to be made: gramophone records of music had to be used a lot, rather than special exclusive recordings, and plays had to be read by the announcer-translators and by any Arabophone amateurs who could be found in London. The history of entertainment on the Service is one of compromise.

The first Arabic play broadcast by the Service was on 26 April 1939: the play was produced in studios outside those normally used by the Service, and acted by outside actors. This was too cumbersome and expensive a way to go on. In the war the Service was thrown entirely upon its own resources for a long time. But in May 1942 the first Arabic play competition was launched, with a first prize of £50. The competition was advertised in the Arabic press as far away as North and South America, though there were no transatlantic entries, and the diplomatic post in Mexico wearily reported that the talents of local Arabs were 'more commercial than literary'. The competition was successful: there were a hundred and thirty-four entries from Egypt, thirty-three from Iraq and sixteen from Palestine, besides others from various parts of the Middle East. The final judges were officials from the Egyptian and Iraqi Embassies: poor Dr Schacht in Oxford ploughed through most of the scripts. All three winners were Egyptian, but the competition benefited the Service, as no less than twenty of the plays submitted were broadcast in all. There was a second play competition in 1947. As in the case of stories, most original dramatic works accepted by the Arabic Service came from Cairo by way of the BBC office there, and through the assistant, Sharara. The playwrights overlapped the story writers: Darwish al-Gamal; Muhammad Fathi Abu l'Fadil; Tawfiq al-Hakim; Ahmad Shawki. Some of these had plays produced from work they had already published.

In London the Service used its own talent as much as it could. Ifadat Tawfiq, who worked in the Service, adapted English novels like *Jane Eyre*, which was produced as *The Orphan* (Al-Yatimah 1948); he also adapted Gurji Zeidan's book on Saladin and made dramatic adaptations from the *Thousand and One Nights*. The productions were amateur in the sense that the parts were read by announcer-translators, by ladies working inside the Service like Mary Barrow (Dib) and Leila Dawton (Tannous), and by any literate Arabophone who could be so persuaded. A 1948 note remarks that 'Each play must be clearly analysed by the producer, in order to get the best performance possible out of amateurs.' Paxton had written in 1945:

We pride ourselves on our productions here and that plays are one thing we do really well. However, if the cast peters out completely we may have to fall back on Cairo productions. . . . Much of our programme output is in the nature of carrying coals to Newcastle, and with the paucity of local broadcasting talent in this country we cannot hope to compete with the local Arab stations who have facilities for using the 'stars' that are not available to us.[13]

Entertainment in the sense of variety programmes was a very difficult bill for the programme to fill. There were some attempts during the war, but programmes like 'Café Chaos' were really propagandist exercises rather than entertainments. After the war there was still very little to fall under this heading, until the big expansions of the programme in the mid-1950s.

Music, on the other hand, was a large and integral part of the programme from the early wartime period onwards. The later music programme benefited from the management of N. Basri. In the war the programme offered on the whole recorded music, but with occasional exclusive recordings by Umm Kulthum, Muhammad Abdul Wahab, Asmahan, or someone near that calibre. It was sometimes proposed to import to London especially one of these top-rank singers with a *takht* of three musicians, but the operation was too expensive. After the Cairo Office was fully set up, recordings were made in Cairo in the BBC studio there, and by the end of the war, as is noted above, about a third of the programme allowance was spent in Cairo.

Basri himself recorded numerous songs; and his knowledge of the music of the regions of the Arab world was particularly useful. In 1951, for example, he ran the following musical series: *Your favourite singer, Announcer's choice, Music from the films, Songs from North Africa* and *Songs of South Arabia and the Persian Gulf*. At this point music occupied something like 20 per cent of the programme. A place was also found sometimes for learned and illustrated talks on the history of Arabic music: such a series was run in 1946.

The place for European music in the programme was almost exclusively as introductory or fade-out music, or fill-ups. Listener reaction showed little interest in European music at this time, with the possible exception of the bagpipes.

VIII

The apotheosis of the earlier programme came two years before the retirement of Nevill Barbour, with thirteen 45-minute transmissions on the Arabic language, transmitted between 7 October and the end of December 1954. Two introductory programmes, produced by Barbour himself, dealt with the origins of the language in the Arabian peninsula and its development as a world language, then with its adaptation to modern needs over the preceding century.

Barbour chose for the format of his introductory programmes a conversation with two orphaned Palestinian children, refugees now living in Jordan in Amman. Barbour's feelings intruded into the script: a passage which had the orphaned Zeinab weeping for her lost Palestinian home was edited out, but another was left to say: 'The Jews in Palestine were always saying "Shalom, Shalom" to one another; it means "Salaam" – though they didn't bring peace to us!'

In the course of this programme Barbour has it said: 'I remember that Abd al Rahman 'Azzam, when he was Secretary-General of the Arab League, said [it was said in a BBC broadcast]: "He who lives among us, shares our aspirations, and speaks our language, is one of us." ' It was the main theme of Arab cultural nationalism: the constitution of the Ba'th party said – 'An Arab is anyone whose language is Arabic, who believes in the Arab homeland or aspires to live therein, and who believes in his connection with the Arab people.'

The rest of the language programmes were an impressive assembly of the work of western orientalists, though the BBC made its own contribution with R. B. Serjeant (who had worked on the programme in the war) on the Arabic of south Arabia, and with Hillelson, on 'Dialects and the Arabic language', which was a repudiation of the idea of Hillelson's teacher, Margoliouth, that spoken dialects are 'a mere patois'. Hillelson also had interesting things to say about the difference between 'orientalist' linguistic studies and traditional Arab scholarship, the 'ulum al 'arabiyah. Hillelson opposed to traditional studies the aim of 'modern linguistic science', which was to ask 'what is the nature of language?'

The only oriental scholars to contribute to the programme were Amjad Tarabulsi (Syria), and Matta Akrawi (Iraq). The rest were British, French, and Italian. The most distinguished of the foreign scholars to contribute was Lévi-Provençal, the great authority on Muslim Spain, who wrote on the languages of Al-Andalus and Morocco. The concluding transmission, on 'The Arabic Literary Renaissance', was by Hamilton Gibb, the doyen of British Arabists.

The Arabic language programmes summed up the philosophy of the earlier Arabic Service, which had been the contribution that British Arabists could make through the British-transmitted radio programme to the realisation of a new Arab cultural identity. By 1954, when the Arabic language programmes were transmitted, it was clear that the new Arab cultural identity was indeed being asserted all over the Arab world, and that the new Arab nationalism was to be, for the time being at least, uncompromisingly hostile to some of the British foreign policy aims which the BBC Arabic Service existed to promote.

CHAPTER 5

FROM PALESTINE TO
THE VOICE OF THE ARABS

I

The decision to retain the Overseas Service after the war was in effect shared between the wartime coalition government, which set up both a Cabinet and a Ministerial Committee on the future of the BBC, and the 1945 Labour government which accepted the main conclusions arrived at by its predecessor about the organisation of broadcasting. The Attlee government's White Paper on broadcasting (Cmnd. 6852, 1946) maintained the existing financial relationships to support the Overseas Services, and gave guarantees of BBC independence, and instructions about how the Overseas Services were to be conducted, which have remained of fundamental importance. The complete objectivity of the news bulletins was expressly protected:

The Corporation's reputation for telling the truth must be maintained, and the treatment of an item in an overseas news bulletin must not differ in any material respect from its treatment in current news bulletins for domestic listeners.

The independence of the Overseas Services was similarly guaranteed, though with the proviso that they must keep themselves fully informed by the government departments about official policy:

The government intend that the Corporation should remain independent in the preparation of programmes for overseas audiences, though it should obtain from the government departments concerned such information about conditions in those countries, and the policies of His Majesty's Government towards them, as will permit it to plan its programmes in the national interest.

The apparatus of 'directives' and the like which had been operated during the war was gradually dismantled in 1944–6 as the various regions to which it had been applied by the Political Warfare Executive were freed from enemy control. This was only of marginal importance to the Arabic Service, as the Maghrebi transmissions were discontinued at the end of 1944, and these were the only Arabic ones supervised by the PWE. Ministry of Information supervision of some sort continued over the Arabic Service until the end of the war: in February 1945, for example, the Middle East Division of the MOI was still advising it about the dispute between France and the Syrians and Lebanese over the 'troupes spéciales', the forces the French insisted on maintaining in the Levant.[1]

In March 1946 the MOI was wound up; the White Paper on Broadcasting was issued on 2 July. Almost simultaneously, Sir Ian Jacob, whose wartime experience had been in the Cabinet Office, became Director of Overseas Services. Donald Stephenson had become Director of Eastern Services (which included Persian and Turkish, as well as Arabic), in the preceding year; J. B. Clark remained as Overseas Controller. This experienced team immediately addressed itself to the job of forming a new peacetime relationship with the Foreign Office, in order to put into effect the provisions of the 1946 White Paper.

In September 1946, at a time when events in Iran were beginning to point towards a major international crisis there, Stephenson sent a brief historical account of the BBC Near East Services to the Foreign Office, together with some pointers towards the way in which the Services might in future work with the Foreign Office, in the light of the recent White Paper. In language which in its references to 'positive propaganda' still reflected the attitudes of war rather than those of peace, Stephenson proffered the co-operation of the Near Eastern Service in working out a new publicity policy for Near East matters. While asserting the complete independence and integrity of the BBC news bulletins, he thought that he could properly accept, on behalf of the BBC Near East Services, a 'commitment to give special approach or emphasis to any aspect of HMG's policy in any country or area.' However, he insisted that 'the execution of such a commitment, in so far as it affects BBC output, rests in the hands of the Corporation and its staff.'[2]

The new post-war relationship with the Foreign Office got off to a halting start. Stephenson and Barbour had had serious doubts about the competence of the Middle East Section of the Foreign Office Information Department under Major General A. J. C. Pollock, which they thought 'an uninspiring collection of dugouts'.[3] Stephenson also complained of deliberate 'extra-constitutional practice' by the Foreign Office directed against both the BBC and the press with the object of exploiting the undefined grey areas. In his words, this policy:

mitigates the effectiveness of Foreign Office–BBC co-operation in this field. Barbour and I are acutely aware of the fact that these broadcasts are not operated out of any altruistic regard for the Eastern audience. They are designed to further the policy and enhance the prestige of this country. Unfortunately, there has been no evidence of any desire on the part of the Foreign Office either to leave the responsibility for effective broadcasting strictly in our hands, or alternatively to take the BBC into free collaboration on the basis of an independent professionally competent medium.

Clark minuted this as 'a trenchant but, I think, accurate, statement.' William Haley, who had been Director-General since 1944, commented that 'the position remains that we are not prepared to accept their directives or to operate outside the terms of the White Paper.'[4]

Haley was here expressing the position which he had taken up as early as the end of 1944, in his negotiations with Sir Cyril Radcliffe at the Ministry of Information. However, in the letter in which Radcliffe had acknowledged the right of the BBC, once wartime conditions had ended, 'not to have any political policy towards any of the countries to which it broadcasts,' he also remarked that:

it must always be borne in mind that political policies are likely to be attributed to it [the BBC] by the people or the authorities in the country at the receiving end. It is very difficult to avoid this result when so many blameless contributions may appear to have political significance, and when allowance is made for the fact that the BBC is known to enjoy the monopoly of foreign broadcasting and to enjoy a special relationship with the government. We cannot help this. But it is an aspect of the matter that it might be advantageous to bring home to those engaged in serving the BBC's foreign-language broadcasts.[5]

Both Haley and Radcliffe talked sense, even if they sometimes sounded like two gods shouting to each other across Mount Olympus. Radcliffe's qualification expressed a real doubt in the official mind, and one that was not entirely unreasonable. There are always going to be occasions when the BBC's broadcasts to foreign countries are taken in those countries to express government policy, when they do not, and this is always going to constitute an area of uncertainty for British foreign policy, though experience has shown the hazard to be a very minor one in practice. The kind of views expressed by Stephenson showed the conscientious determination of BBC officials of his generation to broadcast in the national interest, even if they were impatient of fussy Foreign Office interference in the way they did the job.

The real ground for future conflicts between the Corporation and the government in these matters was the quite different one of the reporting by the BBC in its overseas services of press or parliamentary opposition to official foreign policy. Such reporting was expressly protected by the White Paper's stipulating that overseas news bulletins should not substantially differ from domestic ones, but it could and on one or two important occasions has proved to be a serious political embarrassment to the government. There had been clashes of this kind over the appeasement issue in BBC–government relations in the 1930s, but disputes over the overseas broadcasts had hardly occurred. Perhaps the only wartime example is the protest by Lampson in Cairo over BBC reporting of the *Times* leader against the Chamberlain government's conduct of the war, in May 1940: this protest went no further, since the government it concerned ceased to exist. The repetition of such clashes was not foreseen in 1946.

II

The most contentious issue confronting the Arabic Service in 1946 was that of Palestine. It was not, in the normal course of things, contentious between the BBC and the Foreign Office. But it was an issue which had shown its explosive nature before the Arabic Service had finished its inaugural broadcast on 3 January 1938, and which had remained important for the Service ever since.

The White Paper on Palestine was issued on 17 May 1939. It remained the public basis for British policy until the Anglo-American Committee of Inquiry was announced on 13 November 1945: the decision to abandon the policies of the White Paper was taken in Cabinet on 25 January 1944, but both that decision and the preparatory discussions of the Cabinet Committee remained well-kept secrets. The Arabic Service had therefore for most of its existence been committed to the defence of a future for Palestine based on the goal of an independent bi-national state: the White Paper specifically stated that it was not part of British policy that Palestine should become a Jewish state. Further Jewish immigration was limited by the 1939 White Paper to a total of seventy-five thousand immigrants spread over five years. As a result, the Palestine created by the contemplated end of the Mandate would be a society with a large Arab majority. This represented the action of a British government which had drawn back before the drastically negative reactions of the Arab states and the Palestinian population to the partition proposed by the 1937 Peel Commission. The White Paper formed part of a strategy to defend British interests in the Arab world of which the Arabic Service itself formed another (though a different and minor) part.

It was not hard for the men leading the Arabic Service to defend the White Paper. We know most about the views held by Nevill Barbour, who wrote a detailed survey of the Palestine controversy, *Nisi Dominus* (although he wrote most of it before the war, it was not published until 1946). Chronologically Barbour's book went as far as the Bevin decision to set up the Anglo-American Committee, taken on 13 November 1945. When it was issued it was, therefore, an up-to-the-minute political pamphlet, and not one which he could have published had he been in government service. The dust jacket included a reference to his duties in the MOI, but tactfully excluded any reference to the BBC.

Nisi Dominus uncompromisingly put the Arab case on Palestine, and with equal conviction attacked the Zionist aim of a separate Jewish state. Although he called the 1939 White Paper 'a rather curious compromise', Barbour defended its application during the war period, including the British immigration controls and their part in the tragic sinkings of the refugee ships, the *Patria* and the *Struma*. He also welcomed the setting up of the Arab League, which Barbour said held out a 'dazzling prospect' for the revival of the Arab world. The book candidly adopted the Arab cause. Its conclusion was that to recommend the establishment of a Jewish state in Palestine:

would involve a complete reversal of British policy and be the repudiation of assurances given to the Arabs on many occasions during the last twenty-eight years; it would cause a turmoil in the Near East of which the results cannot be foreseen.

Evidence of such a detailed kind about the opinions of its members is harder to find for other officials of the Arabic Service. The only other member of the Service to write a book containing clear implications about some of his views on Palestine was Emile Marmorstein (1909–1983), the learned son of a scholarly Jewish family, who was one of the main strengths of the Intelligence Section (subsequently Listener or Audience Research) from 1941 until his retirement in 1971. Marmorstein (like Barbour) worked as a journalist in Jerusalem in the mid-1930s. In later life he appeared a 'venerable and rabbinical figure'. In 1969 he published *Heaven at Bay: the Jewish Kulturkampf in the Holy Land*, a book of some two hundred pages dealing with the conflict between secular Zionist and religious values in modern Jewish history and in the state of Israel. Throughout the book Palestine is referred to as 'the Holy Land' and Israel is referred to, when the text demands it, as 'the State'. Although a whole chapter devoted to the clash between secular and religious values in Israel after 1948 is called 'Confrontation in the State', the name of the state of Israel is never once mentioned (except in quotations), either in that chapter or any other.

Nothing in Marmorstein's book identifies him as pro-Arab; but everything in it shows him to have been passionately opposed on religious grounds to Zionism. What few references to Arabs there are partake of the same spirit of irony as informs the book as a whole: for example, referring to the 'Young Hebrew' doctrine of Jewish leadership of 'local ethnic groups' in the Levant, he remarks that 'Arabs could hardly be expected to take more notice of spirited manifestos in favour of Semitic unity than of the confessions of guilt and protestations of love which elderly exponents of Western liberalism have periodically issued' (perhaps he had in mind Arnold Toynbee's Reith Lectures, *The World and the West* (1953)). Elsewhere, however, he made it clear that he disapproved of Arab nationalism just as much as of Zionism. Marmorstein was not a remote scholar, but a man passionately interested in day-to-day political and social life. He is said to have been intensely English in his tastes, loyalties and prejudices.[6]

Barbour corresponded in some respects (as does Perowne to a perhaps greater degree) to the stereotype of the orientalist Englishman whose sympathy for things Arab may have had a romantic or sentimental origin. But the cases of Marmorstein and Hillelson show how very far the early Arabic Service was from being staffed by a pro-Arab lobby in the normally understood sense of the phrase.

The evidence on how the Arabic Service treated the Palestine question during the war is on the thin side for the simple reason that prudence instructed it to avoid scratching at wounds which were hardly beginning to heal. From the point of view of the competition with enemy broadcasts, the BBC found it difficult to cope with the way in which German and Italian propagandists exploited the Palestine issue. A 1941 memorandum dated shortly after Eden's statement on British support for the idea of Arab unity said:

> while the Zionist question and Palestine form the principal theme of Axis broadcasts to the Near East, the subject is passed over in virtual silence by the BBC. This is due to the general character of the directives received by the BBC and to the nature of the information supplied by [diplomatic] posts in Arab countries. There is evidence to show that the effect of the present handling of the subject of Zionism and Palestine in enemy and British broadcasts, taken in conjunction with the published statements of Zionist leaders, is to create suspicion in the minds of Arab listeners. The impression is created that a sort of taboo on the subject exists in British circles and that behind this silence there are being prepared measures which would be far from acceptable to Arab opinion.[7]

It was a suspicion to be amply justified by events.

The task of the British propagandists broadcasting to Arab lands was far from easy. Official guidance on the whole sought safety by imposing silence: in October 1943 Hillelson was still complaining that 'persistent silence on topics with controversial implications might be interpreted as default.' The enforcement of the immigration laws in Palestine against Jewish immigrants coming from Europe was a notorious example of the political difficulties which faced the Service. Government advice on the subject varied at various stages of the war, and was sometimes contradictory. In 1940 the Foreign Office somewhat cynically asked for publicity to be given in the Overseas Service to the detention in internment camps of the passengers of the SS *Sakariya* 'in bulletins to Turkey and the Balkan countries (as a deterrent), and in Arabic (to cheer them up).'[8]

On the other hand, the shadow of American Zionism lay over Palestinian policy even before the entry of the United States into the war. Rushbrook Williams in the Ministry of Information in May 1941 told Hillelson that he was not, for fear of antagonising the Zionist sympathisers in President Roosevelt's entourage, to publicise measures which the British Palestine government took to enforce the immigration laws. Hillelson objected that it made little difference to Zionist feeling on the subject whether the Arabic Service announced the measures or not.[9]

The depth of sympathy in the Arabic Service for the Palestinian Arabs can most easily be seen in the attitude to Haj Amin al-Husseini and the other exiled members of the Muslim Supreme Council in Palestine. In spite of Haj Amin's activities in the Rashid Ali regime in Iraq in 1941, and of his transfer to Germany and subsequent broadcasts from Berlin, Hillelson and Barbour were very reluctant to treat him in broadcasts as an enemy. In February 1942, Hillelson was telling the MOI that:

There is no conclusive evidence that Haj Amin al-Husseini has made violently anti-British statements either during the Iraqi rising or recently in Berlin. The Germans claim him as an ally, but there is nothing on record to show he has accepted this role. However, for propaganda purposes we could interpret his presence in Berlin as evidence of hostility.

But Hillelson was reluctant to behave in this way.

There is no evidence that Haj Amin al-Husseini is a corrupt and self-seeking politician, and many Arabs, especially in Palestine, take the view that his attitude is dictated by disinterested and patriotic motives. Attacks on his integrity might have the effect of alienating those Arabs who regard him as a sincere if misguided patriot, and as a religious person of great eminence.

Nor was Hillelson alone among British officials in feeling this: in fact an attack on Haj Amin was mounted in a BBC Arabic talk on 24 August 1942, but officials in Jerusalem thought it did more harm than good.[10]

Hillelson and Barbour took a rather similar line in a report they made to Military Intelligence on Jamal Husseini, another Palestinian nationalist leader. Hillelson wrote:

I met Jamal Husseini a number of times and believe him to be an honest, fanatical adherent to the cause of Arab nationalism, and I was much impressed by the straightforward way he gave his evidence before the Royal Commission [of 1937]. He always admired Haj Amin, and his political attitude was one of uncompromising nationalism. . .

Barbour wrote:

Personally, I liked him. There is no doubt that he holds his views strongly, but he appeared to me to be an honest man who would, I think, not say that he agreed with you if he really did not do so, and who would, I think, carry out any agreement that he made.[11]

These were charitable judgements to make on two of the main leaders of the Arab revolt in Palestine.

The final years of British Mandate Palestine from the end of 1945 to the termination of the Mandate in May 1948 were not happy ones for the Arabic Service. It was the beginning of a bleak period for British Middle East policy, when the post-war economic exhaustion and the new relationship with the United States were making it impossible to implement traditional foreign policy aims. The failure to renegotiate treaties with Arab powers anywhere save in Transjordan indicated the decline of British power and influence, but the collapse of the Palestine policy was central. The Arabic Service documentation which survives is scanty, but much of what remains complains on the BBC side of the inadequate briefing by government departments, and of a general lack of guidance on what was to be said. Paradoxically, in Mandate Palestine itself, the BBC service became much more important to the Arab population, because of the greatly increased severity of the censorship imposed by the Mandate government, especially after January 1946. The Arabic Service accepted the advice of the Colonial Office to suppress mention of the Reuters despatch by Kimche on British Palestine policy issued on 22 September 1945.[12] But normally the Arabic Service followed the Overseas Service bulletins; and in April 1946, when it was realised that the severity of the Palestinian censorship had increased listening in Palestine, it was decided to give news in fuller detail in the Arabic bulletins.[13]

Throughout the Palestine negotiations the Arabic Service maintained close contacts with the Arab side, especially after the setting up of the Arab Offices early in 1946. Their head, Musa Alami, visited the Arabic Service in July 1946, and in April 1947 the Service made joint arrangements with the Arab Office and the Arab News Agency for coverage of the UN Meetings in New York. In September 1946 the main Arab leaders attending the London Conference, including Feisal of Iraq, Abdullah of Transjordan, Feisal of Saudi Arabia and Abdul Rahman Azzam, the Secretary General of the Arab League, all spoke on the Service.[14] As the Attlee government started to take the conclusive decisions on Palestine, it became increasingly important for the Service to be in close touch with the Foreign Office. In February 1947, at the critical time of the reference of the Palestine question by Britain to the United Nations, Harold Beeley of the Foreign Office included the Arabic Service in the Information Department briefings.[15]

The uncertainty and disarray of British official circles in the weeks following the final British withdrawal of 15 May 1948 are made clear in a memorandum by Barbour, at that time the Assistant Head of the Eastern Service, to the East European Service, dated 3 June (i.e. a week before the first Palestine truce). 'My guess,' he wrote, 'as to the mind of the Foreign Office is the following. I doubt if there is any clearcut plan. The overriding principle is, I imagine, not to do anything which would, in the event of a war, prejudice our having at least that degree of good will in and facilities from the Arab states which we enjoyed in the last war.'[16] This is not the alarmist language it may seem: the Foreign Office and Bevin himself were very concerned about the possibility of Jewish attacks on the territory of Transjordan which would entail British military intervention under the Transjordan treaty.[17]

Given Barbour's known views about Palestine, it is not surprising that he still clung to the remnants of earlier British ideas on a bi-national Palestinian state:

It can be taken as certain that the Arab governments cannot accept an entirely independent Jewish state. . . Anglo-American policy must therefore be to try and induce the Jews to accept something less than an entirely independent Jewish state. . . Even the UNSCOP plan itself envisaged that the Jewish state should be linked with an Arab state in Palestine under an economic board in which UNO representatives would exert a decisive influence. The existing Israel appears on the contrary to have hoped by the use of military force to enlarge its territory, to absorb western Galilee, and to become quite independent. . . The FO's policy must therefore I believe be primarily one of educating the American government and public opinion on the elements of the Palestinian situation, the ultimate objective remaining international trusteeship or possibly a Jewish autonomous area, or if you like 'state', within a predominantly Arab federation, whose federal government would exercise control over immigration.

Nevill Barbour's views as shown in this memorandum are not 'pro-Arab' in the sense of being evidently dictated by sentimental sympathy with the Arabs. They are certainly unfriendly to the idea of a fully independent Jewish state, but so were the ideas of the British Foreign Office as revealed by recent research in its papers. Professor Louis thinks that Foreign Office officials in London reconciled themselves for the first time to the conclusion that there would be a Jewish state in mid-June of 1948: in other words, Barbour's thinking was only a matter of weeks behind that of Harold Beeley and the official British view.[18]

It is a matter of some interest for the history of the Arabic Service, since it would be easy, but misleading, to represent the Service as run by a small clique of prejudiced 'Arabists' whose bias came from their own personal sympathies. In reality the Service made a continuous effort to understand and interpret official British policy. Its problem was that in Palestine official policy had been overtaken by events to a disastrous degree, and that when the whole Middle East was in the melting pot, as it was in June of 1948, the information services which were supposed to interpret government policy had to wait until there was one. It was in those confused and unhappy circumstances that figures like Barbour in the BBC had to guess what government policy was: his doubt whether 'there is any clear-cut plan' was at that moment an entirely justified one.

The first big defeats of the Egyptian army in the autumn of 1948 were as painful a surprise to the Arabic Service as they were to the British government. To the review of the British press which went out on 24 October it was found necessary to preface an apology:

There is no doubt that some of the quotations we are obliged to mention this week will be found surprising and disagreeable by our Arab listeners. Nevertheless, we feel it to be our duty to give our listeners a frank and truthful account of what the British press is actually saying.

And the broadcast went on to quote the *Times* on the Egyptian defeats in the Negev, including its reference to the 'poor fighting spirit of the Egyptian soldier'.

III

In August 1949, a few months after the end of the Palestine War, Bevin circulated a memorandum to the Cabinet about the changed British position in the Middle East. It contains a sentence which is of importance in showing the terms in which British official policy saw the Middle East,

Above: *Four Heads of the Arabic Service:* (left to right) *Hamilton Duckworth (1976–81), Charles McLelland (1971–76), Gordon Waterfield (1959–63), James Thomson (1964–71)*

Below: *Amir (later King) Feisal of Saudi Arabia with Sigmar Hillelson, Director of Near Eastern Services during the Second World War*

Right: *Emir (later King)
Idris of Libya broadcasting in
the Arabic Service in July
1947*

Centre right: *The great
Egyptian writer Taha
Hussein, photographed in the
Arabic Service in 1949*

Far right: *George Masri in
the 1986 Arabic drama
adaptation of John le Carré's*
The Spy Who Came in
from the Cold

Below: *Ahmed Suleiman
(second from right) with
studio guests during a 1960
production of his popular
programme* Fi al Mahdif

Below right: *Hassan Karmi
interviewing the future King
Hassan of Morocco during a
visit to London in September
1957*

Far left: *Musa Bishuti, one of the longest-serving members of the Arabic Service, seen here in 1955*

Centre left: *Fadlo Hourani is seen sifting through Arabic correspondence in October 1944*

Below left: *While judging a listeners' competition in 1987, Rashad Ramadan* (centre) *discusses an entry with colleagues and fellow judges*

Left: *In 1947 the future King Saud recorded a message for broadcasting by the Arabic Service*

Below: *Donald Stephenson* (standing second from left), *as Director of the Eastern Services, seen with the Yemeni delegation to the London conference on Palestine in 1946*

Above: *Edward Atiyah
(second from right) takes
part in an Arabic discussion
programme in 1954*

Right: *Naim Basri, seen here
in 1944, was for many years
responsible for the Arabic
Service's music*

Above right: *Robert
Serjeant, later to be Professor
of Arabic at Cambridge, seen
in 1944* (second from left)
when he was editor of the
Arabic Listener

Below right: *Evelyn Paxton
(standing right) with a
Kuwaiti visitor and members
of the Arabic Service in 1957*

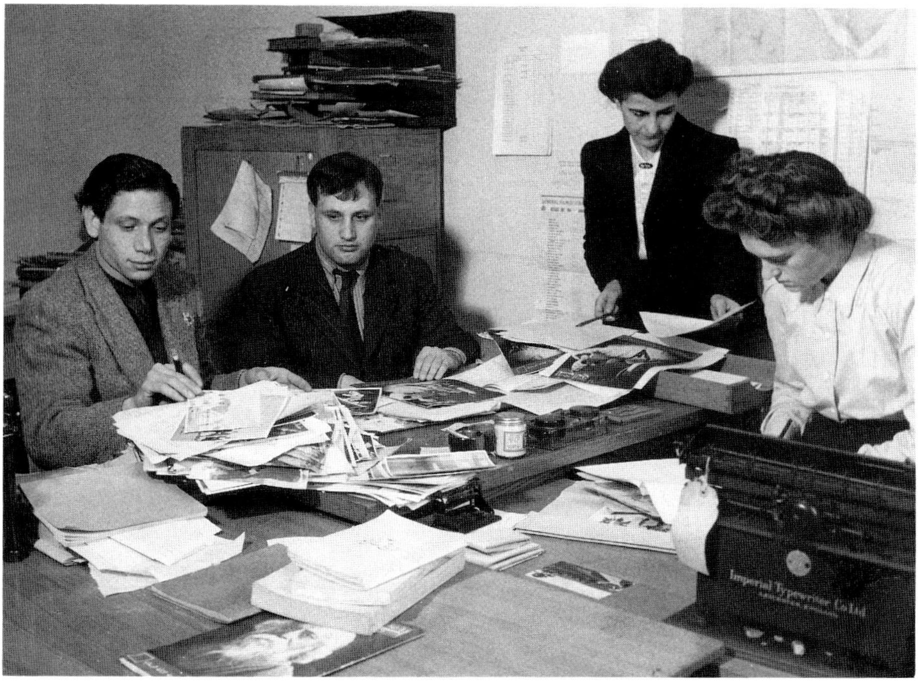
Imperial Typewriter Co Ltd

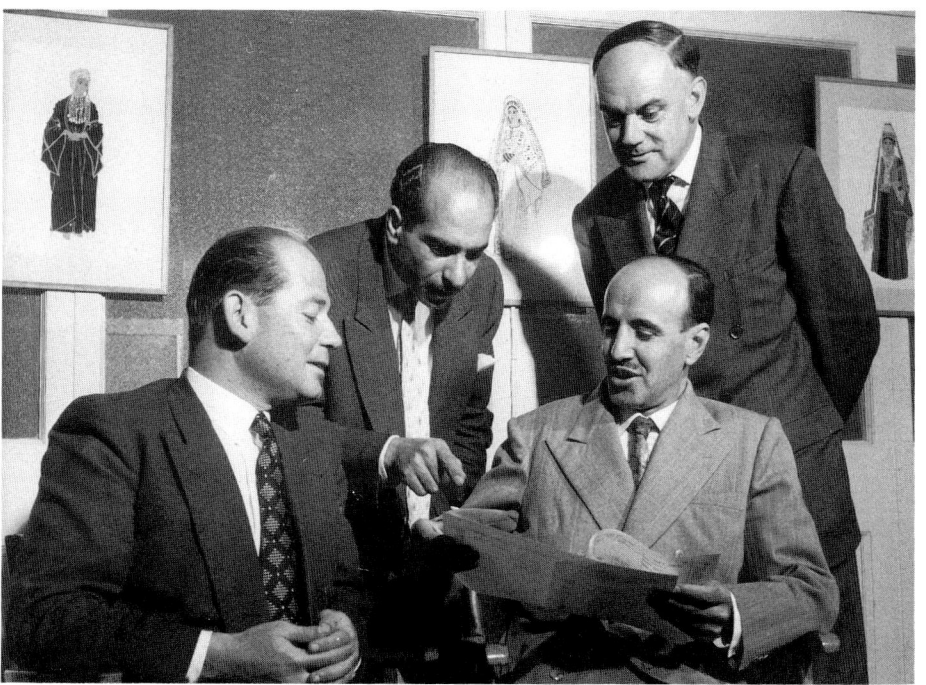

Far left: *At the celebrations of the Service's tenth anniversary in 1948 the Minister at the Lebanese legation Victor Khoury* (third from left), *is seen in conversation with Sir Ian Jacob, later to be Director-General of the BBC* (left) *and Director-General Sir William Haley* (centre)

Below left: *Arab staff of the Arabic Service in 1955, with Naim Basri* (seated centre)

Left: *Nadim Sawalha, actor and broadcaster, seen in 1970 while presenting the popular series* Music Shop

Below: *Fairuz during one of her visits to the Arabic Service, here seen in 1961 with the Rahbani brothers and with the producer Yacoub Musallam*

Above: *Richard Williams,*
a BBC special correspondent,
photographed during an
assignment in Palestine in
April 1948

Right: *Hamilton Duckworth,*
later to become Head of the
Arabic Service, at the 1968
Farnborough air show in his
capacity as Programme
Organiser

Above: *Nuha Batchone interviewing the Egyptian writer Jadhbiya Sidqi* (left) *for the programme series* Woman's Corner *in 1960*

Left: *Ali Nour, Egyptian artist and art editor of the* Arabic Listener *is seen here at work in the Arabic Service in October 1944*

Right: *Eric Bowman, Head of the BBC Arabic Service, 1981–86*

Below: *Muhammad Abdul Wahab, musician and composer, was escorted by Naim Basri* (left) *and Hamilton Duckworth* (third from left), *when he visited BBC Television Centre in 1962*

Left: *James Norris, Head of the BBC Arabic Service, 1986–88*

Below left: *Bob Jobbins, Head of the BBC Arabic Service, 1988–*

Below: *One of the earliest and most popular Arab broadcasters in the BBC, seen here during the Second World War, was Isa Sabbagh*

Right: *Two future Kings of Saudi Arabia seen on a visit to the BBC during the Second World War: the Amir Feisal* (seated) *and the Amir Khaled* (standing second from right) *with the Saudi Minister Sheikh Hafiz Wahba* (extreme left)

Below: *Director-General Sir William Haley in conversation with Isa Sabbagh and other members of the Arabic Service in 1945; the first Arab announcer of the BBC, Ahmed Kamal Sourour, is on the right of the picture*

Above: *The Board Room at Broadcasting House on 3 January 1938 and five men who broadcast inaugural messages for the Arabic Service: Sir Bernard Reilly, Governor of Aden; Sheikh Hafiz Wahba, the Saudi Minister in London; the Amir Seif-al-Islam Hussein of Yemen; Rauf al Chadirji, Minister for Iraq; and the Egyptian* chargé d'affaires *in London, Abdel Rahman Haqqi*

Left: *Singer Sabah (right) in 1986 with the producer of the Arabic Service Arts Magazine, Salwa Jarrah*

Above: *Gordon Waterfield, Head of the Arabic Service from 1959–63, previously Head of the BBC's Eastern Service which included Arabic until 1959*

Right: *Ronald Icke, who retired in 1987 after nearly thirty years in the Arabic Service, mainly in News and Presentation, of which he was Organiser at the end of his career*

and which had important implications for information policy. 'We must never under-rate,' states the memorandum, 'the political and psychological preoccupation of all Arab governments and peoples with the Palestine question.'[19] That Bevin chose to emphasise the importance of peoples as well as of governments, and that he did so in the context of their political psychology and not just of the flow of political events, meant that so long as that view of things prevailed, British official policy had to place a high value on the supply of British news and information to the Arab world. Moreover, Bevin was expressing a collegiate rather than a personal view, and Foreign Office thinking about the Palestine factor in the Middle East changed little after the end of the second Attlee administration in 1951. This meant that the Eastern Service continued in the long term to get some priority in Foreign Office treatment of the BBC Overseas Services.

It was fortunate for the Arabic Service that this was so, since the BBC Overseas Services were under considerable pressure in this period from rising expenses, and successive governments were reluctant to pay a bigger foreign broadcasting bill.[20] In April 1951, in reply to an enquiry from the Foreign Secretary as to what evidence there was that the BBC's overseas broadcasts were in fact effective, the Middle East department said that reports from representatives in Arab countries revealed that large Arab audiences listened to the BBC, and that this fact was reflected in the press and radio of the Middle East countries. The international news broadcasts by the BBC were generally believed, and a large number of Middle East newspapers used the broadcasts as their main source of foreign news.[21]

At this time the fortnightly meetings at the Foreign Office on Eastern and Far Eastern policy which were attended by the BBC were said by their organisers to be a valuable exercise. The BBC, J. S. H. Shattock of the FO wrote ruefully, 'always put their fingers on the subjects which cause us the greatest amount of difficulty.' At the meetings the Foreign Office representatives gave the BBC a certain amount of confidential background information, and they found that their confidences were respected. It may be added that this was not a privilege reserved to the BBC, since it has on many occasions been extended to selected journalists. The BBC representatives showing the greatest interest were the 'Head of the Middle East Department' (by whom Gordon Waterfield, the Head of the Eastern Service, is probably meant), the general diplomatic correspondent, and the general feature writer.[22]

There was no deep disagreement in the Foreign Office about the value of the Arabic Service, nor was there any reluctance to allow the BBC a proper independence in the control of its news presentation and its programmes. An FO circular of January 1949 set out clearly the position about both questions, basing itself on the 1946 White Paper. The circular adds that the Information Policy Department was responsible for justifying to the Post Office and the Treasury the expenditure for the BBC Overseas Service: this financial responsibility was to be of great importance during the debates of the early 1950s. The personal contacts were, of course, of great practical importance: in 1949 the FO directed that complaints about the BBC were to go to G. A. Warner (who had been connected with the Overseas Service since its earliest days), and that Warner should take them up personally with Sir Ian Jacob if he saw fit. A circular of 1951 restated the position, that Foreign Office control over the Overseas Services is limited to prescribing the countries to which programmes are directed, the languages used, and the times of transmission.[23]

In the spring of 1952 the Foreign Office submitted to the Select Committee on Estimates a paper on their relations with the Overseas Services which would have later saved them from much travail, had they stuck more closely to the ideas which they expressed there. The paper emphasised strongly the close co-operation which in fact obtained between the two organisations, and said that 'both the shape and content of the various foreign language broadcasts and the nature of the other activities of the Overseas Services are determined as a result of joint consultation.' The BBC, the paper says:

interpret their obligation to 'plan and prepare their foreign programmes in the national interest' with a high sense of responsibility. . . Any formal policy control by the Foreign Office would not only be inconsistent with the terms of the License and Agreement, but would also undermine the reputation for independence and objectivity which the BBC gained during the war and has since retained . . .

The key to this amicable attitude perhaps lies in the conclusion, which has a caveat that 'the present satisfactory state of affairs rests largely on good personal relations which have been built up over a period of years between the officials of the two organisations, and on the experience and expertise of the principal BBC officials concerned.'[24] The future was to show that failure to preserve mutual trust between the BBC and the government could lead to disagreeable consequences for both.

In the same post-war period a debate was going on within the Arabic Service about the way in which the transmissions ought to develop. Stephenson in typically trenchant fashion wrote in 1947, apropos of recording tours in the Middle East, that recorded programmes ought to be kept within due bounds:

The Arabic Service is primarily a news and information service from London. In the next place, it is a service offering Arabic programmes evolved from our own resources both as to staff and material. Only thirdly is it a medium for the transmission of Arabic programmes originating wholly or in part outside this country.[25]

At a time when a third of the programme allowance was being spent on material put together in Cairo, this was an interesting statement: Stephenson was evidently not keen on allowing the reliance on Middle East material to increase further. However, from 1949 the news and information part of the programme was itself directly influenced by a supply of material from the Middle East, in the shape of the information and commentaries supplied by the Arab News Agency.

The two topics to which discussion always returned were the priority which ought to be accorded to the 'projection of Britain', and the degree to which the Service ought to aim to become an Arabic-thinking service appealing to specifically Arab interests and local Arab concerns, and with its own Arabic style. Paxton in 1949 was arguing for an authentically Arabophone programme, even at the price of some seeming naivety of presentation, and of neglecting British 'Arabist' contributions:

> I have always endeavoured to maintain the balance between talks reflecting Britain and British ideas to the Arabs, and those which deal with things Islamic or Arabic and their influence on the west; also between translated talks written by Europeans and read by the staff, and those conceived, written and delivered by Arabophones. There are occasions when I feel it is better to let an Arabophone research student go on the air, than to broadcast a learned talk by some eminent European scholar who may not be understood or appreciated since his name is probably known to few of our listeners. . . Arabic plays or short stories would seem naive to western critics, but again there is the question of balance; and to give nothing but translations of western material would defeat our object.[26]

On the other hand, some substantial presentation of the British way of life there must be, and as was remarked at the time, an unmistakable flavour of bacon and eggs is likely to hang over an honest attempt to do this. Listener reaction was not always favourable; 'Give us more plays and talks on Arab themes!' was a constant cry from correspondents.

But in spite of the deep disagreements between the BBC and successive governments about the financial support to be given to the Overseas Service, the Arabic Service did better than most. In 1951 it gained an extra hour, and an extra fifteen minutes in 1952, bringing the total broadcasting time to four hours daily. At a time of heavy cuts, when the only other service to be increased was that to East Germany, the 45 per cent increase accorded to Arabic Service output shows the value which the Foreign Office attached to it.

The Drogheda Committee which sat in 1953 to examine overseas information work in general, including the External Services of the BBC, never reported in full. It heard a great deal of evidence, including a paper on BBC services to the Middle East. Its conclusions were part-published in 1954 (Cmnd. 9138), but those relating to the External Services were not implemented, either as to cuts or as to increases. The recommendation to spend £160,000 on increases in the Middle Eastern and Far Eastern services, increasing the Arabic Service transmission by thirty minutes, was not effected, nor was the recommended capital investment in new transmitters.

While Lord Drogheda's Committee was sitting in the summer of 1953, changes were taking place in the field of Middle East information which made the deliberations of that august body out of date before they had been typed. The British government had been locked in diplomatic conflict with Egypt over the future of the Canal bases and the British military presence, ever since the end of the war. In 1951–2 the political disagreement led to something close to guerrilla warfare in the Canal Zone, and to the explosion of popular discontent in the burning of Cairo in January 1952.

The revolution of July 1952 and the seizure of power by Brigadier Neguib and a group of 'Free Officers' made the existing clash with Britain even more acute. But the nature of the conflict was changed by the 1952 revolution. It is true that the diplomatic aims of the Free Officers' government in Egypt were not, so far as they concerned British withdrawal from the bases, so very different from the aims of earlier Egyptian governments. But the Pan-Arab, populist, and, eventually, neutralist policies of the Free Officers made them into a new sort of government, which the British had virtually no experience in dealing with.

The new Egyptian regime launched on 4 July 1953 an instrument which changed the face of Arabic-speaking radio, and which exploited radio propaganda in a way completely new to the Arab world. This was the 'Voice of the Arabs', which expanded rapidly from its first half-hour daily transmission to become the fullest, best-subsidised, and most aggressive political radio service in the Arabic language. From using a power of 72 kW on medium wave in 1952, Egyptian foreign-directed radio acquired a power of 560 kW for short- and medium-wave transmissions by 1956. Since, for the first few years of its existence, British policy in Egypt was one of the main targets of the Voice of the Arabs, the BBC Arabic Service suddenly found itself serving in a new radio front-line.

IV

One of the recommendations of the Drogheda Committee had been to accord high priority to providing the BBC with a high-power medium-wave transmitter in Cyprus. This was effectively to go back to the original recommendations of 1937, and the BBC had complained bitterly for years that nothing of the kind had been done. There was, however, a difficulty which was occasioned by official secrecy. This concerned the existence of the Near East Broadcasting Station (Sharq al-Adna), which had been transferred from Jerusalem to Limassol in the spring of 1948, just before the end of the Mandate, and which was given powerful medium-wave transmitters in 1955.[27] Although technically operated by a commercial company, Sharq was almost certainly controlled by one of the secret agencies: there is, for example, no mention of it in the list of commercial broadcasting stations in the colonies, which was produced by the Colonial

Office for the Beveridge Broadcasting Report in 1949.[28]

As Gordon Waterfield observed in 1950, the Near East Association (as Sharq al-Adna was then known) was a hangover from the war period and was in an anomalous position surrounded by secrecy, which made any planning or co-operation between the BBC and Sharq al-Adna difficult if not impossible. 'It is,' he continued, 'an expensive outfit. At a time when there is a demand for economy in government expenditure it is in a weak position. The time has come for the BBC to put forward plans for a more extensive coverage through Arabic broadcasts of the important Middle East area.' Waterfield argued, and the BBC continued subsequently to argue, that the Corporation could do the work as effectively, if not more effectively, and at less expense. He also argued that it was easier for the BBC, at times of political crisis in the Middle East, to keep in close touch with Whitehall than it was for Sharq al-Adna in Cyprus.[29]

Continued official secretiveness about the files makes it very difficult to know what post-war Foreign Office thinking about Sharq al-Adna was. It is possible that its continued attachment to this wartime way of doing things was simply due to the conviction that Sharq al-Adna was a valuable information asset which did not have to be justified in the parliamentary vote, and which was swept through in the secret estimates. Bringing the Sharq al-Adna station into the open might have had the effect of reducing the total information budget: the Foreign Office may well have thought that one secret transmitter in the hand was worth two public ones in the bush. The events of 1956–8 were to show that this pessimism (if that is what it was) was unjustified, but this could not have been safely predicted in 1950.

It is necessary to discuss these things at some length, because Sharq al-Adna was not merely a convenient, though secret, device to increase the flow of British-inspired information to the Arab world. It was, in effect, the light programme to the BBC's Arabic Home Service, but by 1955 with the advantage of medium-wave transmission which got it blared out in all the taxis of Cairo and Beirut. All the audience research surveys of the period show it enjoying a very high rating indeed in the listening habits of the Middle East area. It operated according to a very successful formula of light music and entertainment interspersed with short news bulletins. It employed some of the best Egyptian entertainers and musicians: it had a studio in Beirut, and used a studio in Cairo until late in 1951. Its personnel was predominantly Palestinian. Its modern equivalent is the French station, 'Monte Carlo', which uses a very similar programme formula, and which is controlled in a similarly indirect way, only by the French government.

The news policy of Sharq al-Adna was explicitly pro-Arab and anti-Zionist in a way that the BBC was not. It also concentrated much more than the BBC on news from the Arab world, and carried less world news.

Its news was important, partly because it issued a dictation-speed news bulletin which was much used by Middle East journalists. Its production has sometimes been referred to as 'propagandist', but judgements of this sort tend to be subjective. Possibly the distinction is that at times of political crisis the BBC consciously strove for objectivity in news reporting, whereas Sharq al-Adna was not constitutionally inhibited, as the BBC was, from having to follow a Foreign Office line. Few people who listened to the station were in much doubt that there was a British hand in its control, though no one, naturally, knew what official body in Britain was responsible. But it should not be thought that the station was operated in a cloak-and-dagger atmosphere: it was not. Ralph Poston, the Director from 1951, was a person of unimpeachable integrity who after his retirement in 1956 was ordained a priest of the Church of England.

In the crisis of November 1951, when the Egyptian government had abrogated the 1936 Treaty with Britain, Sharq al-Adna got into worse trouble with the Egyptians than the BBC did. A difficulty about this was the number of Egyptian performers used by the station who were valuable to it for its power to command an audience. *Rose al-Yusuf* claimed on 6 November 1951 that Egyptian speakers and artistes had apologised publicly for working for British broadcasting. This may be contrasted with Nevill Barbour's report at the same period that the abrogation crisis had enormously increased listening in Egypt to the Arabic Service of the BBC, and that the leading newspapers were continuing to publish the future programmes of the BBC service.[30]

The Voice of the Arabs was only one factor in the deteriorating diplomatic situation between Britain and Egypt, but, especially after the fall of Neguib in early 1954, it became a thorn in the flesh of the British government. The success of the Voice of the Arabs in mobilising popular opinion all over the Arab world against the British and French governments was a commonplace of the time: so far as Britain was concerned the issues were not only the old quarrel about the British troops and the Canal base, but also the question of whether Arab governments should join western defensive pacts against Communism. The cause of revolutionary Arab nationalism was gaining immense popular support in a way which suggested for the first time that Pan-Arabism could become a political reality. In 1954 a BBC representative reporting a Middle East trip wrote sadly that 'In Aden I was drawn inevitably to the conclusion that there, as elsewhere in the Arab world, the British and other western information services are fighting a defensive battle which by and large is slowly being lost.'[31]

The Voice of the Arabs may not have been quite as uniformly vulgar and irresponsible as the British thought[32] but its propagandist tactics still reminded many people in Britain of the German radio of the 1930s and the war period. Ahmed Said, the main announcer and later Director of the station, was encouraged to improvise his anti-imperialist rhetoric in a way that reminded British Arabist listeners of Yunis al-Bahri. In fact at the height of the propagandist struggle with Nasser the BBC Arabic Service reverted in some respects to old wartime tactics, and resurrected against Nasser some of the 'jokes' which had been used during the war against Hitler. That behind the ranting of Ahmed Said lay a hard-nosed politician, Abdel-Kader Hatem, the Secretary of the Council, and that behind Hatem lay Gamal Abdel Nasser himself, only deepened British concern about the broadcasts.

The Voice of the Arabs has to bear part of the responsibility for the conviction that first Neguib and then Nasser were 'dictators' in some way comparable with the European dictators of the 1930s. Several political commentaries on the Arabic Service offended Egyptian opinion at the time by comparisons between Neguib and the Syrian leader Shishakli, both treated as a new type of Middle Eastern 'dictator'. But its importance was far more general than this. The Voice of the Arabs penetrated the consciousness of western political leaders, and made them convinced of its genuine political importance. It did not merely irritate: it intimidated. And the response of political leaders to intimidation is to seek a weapon of the same nature as that which is seen to threaten them.

CHAPTER 6

THE YEAR OF SUEZ

I

In this struggle for hearts and minds, British official strategy had earlier been weakened by attachment to the doctrine that influence in foreign countries should be sought through access to the influential few. This had been said by the Drogheda Report, though it did cite the BBC External Services as a means of appealing to wider public opinion abroad. On the other hand, Foreign Office practice in the Middle East had in this respect differed from the elitism of its publicly stated theory. Its control of the Sharq al-Adna transmitter gave admission to a much wider public than that accessible to any other country broadcasting to the Arab world from the exterior. It is true that there were political limits to the kind of message that Sharq could carry, and that it could not tackle head-on the Pan-Arab challenge of the Voice of the Arabs. But at least it addressed part of the same audience.

It is not so surprising, therefore, that in spite of the Voice of the Arabs the British government failed to show great enthusiasm in implementing the foreign broadcasting provisions of the Drogheda Report. If the Foreign Office had what it probably thought of as its own Middle East popular radio station, the pressure to increase BBC Arabic-language radio capacity was accordingly lessened. In 1954 the Treasury turned down Foreign Office proposals for an increase in Arabic Service capacity. A Foreign Office report of March 1955 concludes that while the BBC is under-funded, its needs are not desperately urgent. The report is, it is true, mildly favourable to BBC Arabic expansion:

The consensus of opinion in the Middle East is that broadcasting is the most effective means of propaganda in the area. This view was endorsed by the Drogheda Committee. There is reason to believe that the BBC Arabic Service is losing ground because of the growth in medium-wave as contrasted with short-wave broadcasting. There is a case, therefore, for providing the BBC with medium-wave facilities in the area at a capital cost of about £80,000. Even if this is impossible we should certainly maintain the existing level of the Service.[1]

Naturally enough, given the lukewarm measure of this support, an interview with Sir Alexander Johnston at the Treasury did not produce much in the way of comfort for the BBC. Robert Marett (the former Secretary of the Drogheda Committee and the Head of Information

Policy) concluded that 'there is a fairly strong (but not overpowering) case for some [BBC] expansion in the Middle East.' On 15 April 1955 Paul Grey, the Assistant Undersecretary, saw Sir Ian Jacob and told him that there was no hope of getting money for the Drogheda recommendations, and that the best to be hoped was a gentlemen's agreement with the Treasury to maintain the existing level of BBC External Services activity over the next few years. In June the Treasury agreed to proceed on this basis, at least for the short term.

It is not easy to say why, in spite of the close personal relations between Sir Ian Jacob with many top officials in the Foreign and Cabinet Offices, in spite of the BBC Chairman, Sir Alexander Cadogan, being an ex-mandarin of the highest grade, relations between the BBC and the government obstinately refused to improve at the end of 1955, and turned rather sour early in 1956. On the BBC side there was resentment about nagging, irrational economies which arose from the failure of the government to deal with the rising expenses of the External Services: on the government side there was mounting impatience with what was seen as the over-extended nature of BBC foreign broadcasting operations, and the obstinate refusal by the BBC to accept their long overdue reorganisation.

A dinner offered to the Foreign Secretary by the Chairman, Director and the main External Services officials at the beginning of December quite failed to warm the atmosphere. The BBC paper which served as the basis for discussion represented that over eight years the overall costs of the External Services had risen by 50 per cent, whereas funding had risen only by 20 per cent. J. B. Clark tried a few days later to emphasise the strength and importance of the Corporation as something 'well established in the fabric of National institution [sic], all parts of which are interdependent', and cited the contribution of the Persian Service during the oil crisis as evidence of the political value of the External Service.[2] But the government was not at all ready to listen to resounding affirmations of BBC ideology: in fact it was about to display impatience and scepticism with the whole BBC way of looking at things.

The idea of a new BBC medium-wave transmitter to reach the Middle East, which was of the most consequence to the Arabic Service, was going ahead only haltingly and slowly. The most obvious site for this was Cyprus, where the Diplomatic Wire Service must have owned the two sites used by the Sharq al-Adna station, but the Post Office were also considering Kuwait (where the Ruler was said to be 'not enthusiastic'), and Aden. The BBC were in the dark about Foreign Office thinking, and gloomy about prospects. Tangye Lean, the Assistant Director of External Broadcasting, wrote to the Foreign Office on 19 January 1956 that:

In the face of other curtailments and restraints, I can see no prospect of our being able to carry out the extension of the Arabic Service in transcriptions and programme time, or the reintroduction of Latin American transcriptions, desirable though we all agree these developments to be.[3]

On 20 February Anthony Nutting, the Minister of State at the Foreign Office, asked Paul Grey in the Foreign Office to satisfy himself that no reallocation could be made in the overseas information vote to meet the special threat of Soviet propaganda. This request seems to have released a small landslide in Foreign Office thinking about the BBC. Grey reported on 20 April in a way which reflects basic changes from his earlier judgements as recorded in the files. He had reservations about the BBC External Service which turned out to be of a fundamental kind:

Apart from broadcasts to iron-curtain countries, it is questionable whether the BBC contribute greatly either to our publicity overseas or to our anti-communist work. Through lack of power they are ineffective in some of the most important parts of the Middle East. We are trying to remedy this; but, though, there are other difficulties, a primary one is, against the continuous pressure of rising costs, to find the money for new capital installations . . . [criticisms of the West European services follow] . . . In peacetime direct sound broadcasting from the UK is probably now only effective when, as in the Middle East and Asia, and behind the curtain, it competes with local programmes on account of the quality of its content. The BBC are, meanwhile, holding on to what is largely a fetish . . .[4]

Radical proposals followed. Grey was aware that these would not pass without comment in Parliament, but suggested remedies:

To suggest that a large part of the Overseas Services should be abolished would cause a certain storm in Parliament and the press; but I believe that it would be shortlived if HMG based their view on the Drogheda Report and announced at the same time that they would provide money for activities in other directions.

He therefore proposed the abolition of foreign-language services in Europe outside the iron curtain countries and the abolition of the Latin-American Service. At the same time he would retain the Middle East, South East Asian and Far Eastern Services, and see to their extension where it was practicable. Sound and television transcription services and exchanges would be extended.

This root-and-branch proposal got the support of Sir Ivone Kirkpatrick, the Permanent Undersecretary at the Foreign Office, and of Nutting. The former minuted on 11 April, 'I agree, but the protests will be loud and angry': Nutting on the same day, 'I agree too. I have always wanted this kind of redeployment. But it can only be sold in Parliament if it is a redeployment.' Nutting would therefore refer to the 'expansion' and not merely to the retention of the Middle East, South East Asian and Far Eastern Services.

That Kirkpatrick, whose experience of the BBC was as extensive as that of anyone in government service, should have given full support to this programme, shows how far the BBC had at this point, some months before Suez, lost the confidence of the government. How far this was due to BBC pertinacity in defending all it held in the External Services, and how far due to government frustration and to the feeling that their information services were useless in fighting a totalitarian propaganda service like the Voice of the Arabs, it is hard to decide. Churchill's feeling – which he held right through the war – that the BBC was at the managerial levels run either by Bolshevik sympathisers ('fellow-travellers', in the vocabulary of the 1950s) or by milk-and-water liberals who were never prepared to say anything definite on behalf of the country, began to re-emerge. On 24 May Douglas Dodds-Parker, the Parliamentary Under-secretary, commented darkly on the BBC Television film of the visit of the Soviet leaders to Britain:

I consider this a disgraceful occurrence in an organisation as big as the BBC. It *cannot* be just the result of Harman Grisewood [the Chief Assistant to the Director-General, whom Dodds-Parker trusted] being away for a few days. Many people, far beyond the confines of the Tory Party, believe that there are sinister extreme-left influences in the BBC who since the war had slanted news against HMG's long-term interests. Ever since I returned to the Foreign Office at Christmas, 1955, there have been several inaccurate items of news about the Middle East which I refuse to accept as merely chance occurrences. It is high time that one or two patriots were put into these key positions.[5]

On 6 June Paul Grey circulated a draft Cabinet Paper on BBC overseas broadcasting which argued the case as he had already argued it in April, and concluded that when the desired cuts in other overseas broadcasts had been made, the first call on the monies saved should go to build up a relay station in Cyprus in order to make the BBC effective in the Middle East.[6]

As in 1940, the BBC was to be made to understand that part of the price it paid for its relative independence of government control was that it had no right to a voice in the decision-making, on the occasions when that control was exercised. It had no precise idea of what Whitehall was thinking. As Harman Grisewood (Chief Assistant to the DG) later in the year observed, decisions were based on 'discussions about which we know nothing and in most cases with aims of which we know next to nothing.' The BBC was kept in the dark, only able to fire off its defensive memoranda into the government lines, and wonder whether the shell was a dud. Sir Ian Jacob fired such a shell on 14 June, when he sent Sir Ivone Kirkpatrick a memorandum on the External Services.

Paul Grey gave the memorandum a grudging reception, though he thought it made:

a good case for the existence of these services. It underlines the weight which the BBC carries as a national institution. It emphasises the authority which the BBC has won and maintained by its policy of presenting sound views and fair comment, and its refusal to descend to abuse and special pleading. It points out the bad effect which economy has had on the services and the need for renovating equipment if the BBC is to hold its own in a broadcasting world in which competition has greatly increased. All this is fairly stated . . .

However, Grey continued to think that the BBC had placed its eggs in too many baskets: the need was to concentrate on fewer services and to make these as effective as possible.[7]

On the Middle East services, Jacob's memorandum argued that:

For a generation successive British governments have shown reluctance to finance propaganda services in Arabic corresponding to the size of the problem and the virulence of our competitors. Broadcasts from this country were only introduced at all in 1938 because of the progress Mussolini had already made from Bari. The BBC's case for a medium-wave relay has been shelved for nearly twenty years on grounds of economy, and the publicity journal, the *Arabic Listener*, was suspended in 1952 for the same reason. Meanwhile the Voice of the Arabs has been built up in Cairo as a powerful medium-wave transmitter.

Jacob continued:

It is not being suggested that Britain's relative weakness in this area can be magically corrected by radio, or that the preservation of the status quo is as simple or cheap a procedure as a campaign of disruption. Nevertheless a long-term broadcasting policy in the area would pay dividends even at this very late stage. The most obvious need is the installation of a medium-wave relay transmitter on Cyprus at a cost of the order of £250,000.

Grey did not take issue with Jacob on the question of the Cyprus transmitter, a proposal with which he more or less agreed. There had been earlier correspondence between Jacob and Kirkpatrick about this, and Jacob had already been asked to cost the Cyprus project for submission to the Treasury.[8] But Grey went on to the issue of confidence, which was gradually becoming moot. It was only by effecting the changes he proposed, or something like them, that, he thought:

We can restore confidence in the BBC External Services, which have clearly been undermined in Whitehall, if not with the public, who have, however, no means of judging how effective they are. It becomes important, however, that an attack on some of the services should not result in our casting doubt on the services as a whole. It is not in our interest that the BBC should be regarded as having lost the confidence of the government.

The Foreign Office, in spite of everything still the proud parent of the External Services, did not want the public to know that it was belting its offspring within doors.

On 5 July, as the Middle East crisis gathered, Anthony Eden, the Prime Minister, said in Cabinet that he was concerned about the presentation of government policy to the public in this country. He mentioned only the independent television companies, and these in the context of home and not of foreign policy. But the reference was symptomatic of a concern which came close to the BBC.

On 10 July the Cabinet set up a committee chaired by Douglas Dodds-Parker to consider overseas broadcasting.[9] The following day Selwyn Lloyd and Dodds-Parker saw Sir Ian Jacob. The Foreign Secretary, Selwyn Lloyd, said he wished for a frank discussion on overseas broadcasting as he thought there was a mutual lack of confidence between government circles and the BBC. This, he said, was not due to any personal cause but because neither perhaps fully understood the other's problem. Jacob, in reply, claimed that the BBC had kept itself well informed about government policy and knew how to put it across. His main complaint was of financial stringency. When the Foreign Secretary spoke of the advent of television in Bagdad as the start of a new medium in the Middle East, Jacob replied that the BBC had been asking for money for this sort of thing for some five years. Every time they looked for development, they found that it was offset by an annual cut being made in their services elsewhere. They had been asking for the medium-wave transmitter in Cyprus for ten years (Jacob had, as it happened, that very day sent the costed project to Kirkpatrick).

Selwyn Lloyd, in a comment very revealing of the mood of the Cabinet, said that his impression of the BBC was that it was too respectable. In most instances it was good, but in others it might be more aggressive, although certain aspects of 'offensive' broadcasting might better be done other than through the BBC. (He did not mention Sharq al-Adna by name, but the implication is clear.) The indications were that the government, anticipating a possible return to something like wartime conditions, was already beginning to talk the language of 'virile' broadcasting which went back to the wartime period. Jacob asked for a five-year plan: for the new Cyprus station he asked for about £250,000 for the capital investment, and £50,000 a year to run it. It could be operational, he said, within three months.

II

On 24 July Nasser announced that he would finance the Aswan Dam without western assistance. On 26 July he proclaimed the nationalisation of the Suez Canal Company, and the acute phase of the Suez crisis began. The effect on government relations with the BBC was immediate. There was a meeting of the Committee on Overseas Broadcasting on 25 July. The notes for it mention the case for redeployment of effort and the special broadcasting importance of the Middle East. A significant note spoke of the tone and content of BBC broadcasts, and asked whether the Committee wished to make any recommendation on policy in this respect, and if so, what machinery should be used for liaison between the BBC and the interested government departments.[10]

On the same day as Dodds-Parker's committee met (25 July), the more powerful Policy Review Committee met under Nutting. The latter had been asked by the Foreign Secretary to consider 'by what means the government could secure a larger measure of control over the contents of broadcasts to the Middle and Far East, against the background that the

BBC was thought to attach too much importance to impartiality.' The possibilities envisaged were 'either to arrange with the BBC that its broadcasts should be used as an instrument of government policy, or to make use of a different organisation and reduce government expenditure on BBC overseas broadcasts.'[11] A slightly different version of the instrument proposed to control the BBC was given by Grey, as 'whether greater control should not be exercised over the external services generally, and whether a senior official should be put in charge of publicity in the Foreign Office.'

These were drastic measures to propose, and they closely resemble the proposals made by the Second Kingsley Wood Committee to the War Cabinet at the end of 1940, which the War Cabinet adopted but put only half-heartedly into effect. There are some very obscure aspects to the alternative courses of action contemplated in the Nutting proposals. In particular, what 'different organisation' was the government going to make use of in order to replace part of the BBC External Services? It is hard to think of anything other than the Sharq al-Adna station, given the extreme urgency of the Middle East crisis. It is very difficult to imagine that the Minister of State, in the midst of the exploding Suez crisis, would seriously have proposed to start setting up from scratch some entirely new broadcasting organisation.

It is also a little mysterious that control over the contents of broadcasts to the Middle and Far East should have been specifically mentioned, since up to then no complaint had been made about the Arabic broadcasts. It is possible that some elements of the government, anticipating a wartime situation, had in mind something like a revival of MOI and PWE control, but the evidence is too thin to be definite about this. It is clear, however, that one strand in government thinking was a desire to reduce BBC independence in the External Services by some new broadcasting policy, and at the same time to cut BBC funding.

If the government was seriously thinking of a big expansion of the role of Sharq al-Adna, it cannot have been fully informed of the limitations of the station and its output. The news policy of Sharq al-Adna had always been to favour the Arab cause strongly, and to speak as fairly of the Egyptian regime as current British policy would admit. When things approached a crisis in 1956 this policy began to burst at the seams. Sharq al-Adna besides extolling the Bagdad Pact began to imply that a *coup d'état* against Nasser in Egypt was a serious possibility. Both the Voice of the Arabs and the Egyptian regime reacted strongly. At some time between the spring of 1955 and the summer of 1956 the Egyptians issued a radio 'ultimatum' to the Arabs who worked for the British Cyprus station, and gave them a week to stop their broadcasting work there. The supply of Egyptian entertainers and artistes was cut off at the same time. Ralph Poston, the Director of the Sharq al-Adna station, went to Cairo, according to Egyptian and other sources, and pleaded against the ultimatum. He was received by Nasser's propaganda chief, Abdel-Kader Hatem, who gave him a friendly reception but would not withdraw the ultimatum.[12] If this had happened before the British government had adopted a position of open hostility to Egypt, what was likely to occur when Sharq al-Adna was ordered to carry out 'offensive' propaganda?

However, a decision taken in principle to increase control over the BBC, and its execution, were two very different things. Paul Grey, when asked about securing a larger measure of control over the content of broadcasts to the Middle East and Eastern Asia, at once warned that:

direct responsibility for the content of the broadcasts could not be vested in HMG without a change in the License and Agreement if not of the Charter; that it would be strongly resisted by the BBC as destroying their present independence and thereby damaging their reputation abroad; and that HMG themselves might find that there would be disagreeable consequences, including responsibility, both in Parliament and abroad, for every word broadcast. Secondly the machinery required to exercise such control would have to be elaborate if it were to be effective.[13]

Relations with the BBC did not improve as the crisis developed. The broadcasts of the Prime Minister and the Foreign Secretary were translated and broadcast in Arabic (as on all the other services) on 8 and 14 August. But the broadcasting time given to the Egyptian 'dancing major', Salah Salem, on 15 August, roused the government to irritation if not to anger: the Prime Minister himself complained about it to Sir Ian Jacob on 20 August.[14]

On 16 August Kirkpatrick wrote to Jacob to ask him to name a BBC representative to a Committee under a Foreign Office Minister (who was to be Douglas Dodds-Parker) 'to achieve closer co-ordination between those departments most directly concerned with the Suez Canal question' – dark words in a dark time. Kirkpatrick asked for Donald Stephenson, but Jacob nominated Hugh Carleton Greene.[15] On 28 August Kirkpatrick saw Jacob, and told him that ministers were 'preoccupied about the state of the Overseas Services.' He told Jacob that 'there were two schools of thought, one of which was disposed to favour governmental control in the Overseas Services and the other, the curtailment of the £5 million grant in aid of the BBC, and its expenditure in other propaganda enterprises.' 'Sir Ian Jacob,' Kirkpatrick related with relish, 'looked stricken like a mother about to be deprived of her child. He denied that the Home Service was lowering its standards and claimed that the Overseas Service was doing its job. He defied any impartial enquiry to come to any other conclusion.'[16]

According to Kirkpatrick's own account it was a tough and threatening interview; there must have been a streak of the bully in his character for him to treat an old wartime colleague in this way. Kirkpatrick felt obliged to warn Jacob that, even though his claims in defence of the BBC might be correct, ministers were becoming increasingly dissatisfied with the BBC in general and with the expenditure of £5 million a year on its overseas services. It was unlikely, said Kirkpatrick, that this subject would be raised in an acute form until after the government had finished with the Suez crisis – this assurance held good only for a few weeks, as the subject was indeed raised in an acute form on 25 October.

It is doubtful whether the BBC's feared even-handedness was practised overmuch that summer in the Arabic Service. A BBC memorandum of September tells how the transmissions defended the British point of view, emphasising the common ground between the Labour and Conservative parties in the August parliamentary debate, the 'futility of Nasser's economic plans' and the difficulties he would experience in running the Canal, the threat posed by the seizure to Asian as well as to western interests. The comments on the Arab staff of the Service are especially interesting:

> Throughout the crisis the staff of the Arabic Service has behaved extremely well. There were a few murmurs at first about the tough nature of the statements which our Arabs were called on to broadcast, but these died down after a careful explanation to all concerned by the Arabic Programme Organiser about the reasons for the British stand.[17]

The Arabic Service broadcast a few feeble anti-Nasser jokes called 'Political asides': for example, a Cairo dog tells another in the street that he had to go out of town to Libya because he 'felt an irresistible desire to bark'.

There were some diplomatic grouses. The Colonial Secretary, Alan Lennox-Boyd, complained to Tangye Lean that the Arabic Service had reported unhelpful speeches by the King of the Yemen and the Syrian Foreign Minister, but had to express himself more or less satisfied with the general tenor of the Service.[18] There were no complaints of substance about the Arabic Service in the dossier of grumbles about the BBC which the Head of the Information Policy Department in the Foreign Office put together in September. It was conceded that:

> the BBC's Arabic Service has represented our case pretty well; the staff have shown themselves co-operative though the Head of the Arabic Service, Mr Waterfield, has made it abundantly clear that he privately thinks there is no alternative to Nasser and that it is a mistake to attack him. If the temperature of the Suez crisis were to fall, I expect this Service to become critical of some aspects of HM Government's policy.[19]

The main complaint of this report is not about specific failures to present government policy properly, but about insubordinate attitudes. The General Overseas Service is criticised because its news staff are 'infected with the same jealous regard for complete independence as the staff of the Home Services'; the GOS is therefore 'the most difficult over which to exercise influence, and the one about which we most often receive complaints from posts abroad.' The complaint about Waterfield gives some idea of the gap between the Arabic Service and the hawks of the Cabinet Office.

III

On 24 September Paul Grey drew up the plan which was eventually to be put into force, for the appointment of a Foreign Office Liaison Officer to the BBC. But the ministers had in mind to bring into operation against the BBC much heavier guns than this. On 26 September the Prime Minister said in Cabinet that he continued to be dissatisfied with the conduct of the Overseas Services of the BBC, and considered that the whole basis of the existing arrangements should be reviewed. The Cabinet approved the setting up of a new Committee of Ministers under the Lord Privy Seal (R. A. Butler), to review the existing arrangements for overseas broadcasting.[20] This was a far less sweeping brief than had been given to Kingsley Wood's Committee in 1940, but the ministers' growing irritation with the supposed failure of the BBC to present the country's policy in an aggressive and virile way will bear comparison with the events of sixteen years earlier. Both Eden and R. A. Butler took major roles in the 1956 attack on the BBC, just as they had done in the earlier one.

The critical meeting of R. A. Butler's Committee took place on 9 October. Doubts about the legal difficulties in controlling the BBC played a part. The Postmaster-General (Charles Hill) had advised that there was no general power at present to require the BBC to broadcast particular programmes or features supplied explicitly by HMG apart from what was covered by the word 'announcement', unless an emergency arose, in which case it could be required to broadcast 'other matter'. These phrases were too obscure to give the government much comfort, and to achieve greater control of the programme content of the External Services would mean a modification of the Licence and Agreement, which could only be done in Parliament, and at the cost of much public controversy.

Sir Ivone Kirkpatrick evidently expressed to the Committee a trenchant, radical view of BBC–government relations which is very striking, coming as it did from the peak of the official hierarchy. He advised that there is no logical half-way house between no control over the BBC and total control, which would expose HMG to the need to answer to Parliament in detail on the contents of the broadcasts.[21] This conclusion had perhaps been suggested by the advice given by Paul Grey, but it goes far beyond anything said in the preparatory Foreign Office papers. It is hard to know exactly how Kirkpatrick viewed the situation in 1956, since the documents are sparse. But it may be that his memories of the confused and unhappy arrangements for controlling the BBC in the war years, in which he had played a major part, influenced him in proffering this advice.[22] His opinion is extremely interesting, as at a critical point of the Suez affair he was advising the government that there was no real alternative between either leaving the BBC in the constitutional position in which it was, or imposing on it a control at least as drastic, perhaps more drastic, than had been imposed on it between 1939 and 1945.

Nevertheless, neither Kirkpatrick nor the Committee gave up the idea of intimidating the BBC, so that in the short term at least it would more or less do what the government told it. On 24 October R. A. Butler reported to the Cabinet in a rather confusing way, pinning his account of the Committee's work to the fact that Sir Ian Jacob was shortly leaving the country for Australia, and arguing that it would be useful if the Committee's provisional conclusions could be disclosed to Jacob before his departure, so that his reaction could be reported to the Cabinet. This tortuous piece of reasoning prefaced the recommendations of the Committee, which were first that the BBC grant-in-aid of the External Services should be reduced by £1 million (that is, nearly a fifth of the whole grant), which was to be achieved mainly by eliminating the European language services. Second, part of the saving should be devoted to intensification of BBC services to the Middle East and South East Asia; and, third, another part of the money saved might be used to increase the effectiveness of our information services by other methods over which the government would retain more direct control, such as the production of television material by the Central Office of Information. [23]

Butler's Committee would not seek to impose any direct control over the BBC's External Services, but would require the appointment of a Foreign Office Liaison Officer to advise the BBC on the content and direction of their overseas programmes. The advice of Kirkpatrick and Grey had therefore been accepted. It may be asked, however, whether the proposal to make drastic reductions in the existing External Services was made entirely on the merits of the courses of action proposed, or whether they were not being poured over the BBC as a bucket of ice-cold water which would have the effect of bringing the Corporation to reason. That the second was the case is suggested by the departmental minutes, which referred to:

the recommendation made in his [the Minister of State's] note about the expenditure and deployment of the External Services, partly as a means of administering a shock to the BBC and inducing them to reconcile their independence with the need for greater care in conducting their services in the national interest. [24]

The amount of time, trouble and political effort the Cabinet was willing at this point to expend on BBC overseas broadcasting is striking. It was a critical juncture of the Suez crisis, when a military solution of the problem had been virtually decided on and would be put into effect within a few weeks. The whole affair gives some idea of the importance of broadcast information to the government. Eden's own ideas about what to do with the BBC were probably more like those of Churchill in 1940 than they were those of Butler and his Committee. According to Harman Grisewood, Eden had at this point instructed the Lord Chancellor to prepare an instrument which would take over the BBC altogether and subject it wholly to the will of the government.[25]

On 25 October Nutting saw Sir Ian Jacob and acquainted him with the Committee's provisional decisions as approved by the Cabinet. Sir Ian took the interview badly. He protested strongly at the way the government suddenly presented these requirements without any prior consultation with the BBC; they would, he said, have the effect of destroying a large and integral part of the Corporation's organisation built up to carry out work on behalf of the government; and he would have to consult the Chairman and Governors who would certainly resent them. They would involve terminating contracts with people who had worked for the BBC for twenty years. The Corporation should at least have been asked to produce their own plan, and he suggested that at least it should be requested to make a saving of a certain order, and the way in which it might be done should be left to them.

The next day Douglas Dodds-Parker (who had also been at the meeting) sent Sir Ian the draft of a Cabinet letter which placed the decisions in writing, though without (since it was a draft) committing the government or obligating the Corporation. The draft letter ended 'I should be grateful for confirmation of the Corporation's agreement to this proposal.' The content of the letter was according to the decisions reached in Cabinet on 24 October. There was however a major change in the proposed financial arrangements, a change very mysteriously reached between the interview of 25 October and the despatch of the draft letter on the following day. Nutting, following the Cabinet decision, had told Jacob on 25 October that the cut in BBC External Services financing would be of £1 million: overnight this cut was halved and became one of £500,000.[26]

Once more, some parallels suggest themselves with 1940–41. Just as Monckton and Duff Cooper had been unwilling to impose the Cabinet's will unilaterally on the BBC in 1941, and had subsequently lost themselves in complicated negotiations to get the BBC's consent, so in 1956 Butler and Nutting (Monckton had actually been suggested in 1956 to take part in this mission, but seems to have avoided it) flourished what they knew to be an unacceptable solution for the future of the External Services in Sir Ian Jacob's face, and asked him to agree to it. This could only lead to a period of BBC–government bargaining. If the intention had been to administer a short, sharp shock to the BBC, this was an odd way of doing it.

Sir Ian Jacob, helped by his impending departure for Australia, decided on avoiding and delaying tactics. He was too old a hand to allow Butler and Nutting to 'see his reaction' on paper. Angus Rae in the Foreign Office minuted on 26 October that Sir Ian Jacob's secretary had telephoned to say 'no comment' on the draft letter sent him that day: 'The secretary said that she supposed that the BBC would now be getting the letter in final form. I hedged, and did *not* say that I thought that there were a number of Cabinet hoops to be gone through first.'[27]

IV

The press reviews which went out on the External Services in the Suez period carried a lot of material which was very unwelcome to the government, especially because the latter wanted to avoid giving the impression abroad that the split in the country over the Suez issue was as deep as it was. Even though the BBC Board were 'anxious to do nothing to underline the existence of party division and disunity at a time of crisis', the issue could not be ducked. It came to a head over the *Manchester Guardian* leader of 31 October, the summary of which in the External Services press reviews at a time when British troops were preparing to go into action gave deep offence to the government.

When the final military crisis came the Arabic Service, so far as can be ascertained from the programme summaries, broadcast programmes which adhered to the policy of the External Services as a whole, and which must have made clear to its listeners the extent of the division in the country over the Suez action. It had already translated a talk on 'The BBC and politics' by John Sherwood, which went out on 1 October and was repeated on 10 November. On 30 October the Arabic Service put out a talk on the freedom of the press by the *Observer* journalist, Robert Stephens, who was not noted for following the government line over the Suez dispute.

Wednesday, 31 October was the day when the Anglo-French bombing of the Egyptian airfields began. A review of the Middle East situation in the British press went out on the Arabic Service that evening. It was the same press review (compiled by A. S. Parker) that went out on the other services. It included mention of the *Daily Herald* headline, 'This is folly', and a brief quotation from the *Guardian* leader of the same morning. The Conservative press and *The Times* were, of course, also reported. The text of the report said that the *Guardian* 'condemned the Middle East ultimatum in less violent fashion [than the *Herald*], but left no doubt that it considered a dangerous mistake had been made.' The report was stamped and signed in the Arabic Service, 'Passed for policy'. There was that evening a talk on Sir Anthony Eden's statement by David Mitchell, a talks writer who on occasion took a fairly strong anti-Nasser line.

On 1 November, as the bombings continued, Mitchell put out a press review, 'The current situation in the Middle East as reported by British newspapers'. On Friday, 2 November Roy Defrates (another member of the BBC topical talks staff) edited a parliamentary report, 'The defeat of the vote of censure', which must have described the scene in the House of Commons on that memorable day. On Sunday, 4 November Sir Anthony Eden's broadcast went out in the form of a news talk by Mitchell. On Monday, 5 November, the day of the Port Said landings, David Mitchell broadcast a news talk, 'Eden, Gaitskell and British Opinion'. It has been said that William Clark had telephoned from the Cabinet Office urging that 'the more inflammatory parts' of Gaitskell's broadcast of 4 November should not be transmitted on the Arabic Service: if such a request was made, we do not know whether it was complied with.[28] There was a press review that day, although the normal Monday programme, 'Arab affairs in the British press', was not resumed in the Arabic Service until 10 December, and when it was resumed took a strongly pro-government line.

The tone of the Arabic Service broadcasts in these critical days is not easy to recover, but we have a few hints. It was very difficult to find commentators in the middle ground, but they were found. The journalist Edward Hodgkin of *The Times* wrote for the *Political Question and Answer* series broadcast on 10 November (after the cease-fire and the UN intervention) a reply to the question: 'What will the effect of the Anglo-French action in Egypt be on the United Nations organisation?' His text is a model of discretion, though far from the British official line. It begins:

Although the great debate is still going on in Britain as to whether Sir Anthony Eden and his Cabinet [the avoidance of the term, 'the British government' is interesting] were justified in acting as they did when they moved against Egypt, there is increasing attention being paid to the long-term effects of this action, particularly in respect to the United Nations.

Hodgkin's stress in the broadcast is on the positive and hopeful elements in the idea of the UN force to be assembled for the Canal, and its significance for future international co-operation. He emphasises the general consensus at UN to set up the force:

This is all gain. It was important that the prestige and self-confidence of the United Nations should have received a boost just at the moment when events in Suez and Hungary seemed to some people to show that the United Nations was impotent. Now, however, although the Russians continue with cynical brutality to flout United Nations resolutions over Hungary, the ceasefire in the Middle East and the establishment of the police force there have restored much confidence in the United Nations.

The Pro-UN line of the broadcast would not have given much pleasure to Conservative hawks of the time, but the reference to Hungary is important.

Another talk in the Arabic Service *Political Question and Answer* series, a week after that of Hodgkin, was written by N. Leadbitter of the BBC External Services staff. It is not so clear-sighted as that of Hodgkin, and gives away some of the confusion which was felt at the time. It begins on a pro-government note. The question was 'Did the UN stop the fighting in Egypt?':

The questioner assumes that the Anglo-French action was aggressive. It may be that this is widely believed. Nevertheless the British government would strongly reject such a description of their action. The British Prime Minister has repeatedly described the Anglo-French action as a police one, with the sole intention of stopping the spread of hostilities. Had no such action been taken, the chances were that fighting would have spread across Egypt and possibly across the Arab world as well . . .

But Leadbitter's positive attitude to the UN force is the same as that of Hodgkin:

One can therefore say that the action of the UN has produced a situation in which the problem of what has been called aggression by the British and French against Egypt can be solved . . . It is important as an experiment to maintain international law and justice . . .

Leadbitter was trying to have his Suez cake and eat it with UN icing.

V

Ministerial and opposition broadcasts constituted yet another bone of contention between the BBC and the government. This involved the interpretation of procedure for ministerial broadcasts laid down in the Beveridge report, and the so-called 'three days rule' regarding broadcasts concerning matters under debate in Parliament. It has no direct bearing on the broadcasts in the External Services, but it was another vexed question which at this time helped to strain relations between the Corporation and government.

BBC tactics against the threat to the External Services were worked out by Harman Grisewood (Chief Assistant to the DG) and Sir Norman Bottomley (Director of Administration and Acting-DG), who were keeping shop in Sir Ian Jacob's absence. On 9 November a letter signed by Bottomley complained that the BBC could not reasonably be expected to deal with a set of decisions arrived at in discussions in which it had played no part, and geared to government 'policy objectives' of which it knew nothing. Technical considerations about the use of short-wave frequencies and the utilisation and modernisation of transmitters were mentioned. The letter reserved comment about the list of services to be eliminated. Grey in the Foreign Office minuted Bottomley's letter:

The BBC are keeping up the pretence of a grievance because they were 'not consulted' and consequently have no idea what the government is driving at. This is hypocritical. They know only too well and there is, in essence, nothing new in the government's demands for a reorientation which was foreshadowed in the Drogheda Report, and, as regards the urgency of the Middle East, must be obvious to a child of ten.[29]

The BBC had already done what it could about 'the urgency of the Middle East'. Early in October a low-power 20 kW transmitter had been despatched to Cyprus in order to act as a medium-wave relay for the Arabic Service: unfortunately it arrived damaged, and could not be put into immediate use.

But the Sharq al-Adna station had, at the outbreak of the shooting war in the Canal, fallen to pieces in its operators' hands. Details of the conduct of the British propaganda war in Cyprus are hard to come by. It was in the hands of Ralph Murray, the former Minister in Cairo (and later a governor of the BBC), and of a distinguished soldier, Brigadier Bernard Fergusson. The station was formally requisitioned by HMG on 30 October. When the instructions on what they were to broadcast were given to the Sharq al-Adna staff they appear, although they were mostly Palestinians and not Egyptians, to have refused to work any further for the station. Moreover, Ralph Poston, the Director of the radio station, was also so recalcitrant that according to some reports he was placed for a time under house arrest by the British military authorities in Cyprus. This fiasco is not so surprising in view of the earlier history of the Sharq al-Adna station, but it came as an unpleasant shock to the British government.

A new Arabic propagandist broadcasting station, the 'Voice of Britain', was set up to replace the defunct one, and the thankless task of directing it was after a time assigned to a Foreign Office official, Sidney Hebblethwaite. Its staffing was necessarily makeshift, and it pursued a somewhat inglorious life into the spring of 1957.[30] Part of the new station's transmissions consisted of relays of the BBC Arabic Service, but the BBC's wish to take over the whole Cyprus radio operation was denied for the time being.

It was not in the power of the BBC to do much to help the government over the Sharq al-Adna business, once it had been decided to replace it by a new station, but it did what it could. The Arabic Service transmissions had already been lengthened by half an hour on 5 August, in pursuance of a decision taken in April. When the military part of the Suez operation began, the news bulletins in Arabic were lengthened, and on 5 November a new midday news bulletin was introduced. This was done in spite of the fact that four Egyptians had resigned from the Arabic Service out of a total Arabic staff of twelve.[31]

John Titchener, the Foreign Office Liaison Officer appointed to the External Services, arrived reluctantly from Teheran and took up duty in Bush House on 12 November, the duty having been exercised from 2 November by a deputy. An ex-SOE and psychological warfare man, Titchener was not happy in the BBC. In December Grey commented on a Titchener minute about:

the extraordinary mentality of the BBC as here revealed. They carry their resentment of criticism and outside influence, even in the External Services, to a quite ludicrous point. They make it clear that when you discuss the actions of the BBC you are treading on holy ground.[32]

It was a clumsy arrangement which lasted only for a few months. Grey had done his best to bully the BBC, stating at one point to Bottomley that in such a situation as the military action against Egypt it was not necessary to tell the whole truth, and that certain news items should be suppressed in the Arabic bulletins.[33] But it is very doubtful if he got his way.

On the main issue of the financing of the External Services, it gradually became clear that this was one of the many things about which the government had been hasty in 1956. The External Services came under fire in the House of Commons on 12 and 14 November from Conservative MPs, notably from Peter Rawlinson, who thought that they should speak in the name of the government of the day, and from Sir Lancelot Joynson-Hicks, who asked why the subvention for the External Services should not be stopped. The government defended the BBC, perhaps somewhat hypocritically, in the Commons: on 14 November it had no doubt that 'if any improvements or changes are necessary the Governors and the BBC will be among the first to see that these changes and improvements are carried out speedily': the Minister refrained from saying how brutally the government had suggested improvements.[34]

Negotiations between the government and the BBC continued after Sir Ian Jacob's return. Douglas Dodds-Parker had still been maintaining on 20 November that the government could not continue to meet the continually rising costs of the External Services of the BBC deployed on their present pattern, and still held out for the reduction to £4.7 million.[35] But the urgency had gone out of the government case. R. A. Butler saw Sir Ian and Sir Alexander Cadogan on 14 December: the upshot of the discussion is unknown, but things continued to calm down. On 31 December, seeking to deal with the choleric Joynson-Hicks, Cosmo Stewart in the Information Department concluded:

Given the basis upon which the external broadcasts of the BBC are conducted, I do not see what answer can be returned except to explain this basis and the difficult problem which was set the BBC by the acute controversy which raged in Parliament and the press about our intervention in Egypt. Whether this basis is the right one has of course been under consideration for some time in the Ministerial Committee on Broadcasting. So far as the Middle East itself is concerned, special measures have had to be taken by the institution of the 'Voice of Britain' as the direct mouthpiece of HMG. But the tentative thinking of the Committee seems to be that, so far as the rest of the world is concerned, the principles on which the BBC co-operate at present, though not ideal, are probably the only practicable ones.[36]

It was the voice of weary acceptance of the status quo.

By February 1957 a new government committee on information services under Charles Hill was being set up, and the government's threats of the preceding year had receded into the background. On 8 February, in reply to a parliamentary question, Ian Harvey said that the BBC had made an estimate of £5,700,000 revenue expenditure for External Services for the approaching year. 'Factors such as the rise in costs and the redeployment which have taken place since 1950 make the figure theoretical and somewhat arbitrary.'[37] This did not sound like a government pledged to savage cuts in the BBC budget. On 18 February Hill said in Parliament that:

One decision in regard to overseas broadcasting was taken without waiting for the result of the [Information Policy] Review, and that was the increase in the BBC Arabic programmes from four and a half hours to rather more than nine hours a day.

The Suez controversies were already over, and new policies were being made which would change the BBC Arabic Service in a fundamental way.

Looking at the course of the Suez affair as it affected the External Services, Gerard Mansell's judgement can be accepted, that the government, 'having baulked at taking the final step of placing the External Services under its direct control, did what seemed at the time to be the next best thing.'[38] In fact the Cabinet hardly considered seriously the step of imposing direct control on the External Services, which they well realised would in peacetime have presented parliamentary hazards they could not even consider. Eden's well-known petulance played some part in the trials of the BBC in 1956, as it had in 1940–41. But Eden's political intentions about the BBC in 1956 may have been far more drastic than those of the Cabinet as a whole; whether he would have succeeded in carrying the Cabinet with him on the subject cannot be known.

Sir Ian Jacob's verdict, reported by Mansell, that the Suez episode had no particular effect on the relationship between the External Services and the government, can be accepted if we see the reorganisation of the External Services which took place in 1957–8 as something which had been bound to come, and which was not particularly affected by the Suez Crisis. But it can also be said that the Suez episode showed how a body of men inspired by an idealistic view of their role in society could stand up successfully to the most intense political pressure. Sir Ian Jacob would not, I imagine, have been especially happy with the suggestion that St Thomas Becket was his patron saint. But there are moments when a comparison between the BBC and the medieval priesthood is hard to resist. That both Sir Ian Jacob and Sir Alexander Cadogan had, like Thomas Becket, given distinguished service to the lay power, makes the comparison even more piquant.

There does not seem to be much evidence that the Arabic Service did anything but loyally try to present the British government's policies in the best light it could during the Suez crisis. The only important instances in which it broadcast things unwelcome to the government occurred when it fell in with the rest of the External Services in transmitting extracts from the speeches of the Leader of the Opposition, and from that part of the press which denounced the military action.

Suez was, however, a watershed in the history of the Arabic Service. The importance of maintaining a full service of British news and information in the Middle East had been much strengthened by the events of 1956, and it is not surprising that the government decision to double the transmission time of the Arabic Service was taken early in 1957. It was an implicit admission on the government's part that the BBC's policies, even if they stubbornly baulked at the acceptance of anything resembling official control, represented the best means of getting a hearing for Britain's point of view in the Arab world.

CHAPTER 7

THE EXPANSION
OF THE ARABIC SERVICE

I

At this critical moment in its fortunes the Arabic Service was led by Gordon Waterfield, who as Head of the Eastern Service was also responsible for Israel, Persia, India, Pakistan and Ceylon. Nevill Barbour was Assistant Head with responsibility for Israel and Persia as well as for the Arab World: he retired in 1956. Waterfield had spent many years with Reuters, seven of them in Egypt. He was a member of a family known for its intellectual cultivation, its liberal sympathies, and its European outlook: his mother had been a renowned *Observer* correspondent in Italy at the time of the Fascist regime, and he himself had been Reuters correspondent in Rome before the war. His culture was a very broad one, and although he entertained a deep respect for the Arab world, he did not view it with the passionate partisanship of someone like Barbour.[1]

On a practical level Waterfield was well aware of the trust which the BBC Arabic Service had gained in the Arab world over a long period by its proved reliability and truthfulness, and also by its willingness to repond to listeners when they wrote, especially to the programmes like *Listeners' Forum* and *Question and Answer*, but also outside that framework. Living in societies in which people became frustrated by there being no one to turn to with questions about general knowledge and everyday life of a non-traditional sort, the BBC had become part of their way of life and thinking, and they often came to regard it as a sort of godfather.

Waterfield agreed with Barbour that radio communications had been and continued to be a big element in forming the general consciousness of a common cultural Arab identity: like Barbour, he saw this as a positive and not as a negative influence. Like Barbour, he did not see Arab linguistic and cultural nationalism, any more than he saw Islam, as necessary threats to western interests and the western way of life. Waterfield said that:

the Arab world has been so overwhelmed by Western ideas, customs and techniques that if it is to achieve a true renaissance it must return to its own history, religion and culture, to find strength, confidence and inspiration.

Although, in the lecture from which these remarks came, he was addressing Frenchmen, some of whom saw Islam as an enemy to progress in Africa, Waterfield defended the practice of the BBC and French overseas radio in broadcasting Koranic readings, in spite of the protests of the bishops. He held an optimistic view of the possible future of Islamic modernism, and thought that Muslims of our own time had a good prospect of re-interpreting their faith in the light of modern thought without abandoning or westernising its basic beliefs. This view is far from the fear of a 'revolt of Islam' which had so dominated Lord Cromer's thinking on the subject, half a century earlier. Today Cromer's view may be returning, but Waterfield's reflected the contrasting views of H. A. R. Gibb, the then acknowledged master of British Arabists, whose most influential work on Islamic modernism was published in the closing years of the 1940s.

Waterfield's view of nationalism, including Arab nationalism, was implicitly Whiggish and sceptical. But his own liberal outlook, and a good broadcaster's sensitivity to the views of his audience, made him sympathetic to the legitimate grievances of people who as he saw it 'have suffered a great deal at the hands of the West and who are, for a great part of the time, in a high state of emotion':

Many of the questions the BBC receives from [Arab] listeners are not easy to answer with a clear conscience. Many Arabs feel that their aspirations with regard to independence in North Africa, with regard to sovereignty in the Canal Zone, with regard to the return of Arab refugees to Israel and other matters related to Israel, are being blocked by the great powers at the United Nations.

It is not surprising that some Foreign Office officials in 1956 thought that 'when the temperature of the Suez crisis' fell, they might come in for some criticism from a Service directed by Waterfield, though their apprehension turned out to be exaggerated.

Some expansion of the Arabic Service had been approved in principle by the government before the end of 1955, and Treasury approval was given for the appointment of additional staff in June 1956.[2] With the Suez crisis discussions which had hitherto gone on at a stately pace suddenly became hectic. By September the doubling of the Arabic output was being urgently canvassed, and in the New Year of 1957 Foreign Office approval was given for the increase to $9^{1}/_{2}$ hours daily.

The consequences for such a small organisation were dramatic. Staff numbers had fallen in the economy years of the early 1950s, from eighteen in 1950 to twelve in 1956, and the resignations of November reduced this for a short time to eight. By 31 March 1957, the date of the expansion of transmission to nine hours daily, the Arabic Programme staff numbered twenty: most of the newcomers were taken from the former staff of Sharq al-Adna. It was a transformation of staff and output more radical than any that had taken place since the critical days of the war. Having been discussed for many years, it finally took place hurriedly and under circumstances which no one could have anticipated.

It was to take the Arabic Service some time to reconsider its aims and methods under this new dispensation. There was also the physical change of location which took place in the latter half of 1957, the period when the External Services finally vacated 200 Oxford Street, where they had been partly housed since the wartime period, and were concentrated in Bush House. The reorganisation of Bush House news room, allowing the news editors to work in the same room as the teleprinters, gave the Arabic Service as well as the others the benefits of faster news editing.[3]

For a time the strategy of the expanded Service was to remain in some doubt, because of the reluctance of the Foreign Office to renounce the option of sponsoring a new Middle East popular commercial radio station. Sharq al-Adna clearly could not be revived in its original form, but the Foreign Office was reluctant to abandon the idea of some kind of new station similar in method to the old one, to be operated by an organisation which would not be the BBC.

In December 1956 the possible future purchase of a big new transmitter to be installed in Cyprus for a management which was clearly not to be that of the BBC was under serious discussion.[4] Doubt was expressed as to whether the Treasury would approve such a new transmitter, evidently additional to what was already in place on the island, and to the low-power transmitter which had already been sent there by the BBC. At the time of these discussions the Voice of Britain programme was being put out over the Sharq transmitters, and it may be presumed that the proposed new sender would have been placed at the disposal either of the Voice of Britain station or of some successor to it which was being contemplated by the Foreign Office.

That the Foreign Office continued to contemplate a successor to Sharq al-Adna was shown in the White Paper on government information services published in July 1957 (Cmnd. 225):

In the Middle East there would be an advantage in having a 'light' programme, locally produced, commercial in character and likely to make an appeal to the largest possible audience. The government are considering whether a programme of this kind can be provided.

So long as the BBC knew that such an alternative was being considered, it was very difficult for them to come to definite decisions about the nature of the extended Arabic Service which they had already launched. This passage in the White Paper also, incidentally, virtually acknowledged publicly that the government already had experience in managing such a station and such a programme, and makes it hard to understand the elaborate fiction which was maintained then and down to the present, that Sharq al-Adna had been nothing to do with them.

The Director of the Voice of Britain had not been keen on prolonging the life of his charge unduly. In January 1957 he had recommended that the staff and the music library of the Voice of Britain (the former Sharq al-Adna) be brought as soon as possible to London, and that all broadcasting should be done from Britain. The amount of equipment involved was impressive. Waterfield understood that there were two thousand tapes and thirty thousand discs to be brought to London, and according to the figures he had been given, which he found it hard to credit, the total weight of the consignment would be some $16^1/_2$ tonnes.[5]

Partly because of the haste in which decisions had been made, partly because of the continued uncertainty as to whether the Foreign Office might not again pursue the alternative of a popular commercial service, the expanded Arabic Service set up on 31 March 1957 remained on a slightly provisional basis for over a year. As late as September 1957 a senior Arabic Service officer wrote:

It is clear that before many months are out the new Arabic programme, of which the White Paper speaks, will be heard from Cyprus. This means that a firm commanding a great deal of capital and prepared to spend any sum necessary to secure adequate staff and programme material will be in the market. They will clearly outbid the BBC . . . In a short space of time, therefore, we shall suffer competition in which the Corporation will be unduly handicapped.[6]

The ghost of Sharq al-Adna had returned to plague the BBC, which feared this new competitor for a mass audience. More important, until it was clear that a new Sharq was not going to appear, the BBC could not make a decision as to whether it should itself go for a mass audience or not. The Corporation at last had the medium-wave transmitters within reach of the Middle East for which it had been asking for thirty years, but until the nature of the new audience was clear, it could not identify the right programmes for the transmitters to carry.

II

At some point between the autumn of 1957 and the summer of 1958 the Foreign Office shelved the notion of sponsoring a new commercial broadcasting station for the Middle East in the near future. The Arabic Service was enabled for the first time to consider its new position, and to make a bid for the funding and resources it needed. The man responsible for insisting on a complete reassessment was Tangye Lean, the Assistant Director of External Broadcasting. Under his supervision nearly forty individual contributors supplied material for a more thoughtful and thorough review of the Arabic Service than any made previously.

Behind Tangye Lean's Report lay a government decision (perhaps a provisional decision) to rely henceforward solely on the BBC for the diffusion of radio information in the Arab world, thus returning to the pre-war situation. Between the lines of the Report can be read a certain nervousness about the implications of this choice. The Voice of the Arabs had carried neutralism and Pan-Arabism all over the Arab world, and the establishment of the United Arab Republic early in 1958 had already led to Egyptian dominance of the Syrian radio services. The British government wanted to have 'a voice in the bazaar',[7] and the political argument for countering the Voice of the Arabs and 'stopping Nasser's mouth' had led them to decide on a big expansion of the Arabic Service and on the provision of further transmitters to carry it. But, having decided to spend this money, was the government going to expect from the BBC 'offensive propaganda' which its constitution inhibited it from offering and which was in any case going to be ineffective against the Nasserite tide? 'Failure to recognize the limitations imposed on the BBC by its national status would lead to extravagant hopes and much unreflecting criticism . . .'

There is clear-headed discussion of this, both in Tangye Lean's preliminary guidance paper (an 'Outline for Arabists'), and in the Report itself. The 'Outline' asks for:

a frank discussion of the extent to which our failure to stem the tide in the Near East is due to our own failures and limitations as broadcasters. There are situations which can be promptly heightened and speeded up by broadcasting (e.g., the rise of Hitler within Germany or the resistance of the populations of occupied Europe), and these are the result of a general predisposition among the ordinary people who make up the audience to accept the message of the broadcaster. There are other situations which are not susceptible to such influence because the ordinary member of the audience, however mistakenly, is 'deaf' to the message even though it is presented with inexhaustible resources (e.g., the failure of RTF in North Africa, of Moscow in Eastern Europe, and of the Cyprus Broadcasting Station in Cyprus). Do we find ourselves in one or other of these situations in the Middle East?

Accompanying this analysis, which reflects Lean's great experience as a wartime propagandist, was a warning about:

the risks of too great an overt display of propaganda effort, which can, in excess, acquire odium both for Britain and for the BBC. Odium of this kind is most easily incurred when the reality of what we have to offer does not measure up to the obvious technical effort we are putting into advertising it.

The Report dates the significant radio challenge of the Voice of the Arabs not from its inception in 1953 but from Nasser's decision in 1955 to opt for all-out neutralism and the acceptance of aid from the Soviet Union:

To the cause of Arab nationalism radio brought two inestimable advantages which could be used to their full effect only by Arab nationalism and not by the West: the power to address and inspire all Arab peoples with one voice simultaneously, and the power to mobilise the illiterates.

These modes of address were closed to the Western broadcaster, because of the emotional climate of the audience and his own status as an 'outsider'. The message of Cairo radio, the Report says, can be condensed into the statement that 'The Arab peoples, sharing their common religion and language, are to unite into a great modern power which will throw off the colonial oppressor – whether British, French, or American – and extermi- nate their common enemy Israel.'

The Report discusses the output of the BBC Arabic Service and its political characteristics. It mentions the framework of policy laid down in the 1946 White Paper, which requires, according to the Report, 'ob- jectivity in news and the acquisition of friendship and respect in talks and programmes.' Equally, it says, 'the obligations make it difficult to re- spond to occasional demands that abuse and incitement should be met in kind, and they rule out certain tactical manoeuvres which broadcasts concentrating exclusively on popularity have been tempted to use.' At this point Tangye Lean and his colleagues seem to be telling the government through the Report that the tactics which had been permissible at least to a limited degree in wartime, were excluded by the Charter and the 1946 White Paper in peacetime.

'In the atmosphere which is now prevailing,' the Report continues, 'the major political task of the Service is to win a fair hearing for the British (and Western) case.' This duty was envisaged first in a positive and then in a negative light. The positive duty was to represent British policy cor- rectly. When the Service treated controversial matters its first duty was to insist that political problems are discussed in the correct terms which establish their own version of the question at issue, which meant empha- sising the positive and constructive elements in British policy. Secondly – and this meant harking back to a much-discussed theme of wartime days – there was 'an increasing need of the more negative type of correction which consists of naming a statement or theme of the opponent, denying it in specific terms and stating what is the truth.' This however was an option which should be accepted only cautiously and occasionally:

Not only is it a major principle of propaganda that the case should be framed positively rather than defensively and the initiative should not seem to pass to the opponent, but there is a special need for caution in Arabic. Too many 'negative' denials could undo the primary object of winning Arab friendship.

Not only is this excessively schematic, but its vocabulary and arguments recall the tactical debates of wartime propaganda experts. There is some contradiction between the tone used in this part of the Report, and the preceding emphasis on the principles of the 1946 White Paper and the Charter. It strikes a note not much heard in the Arabic Service between the war and Suez, and perhaps Tangye Lean's long and intense experience of wartime broadcasting came rather too much to the front of his mind at this point. It may be that, in his anxiety to assure the government that the BBC was going to do justice to the British case against the misrepresentations of Cairo radio, he reverted to earlier mental habits.

On the other hand, the sharpness of the political analysis in the Report is striking. It was written at a time of crisis for the western powers almost as acute as that of 1956. The Iraqi revolution of 14 July and the murder of the Iraqi leaders most friendly to Britain had been followed by the landing of American troops in the Lebanon and of British airborne troops in Jordan. At the height of the crisis Gamal Abdel Nasser had been treated by the USSR and many other states as the most important leader in the Arab world. But at this nervous stage the Report counselled an information policy dictated by prudence and restraint.

The Report said:

The most striking political contrast between the pre-war and post-war periods has been the arrival of massive inter-continental broadcasting support for revolutionary Arab nationalism. Not only was this absent from the pre-war scene: the short-wave audience was unsuitable ground for revolutionary incitement. But there is now a clear limit (set by the xenophobia of the masses) to the ability of the West to get in among these popular passions and neutralise them. What can be done is to counteract and rebut much that is said against us, to retain the respect in which we are held (for technical, cultural and perhaps above all for fundamental political reasons) and to restore and strengthen the friendship which exists in spite of everything. With the Voice of the Arabs in the centre of the stage and Radio Moscow coming in from the wings, there is simply no chance of 'putting the Arabs back in their place'. With flattery growing daily louder in their ears, the only result would be to fix their allegiance elsewhere.

The Report had already implied that 'offensive propaganda' was rendered impossible by the constitutional restrictions placed on the BBC; it went on to imply that such propaganda was in any case inappropriate and fruitless.

The 'Output Themes' of the BBC Arabic Service as described in the Report are interesting because they attempt to make explicit the post-war political philosophy of the Service. They reflect the special preoccupations of the time, but they are not discreditable to the BBC. The first theme is 'Liberty in its various forms, with democratic standards of justice, honour and good faith. The British way of life, particularly in this democratic sense.' Secondly, 'The British contribution to the Arab world. The past (irrigation, industry, health, educational institutions etc.) and the present. British support for Arab strength and independence. The truth about Western progressive intentions in Algeria, the Persian Gulf and Aden.' Third, 'the exposure of Soviet and other dictatorships . . . the meaning of the Hungarian revolt and satellite status.' Fourth, the British Commonwealth particularly in the sense of its systematic development to full Dominion status, as in Ghana, Malaya and Nigeria. Fifth, western efficiency: health, sanitation, technics, industry, welfare standards. Sixth, 'Revolutionary Arab nationalism in perspective':

While it is worse than useless as a rule to attack this theme frontally, it may be possible in the long run to encourage a sense of perspective . . . by highlighting with apparent innocence some of the crudities and inefficiencies of the regime.

The example given, of attacking the Iraqi post-revolutionary trials in which officials had been prosecuted under retroactive legislation, would not today seem unnatural to a liberal-minded British journalist. Lastly, the output was concerned with 'the Arab desire to strengthen its technical, cultural and intellectual contacts with the West [including English by radio].'

The most notable political change to be detected in the Report, if it is compared with pre-Suez BBC attitudes, is the switch in emphasis from purely British to western interests. The events of 1956 hang heavily here, in that the United States is not heavily emphasised in the definition of western interests, but France and Israel are. Of 'Commitments to Allies and Policies', the Report says that:

Overtly associated with national policy, as the BBC is, there can be no question of seeking favour with the Arab audience by jettisoning Israel or attacking French policy in North Africa. On the contrary, we often have a difficult role to fulfil in this field as mediators . . . the countries of the west must now stand or fall together. The Arabs now rightly view Britain, France and the US as a single bloc, and the BBC would see more advantage in collaboration between their broadcasting agencies than in civil war. If it were proposed, for instance, to extend medium-wave broadcasting from this country to French North Africa, it would seem for consideration whether the possibility would require discussion with the French government.

In broaching the subject of Anglo-French relations over North Africa, the Report touches one of the most delicate issues in which the BBC was involved, one which stretched back to the wartime tensions between the British and the Free French. When the Report was being written the Algerian revolt was at its bloody peak, and had already led to the installation of the de Gaulle regime in France in May 1958. The setting up of a BBC medium-wave transmission to North Africa would have been a very controversial issue between the governments: not surprisingly it was not attempted, nor has it been undertaken since. It is, indeed, extraordinary, at this most sensitive moment for French government in North Africa, that the Report mentions it as a serious possibility at all.

The Tangye Lean Report still treats the option of a future commercial Arabic radio station under official British auspices as a possible one, although clearly such a station would not be operated by the BBC. The differences between the policies open to such a station and those of the BBC are discussed, particularly the adoption by a commercial station of a 'neutral' political standpoint hostile to Israel and France, and uncritical of the UAR and other Arab nationalist regimes. Such a station might, the Report thought, be commercially viable, or at least might make enough money from advertising to limit the subsidy required:

The Arab press would see to it that the national origins of such a station were known, but it might well be accepted as an alternative to the BBC and penetrate further down the social scale than would be possible for a station accepting its national responsibilities.

But whether the political consequences of setting up another Sharq al-Adna were acceptable, the Report declined to consider: this was not a matter for the BBC.

The bid made in the Report for more money and resources was substantial. The output of the Service in November 1958 was 9½ hours daily, split into an early morning, a late morning and an evening transmission. The proposal was to retain the early transmission (0345 – 0545 GMT), to start the second morning transmission later (1100 GMT) and then to run it continuously so that the main block ran from 1100 to 2030 or 2100. This proposal of a twelve-hours daily transmission was accepted, and was put into effect in 1959 after the government had announced its approval in the White Paper on Overseas Information Services published in March (Cmnd. 685). It amounted to a quadrupling of the transmissions of the Arabic Service relative to their length at the end of the war in 1945, and to a doubling of the transmissions relative to their length at the beginning of 1956. To a large extent this was achieved at the expense of other foreign-language services. In 1956 the only Service allotted more hours of transmission than the Arabic Service was the German Service with 29¾ hours to the Arabic Service's 28. From 1957 the Arabic Service was allotted more than double the output of any other foreign-language service. By July 1958 it employed twenty-eight Arabic staff, an increase of seven over the staff serving at the moment the Service went up to 9½ hours in 1957.[8]

Other back-up facilities were asked for, including substantially more money to acquire a better light music programme. This was not a frivolous matter, if the new output was genuinely to include a sort of light programme. The Cairo Office, the main source of entertainment recordings until then, had had to close in November 1956. A new office had been opened in Beirut, but the cost of hiring artistes in Beirut was much higher. There was a gap to be filled if the new Arabic programme was going to be in some measure a replacement for Sharq al-Adna as well as a continuation of the old BBC programme.

To improve the news facilities and to put out two new bulletins of exclusively Arab items of news, a fuller service from the news agency, the Arab News Agency (which had been a main provider of news since 1949), was asked for, a fuller monitoring service of the radio production of certain Arabic-speaking areas, and three new BBC External Service news correspondents to cover the Muslim world from the Maghreb to Pakistan. These were costly proposals, the estimate being an annual cost in the region of £33,000, approximately the equivalent of what was requested additionally for the light music programme. But the requests for better news services were all met, and by the end of 1959 a news room had been set up in Beirut for the Arabic Service, and two new External Service correspondents appointed, one to operate in North Africa and the other from Aden.

Together with one or two supplementary requests for money for a revived Arabic magazine to replace the defunct *Arabic Listener* (this was duly done, and the monthly *Huna London* appeared) and for Audience Research, the total additional annual cost asked for to improve the Service was estimated at £105,000. Since the annual cost of the whole Service had been in the region of £74,000 in 1956, and the estimated additional cost of the 1957 expansion to a nine-hours daily transmission had been £36,000, the 1958 proposals amounted to a request for the doubling of the annual cost of the Service, as it stood at November 1958.

III

The conclusion of the Tangye Lean Report says that the Arabic Service programme as modified by the proposals of the Report would become 'a light programme interspersed with spoken word material of a high standard but of very general appeal to those who are not insistent on closing their ears to the Westerner.' The insistence on its being a 'light programme' is of great interest: the Arabic Service had never thought of itself in this way before. To whom was the new programme to address itself? Was it to be a popular programme which would become the legitimate heir of Sharq al-Adna? Or was it to be a further development of the old 'news and information service from London', enlivened by an increased proportion of musical and entertainment material?

The final paragraph of the Report, having proposed the Service as a 'light programme', briefly raises some entirely new, radical possibilities for the directions in which it might develop. The first, which it mentions only to reject, is splitting the Service into segments directed at different Arab geographical regions. Another possibility 'might be to address the Arab world at different cultural levels: i.e. with a light programme and cultural or technical programme, more strongly flavoured with British abilities, arts and technics.' The Report concludes that:

this alternative [of a light programme balanced by a technical and cultural programme] already exists as the light programme (especially in the revised form proposed above) and the General Overseas Service, which is beamed on the area, giving much of the information needed by advanced students and intelligentsia.

This does not seem to be a very coherent argument, and it is not surprising that no more was heard of it. The casual throwing into the argument of such unannounced and new topics, at the moment of making the final judgement, shows how uncertain BBC management still was, at this late stage, as to how the greatly expanded Service was going to be articulated.

The great question, not unambiguously decided in 1959 in spite of the conclusions of the Tangye Lean Report, was whether the Arabic Service was to become a popular Service for the Arab masses, a real light programme. Politically, one may cynically argue, it was important for the BBC to convince the Foreign Office that the Service would become so, in order to rid itself of the threat of a new British-sponsored commercial station, another Sharq. But in fact the opposition inside the BBC to the popularisation of the Arabic Service programme had in the past been very vehement, and there is little reason to think that this had changed by 1958. John Rae, the former Middle East Representative, had argued forcefully in 1956 for 'a well-advertised Third Programme for the Middle East'. He conceded that the majority of Arabs now possessed or had access to a radio set, but because most were illiterate or semi-literate, because of their backwardness and poverty, they did not count politically. It was useless, he thought, to dispute the air waves with Nasser's Voice of the Arabs, and he believed that we should virtually ignore the mass audience, directing all our efforts at the middle-class intellectuals, the 'youthful, earnest intelligentsia'.[9] It was Perowne's argument of the priority of the effendi over the man under the palm tree.

The arguments for the conversion of the Arabic Service to a light programme were the political need to counter the mass appeal of the Voice of the Arabs, the proven success of the entertainment programme put out by Sharq al-Adna in the past, and finally a new technical factor which had not even begun to be evaluated when the Tangye Lean Report was compiled, the advent of the transistor radio. The Report talks of 'gathering round' radio sets, and clearly does not contemplate the avalanche of cheap and entirely portable transistor radios which was already beginning to deluge the world market, so that within a few years pastoral tribesmen would normally hook a transistor to their saddles. The size of the potential audience therefore rose in a dizzy manner. Within ten years of 1955 the number of radio sets in the Arab world was multiplied by a factor of five; by 1967 the factor was sixfold. Broadcasting on the medium wave thus became associated with the 'mass media' in a new way. The old calculation of the 1950s that the Arabic Service could reach a normal maximum audience of a million, in time of crisis three million, gave way to new figures which rose in geometric progression.[10]

The Report argues that the Arabic Service was already a light programme in the autumn of 1958 when it was compiled, and to some extent the figures it gives bear this out. Music accounted for some 37 per cent of the programme, news for about 25 per cent of the programme, talks and commentaries for $7^{1}/_{2}$ per cent, and variety and light magazine programmes for about 10 per cent. So almost half the programme was 'light' if we account all the music played to be in this category: news and information took up roughly a third. This was a very different balance from the historical one, and it was to be greatly modified after 1958.

Those who ran or helped to run the Arabic Service were mostly (though not all) unlikely impresarios. Gordon Waterfield's background was journalistic and literary; 'Tommy' Thomson's background was also journalistic; J. H. Whitehead was a former Classics lecturer; Hamilton Duckworth an Arabic scholar and a man very difficult to associate with variety programmes; though it is true that Duckworth's predecessor as Head of Service, Charles McLelland, went on to be Controller, Radios 1 and 2. But the great liberty given to producers in all branches of the BBC meant that, staid and solid as many of the administrators may have been, if they could find the right Arabic staff they could get a lively programme.

By and large the Tangye Lean Report was accepted by the government. In March 1959 a government paper on the Overseas Information Services (Cmnd. 685) stated that the Arabic Service had been reviewed in consultation with the Corporation, and that as a result the daily transmission would rise to twelve hours, there would be increased coverage of events of local significance, greater local appeal in entertainments programmes, and general improvements in quality. To strengthen the Arabic and some African Services, a new relay transmitter was to be built in Berbera, Somaliland Protectorate (this was an ill-fated venture, as soon after independence the Somalis required its closure in 1963).

The BBC showed its awareness of the increased importance of the Arabic Service by constituting it as a separate regional service, no longer part of the 'Eastern Service', on 1 January 1959. Its first Head was Gordon Waterfield. With the further development of the Service the BBC had to express itself satisfied. In the 1965–6 *Report and Accounts* (Cmnd. 3122) the Corporation said:

The Middle East is one of the areas where the situation is satisfactory. The Arabic Service and World Service are available on medium waves to a large part of the Middle East, the Mediterranean and North Africa, and recent audience surveys have shown how successful this investment has been.

Tangye Lean at the same time wrote in the *BBC Handbook*: 'Organisationally, the success of the BBC in Arabic has been a significant one because the standards of BBC output have been backed up by the government with appropriate resources.' Tangye Lean could retire from the BBC secure in the knowledge that the great pains he had expended on the expansion of the Arabic Service had not been wasted, and that he left it in what seemed at the time to be an unassailable position.

CHAPTER 8

THE PROGRAMME
AND ITS PUBLIC: II

I

When in 1957 the Arabic Service gained medium-wave coverage and an increase in transmission time to 9½ hours daily, it also changed the balance of its programmes. Part of this, no doubt, was the provenance of much of its newly recruited staff; coming from the 'light' programme of Sharq al-Adna, they strongly influenced the BBC programme to which they went. The Arabic Service also gained, at this time, its first woman announcer, who soon got a share of the fan mail.

By the autumn of 1958 over 37 per cent of the output of the Arabic Service was, as has been said above, in the form of music. News and news talks took up 32 per cent; variety and light programmes over 10 per cent, features and plays about 6 per cent, and general and cultural talks under 5 per cent. This represented a big change from the earlier programme format. It came close to reversing the wartime arrangements under which news and commentaries had occupied 37 per cent of the programme and music about 21 per cent: general talks of a formidably highbrow tendency had in the wartime period taken up about 20 per cent. The idea, cherished by some BBC officials, that the Arabic Service should become the Third Programme of the Arabic world, had been decisively defeated in 1957 in favour of a relatively popular solution.

The popularisation of the programme was due partly to a political decision made following the demise of Sharq al-Adna in 1956, partly to the recruitment of the Sharq broadcasters, and partly to the changed nature of the competition on the air waves. At the end of the war, apart from British-inspired or controlled stations, there were only nine or ten stations broadcasting in Arabic. Apart from Cairo the standard of these stations was low, and no one could compete with the BBC in the treatment of news. But the post-war expansion of broadcasting in and to the Middle East was rapid. By 1949 the number of stations broadcasting in Arabic had doubled, compared with the number four years earlier. Paxton – still thinking largely in terms of talks – had written in 1947:

The listeners to our programmes would appear to be chiefly lower-middle-class merchants, students and so forth, who are either suffering from the lack of local broadcasting or are deprived of the kind of programme they require by their local station. In either case their tastes are strongly nationalist and their chief desire is to hear talks and plays [sic] on Arab rather than British culture and achievements.[1]

This judgement acknowledged, implicitly at least, the need to move to a more popular programme, but did not show any great sense of urgency.

The competition from nations broadcasting in Arabic but located outside the Arab world increased drastically in the 1950s. By 1950 there were ten external broadcasters in Arabic, by 1955 fifteen, and by 1958 twenty-two. By the last date the major broadcasters in Arabic were, apart from the BBC, the Voice of America (whose most important announcer was the former BBC figure, Isa Sabbagh), France, Spain, the USSR, Israel and Egypt. Of these much the most formidable competitor was the Voice of the Arabs in Cairo. Egypt had always enjoyed far greater broadcasting expertise than any other Arab country. It offered at this stage a political message which was acceptable all over the Arab world, and combined it with entertainment and programme management of a good professional standard.

The broadcasting standard of some of the other Arab stations was modest, sometimes for political reasons. In Bagdad in 1954, for example, a British observer noted that the local station never mentioned Iraq except in official communiqués from either the Cabinet or the Palace. Apart from these, and from the weather forecast, 'nothing but foreign news is ever read, carefully datelined from abroad, and Iraq might just as well not exist.'[2] This political sterilisation of news was and is a widespread phenomenon in the Arab world, and one which gave (and gives) the BBC one of its main chances. It often happens that stations which in other respects reach a good professional level of broadcasting treat the news of their own country in a formal and boring manner, offering no political comment except that which comes from official sources.

On the other hand, the Egyptian influence in the Arab radio world spread very quickly after 1956, and so did Egyptian broadcasting techniques: for example, after the political union of Egypt with Syria in 1958 the Damascus radio station was swiftly reorganised on Voice-of-the-Arabs lines, with the Egyptian propaganda chief, Abdel-Kader Hatem, in charge of the operation. This led to the transformation of Syrian broadcasting. And after the 1958 revolution in Iraq Abdul Karim Kassem carried out a similar transformation in Iraqi radio and television, also inspired by the Voice of the Arabs in method, but devoted to the glorification of the Iraqi leader of that time.[3]

In the mid-1950s the number of potential listeners started to increase with very great rapidity. There were reckoned to be less than a million radio sets which could pick up BBC Arabic programmes in the Arab world in 1953. By 1955 this figure had risen to substantially over two million; by 1965 it was well over twelve million. The audience for a more popular programme was there, if the BBC could reach it. The expansion of the Arabic Service and the popularisation of the programme did in fact bring the programme to the intended audience. Listeners wrote to the Service in immensely increased numbers. In the mid-1950s letters had been arriving in London at the rate of nine or ten thousand a year; in 1961 there were over twenty-six thousand such letters. At this stage the scale of listener reaction had increased in roughly direct proportion to the increased number of hours broadcast: later in the 1960s better programme management meant that the letters continued to increase, in spite of a reduction in the hours of transmission. About two thirds of the letters were either requests for musical items or responses to programmes like *Question and Answer* or *Listeners' Forum*; those that made serious comments or suggestions were carefully analysed and translated.

The great increase in Arab staff which came with the expansion of the programme to nine and a half hours in 1957 and to twelve hours in 1959, meant that the Arabophone programme producer became the rule rather than the exception. By the end of 1964 there were sixty people on the Arabic Service monthly establishment. The result was to transform the output and to make the elements in it which were planned and executed in Arabic into the greater rather than the lesser part of the programme. The great freedom which the BBC gave to producers accentuated the process. There was a great deal of consultation between senior staff and producers, but 'control' was not a word which the producers naturally used to describe the relationship. The result was a programme which to a very large extent was conceived, planned and executed by native Arabic speakers. This did not change very much when the daily programme hours were cut to ten in 1967, nor when they were reduced further to nine in 1976.

But what was going to be the nature of the programmes which this more authentically Arabophone service was going to put out? This did not become entirely clear until after the 1967 Arab–Israeli Six-Day War, but one factor was to impose itself gradually over the whole period. The rise of television and of other leisure pursuits in the Arab world led to a change in the psychology of radio listening. As Bowman, the Head of the Service, wrote in 1985:

When the BBC started broadcasting in Arabic, we could afford to run a network rather like the old Home Service where the listeners switched on and over the course of several hours were exposed to a whole range of information and cultural activities. Now we have to think in quite short time segments – probably about an hour – in which to inform and entertain the audience.

The assumption of a very limited attention span in the audience was in the long run to transform the whole output.

II

News and news commentaries did not remain a closed area in which the British members of staff ruled supreme. Programmes like *Round the World* (which had a venerable history in the Service, but survived into the late 1960s), and its successors *The World at One* and *The World at Six* were the basic news presentations, and were more often produced by Arabophones than not. So was another survivor of older times, *On the Margin of the News*, and some innovations of the 1970s like *Focus* and *Economic Bulletin*.

News was British-controlled in that the External Services and the BBC news organisation were the basic news-gatherers, reporters, and news-sifters. Particularly in its use of despatches from correspondents, the Arabic Service took the basic constituents of its news from the External Services news desks. This was especially important in the Middle East wars of 1967 and 1973, when the documents show clearly that the news put out by the Arabic Service was the news fed to it by the duty editor of the External Services. Some additional news was fed into the programme from the despatches of the BBC correspondents which came direct to the Service. The flexibility with which correspondents abroad could input despatches was radically changed between 1967 and 1975. Before 1967 they had been dependent on two or three circuits a day, arranged in advance, over which they could transmit their reports. The introduction of facilities for inputting despatches by telephone transformed the task of the foreign radio correspondent, enabling him to feed material into the news desk at any time of the day or night.

The Arabic Service ran one or two programmes like *Arab News Letter* or the later *Week in the Arab World* and *Round the Arab World* which took some news from sources different to those used by the External Services as a whole. But this was simply to put into the programme the kind of news which it was known would be of interest to the Arab world, and of far less interest outside it.

One or two of the older political programmes which survived into the 1960s and '70s or later preserved the old arrangement of being put out for reply by a British journalist or commentator (where this was necessary), or of being compiled by a British member of staff. *Arab Affairs in the British Press* was usually treated in this way, and so was *Political Question and Answer*. One long-lived British contributor was a mysterious N. K. Boot, who began to contribute in 1955 or 1956. I understand that this pseudonym (which perhaps covers more than one journalist) derives not from the eponymous journalist in Evelyn Waugh's *Scoop*, but from the Arabic for 'spider', which transliterates 'ankabut'. But there was also more space for Arabophones in the current affairs talks, for example, for Sudanese or other Arabs working in the United Nations to talk about contemporary affairs from a UN point of view.

Changes in the politics of the Middle East affected programming indirectly but decisively. The 1967 war can probably be reckoned to be the watershed of the post-Suez Arabic Service. Politically the date is critical in the history of the Arab world: besides effecting a decisive change in the Middle East territorial balance it marked the end of the old-style Nasserist pan-Arabism and the emergence of a new Palestinian movement; it also sealed the fate of unfortunate Lebanon. The modernised PLO terrorism after the Six-Day War changed the way in which western news media looked at and reported the Middle East. Terrorism in western airports and cities brought with it a completely different treatment of the issues: it marked the end of the old Middle East journalism.

To the Arabic Service, in which Palestinians were so heavily repre-sented, the years after 1967 brought especially difficult problems of ob-jective presentation and newsreading. Only once, during the fighting between the Jordanian government army and the PLO in the autumn of 1970, was it alleged that Palestinian news announcers had phrased or enunciated the news in a way unfavourable to King Hussein. It could not, when an enquiry was made, be shown that the text of the news put out in Arabic was less than entirely objective. If the enunciation of words or phrases by individual announcers had seemed in some way partisan, that was against BBC policy, but was hard to control in practice. The impor-tance of maintaining an impartial tone in the newscasting became clear in the enquiry.

In 1972 it was the turn of the Egyptians to accuse the Arabic Service of prejudice. The Sadat government, which was feeling vulnerable after its expulsion of Russian military men that summer, and which was nervous of Army unrest, was furious when the BBC used a story about an abortive military coup against the regime: that the Arabic Service carried the Egyptian government's denial, which was issued twenty-four hours later, did not excuse it. In November 1972 the Egyptians protested angrily to the British Embassy in Cairo, and threatened (as in 1951 and 1956) to take action against Egyptian artistes and performers who worked for the BBC. There was even a period in which the Arabic Service was jammed. But, as the 1973 *Handbook* observed, there was never any interference with the work of the BBC Cairo Office, and the storm blew itself out in the following March.

The end of the 1960s was also a watershed in the history of the External Services generally: the administrative reorganisation of 1968–9 was de-scribed by the Managing Director, Oliver Whitley, as 'nothing short of a revolution'.[4] This major reorganisation of the Services as a whole did not fail to have an impact on the Arabic Service.

The capacity of the news service to react swiftly and to reflect the British official response to events in the Arab world was sometimes of political importance. In 1970 when the PFLP agent, Leila Khalid, was being held in London, and British hostages in Jordan were being threatened, the British

Cabinet put out a statement at 6.30 p.m. on 7 September which was translated and broadcast in Arabic at 7 p.m. Similarly, at the height of the crisis of the October War of 1973, on 8 October Mr Heath made a statement at a meeting with the Chairman of the United Arab Emirates, that Britain's efforts at the Security Council would be directed towards getting a resolution for a cease-fire, without discussion of who started the fighting, and based on the British belief in the necessity of implementing the Security Council's resolution no. 242 on the Middle East. This statement was put out in Arabic on *Radio Newsreel* at 9.25 that evening.

III

The most striking absentees from the programme after 1957 are the British official or former official and the British orientalist. Either might make a very occasional appearance, but months might pass without a translated talk by an Oxford Professor of Arabic or a British ex-Excellency. Translated scholarly talks were more likely to concern sociology or town-planning, than the early Arabic poets. The Arabic Talks and Magazine Unit of the 1960s looked at things in a very different way from the Programme Assistants of the 1940s. The programme's attitude to cultural matters had undergone substantial change. Most cultural talks were either produced in Beirut or Cairo, or grew from visits to Europe by Arab scholars or research students, or were offshoots of the migrating scholarly population which frequented cultural conferences in the East or the West. Even when western Arabist scholars were saluted or commemorated, the speaker was far more likely to be an Arab scholar than a British one. Conservative BBC administrators like Hamilton Duckworth complained of the confused ideas of the Arab intellectuals who broadcast on the programme, but they would probably have made similar complaints about the contemporary British equivalents. Old-stagers like Marmorstein accused the programme of triviality which had come upon it from following intellectual fashion. These changes emerged gradually in the post-war period, but by the time of the fully expanded programme they were complete.

The projection of Britain (POB) was approached in the 1960s in a more light-hearted way reflecting the increasing self-confidence of post-war British society. Programmes like *Fi al-Madif* ('In the Guesthouse'), *Here and There*, and *Laugh with the English* looked at Britain in an ironic and sceptical way which was far from the solemn affirmations of earlier POB programmes. This was the decade of *That was the Week, that was!* and of Tony Hancock and David Frost, and 'satire' made its mark on the Arabic programmes. What might be described as 'gallows humour' has an Arabic equivalent which producers were quick to seize on. Nor were they unaware of the world export value of the Beatles. The release of *Sergeant Pepper's Lonely Hearts Club Band* was immediately greeted on the Arabic

Service by a special talk. There was also a new programme, adapted from the programme of the same name on the Light Service, *Roundabout*, which strung together miscellaneous topical and curiosity items on British life with a mixture of Arabic and western music and songs. Quite a lot of odd topical observations on British life also went into *Pick of the Week*. *On Life's Stage* was a programme with a more 'cultural' bias which took in the lives of the British poets. *Kaleidoscope of Britain*, the POB programme of the early '80s, was rather less irreverent than some of its predecessors.

Air communications and new prosperity produced new dimensions in Anglo-Arab relations. With the late 1960s the great march of the Saudi and Lebanese ladies upon Harrods and the Marble Arch Marks and Spencers began: while this invasion was taking place their husbands were taking their medical problems to the London Clinic. There had always been programmes like *London Diary* and *London this Week*: in the late 1970s the proportions of the Arab influx into London justified programmes like *Tourist Magazine*, with items on London shopping and fashion design. There were also from the '60s onwards programmes of interviews with Arabs in London, like *Ahlan wa-Sahlan* and *In Town this Week*. In 1978 there was a programme, *With the Arab families in Britain*. A certain number of outside broadcasts took Arabic Service reporters into the streets of British towns: Stratford on Avon was an obvious target, but one wonders what Arab listeners made of 'Towns with one predominant industry – Spalding'.

British education had become, especially before the great rise in university fees for foreigners in 1979, one of the most important commodities which Britain had to offer the Arab world, and also one of its most important social models. The social life of Oxford and Cambridge continued to attract programmes, though these were now more likely to be about the admission of women to the previously male colleges than about traditional roles. But Oxford and Cambridge were of minor importance beside the enormous demand for technical and scientific education, and also beside the provision of new educational models like the Open University. These things were reflected over a wide range of programmes, particularly in those directed at Arab youth, like *The Rising Generation, Tomorrow's Citizens* and *Youth Magazine*.

Trade and Industry and 'British Enterprise' programmes, and science and technology talks, continued to be a staple diet of the Service, and were never put out less than weekly; by 1985 such programmes occurred no less than ten times a week. The contact between the Arabic Service and British firms operating in the Middle East became close; projects and products were normally mentioned by name in the programmes, and in the 1980s firms were given what was virtually free advertising space in the Service's equivalent of the *Radio Times, Huna London*.

Of the programmes about Anglo-Arab life the most fascinating is the drama series about a Jordanian medical student living in Britain written by Tom Stoppard, who later became a dramatist of world reputation, but was signed on before he was either famous or rich by Leila Tannous in the mid-1960s, to write a series which went to approaching a hundred and fifty episodes. *A Student's Diary* was a competent and amusing look at the new Arab student, in digs in Kingston-on-Thames or Hull, who was trying to cope with the society of the mini-skirt and the Beatles. It was saluted ironically by an aging Emile Marmorstein (who had been working on Arabic audience research since the beginning of the war) as something for which it was easy to predict a favourable audience response, since its 'reflection of the camaraderie between the sexes attractively confirmed the romantic visions of Western student life that are cherished by such a large section of literate Arab youth.' It is pleasing to think of that rabbinical figure, Marmorstein, assessing Tom Stoppard's prentice efforts at an Arabic radio soap series.

One new manifestation of British cultural life in this period was the festival. At Edinburgh, at Aldeburgh, at Bath, in towns of cultural importance all over the country, drama, poetry, the visual arts were encouraged and displayed in new ways and to new audiences. In the Arab world these manifestations awoke answering responses like the festivals in Baalbek, Carthage and Hammamet, in which British artists and producers often took a main part. The Arabic Service was able to respond to these new tendencies in British and Arab cultural life, and Leila Tannous, particularly, produced a great many programmes about them.

One offering which was bound to be eagerly received all over the Arab world was the English lessons. Tapes of these were at one time distributed without payment. However, the FCO and British Council policy of the 1970s was that lessons were to be offered by British agencies fundamentally on a commercial and paying basis, and that it was not the function of information work to distribute them free. *Let's Speak English* and similar courses remained a basic, though a minor constituent in the Arabic programme. In 1980 the BBC had compiled on its behalf English lessons which broke new ground in language teaching (*Follow Me*), and these were sold to several Arab countries.

Viewed overall, British life was reflected in the programmes of the '60s and '70s in subtle and multifarious ways which testify to the awareness and sensitivity of the young Arab producers and reporters in the Service. They also reflected the ways in which current British domestic programmes and radio methods influenced the External Services. The variety of the responses shows how inadequate attempts to define the 'projection of Britain' have been, which fail to think about the interaction of two cultures, and not just of the 'projection' of one.

IV

After the expansion of the programme, light entertainment and features were each accorded their own Arabophone head (in 1964 these were A. R. Rifai and I. H. Rizq, respectively). Variety programmes like *Shahr al-Asal* ('Honeymoon') had a bigger place in the programme in the decade after 1957 than at any time before or after. Many of them were made in Beirut by independent Arab companies, or occasionally in Cairo. Others were produced in London, especially by two talented and amusing Egyptians, Anwar Sheta and Fuad Gemie. Nevertheless, the proportion of variety items in the programme was declining even before the cut in broadcasting hours was made in 1967: in 1966 variety took up only 4 per cent of the output. After 1967 variety programmes virtually disappeared. In the early 1980s people became conscious of a certain solemnity which had crept over the programme, and by 1986 the *BBC Handbook* reported a 'livelier style' of music and entertainment programmes.

After the programme had been reduced from twelve hours daily transmission to ten in 1967 it moved away from entertainment towards a much more topical and current-affairs basic diet, and this trend continued when transmission time was further reduced to nine hours daily (which has remained the norm down to the present day) in 1976. One reason for the more sober nature of the programme after 1967 was, initially, the gloom which settled over an Arab staff in which the Palestinians were numerous, after the disasters of the Arab–Israeli war of that year. There was no Christmas party for the Arabic Service in 1967, because the staff declined to hold it. But the drift back to current affairs was also a return to the original nature of the programme in the 1940s – to a 'news and information service from London'.

Listeners' Forum and *Question and Answer* continue to the present day in very much the same format with which they started forty years ago. It is almost impossible to abandon programmes which provoke such a large proportion of listeners' correspondence. On the other hand the women's programmes like *Woman's Corner* and *It's a Woman's World* failed to survive the 1970s: whether their abandonment was due to fear of feminist resentment of discriminatory programme forms or to the dissatisfaction of managers with the programmes themselves, it is hard to guess. Children's programmes also became few and far between. *The Family Programme*, introduced in 1986, filled this gap.

Sports programmes had their ups and downs. The attitude towards them changed after the late 1960s, when the Arab world acquired its own inter-Arab games and sports events, and sports reporting ceased to be a matter of reporting mainly European events. In North Africa a huge footballing public developed, for example. That in many Arab countries the local viewers are discontented with the television and radio coverage of sport which is available to them, makes this a market in which the BBC has enormous advantages, when it cares to use them. *Sports Magazine* and its predecessors did well, though there were gaps in the sports expertise available to the programme at various times. Musa Bishuti had been a notable presenter on the sports programme.

With medical programmes the demand was always enormous: a large percentage of the letters to *Question and Answer* has always been concerned with medical queries, and programmes like *With the Doctor* and *Medicine Today* were virtually guaranteed an audience. The great transformations of medical care in the Arab world in the 1970s, especially in some areas like Saudi Arabia and the Gulf, made medical reporting a quite different affair. Some of the most advanced hospitals are now located in Arab countries and some of the most interesting medical conferences now take place there, and this is bound to be reflected in the programme.

Other new features were modelled on domestic service originals. *This Morning* was a general ragbag programme with a mixture of topical items on British and Arab life, which went out first with the early morning transmission. *Pick of the Week* was a retrospective programme of much the same kind, again with a mixture of British and Arab items. In these programmes the motor-racer Jackie Stewart rubbed shoulders with visitors to an orientalist congress in Paris, and reports on the British educational 'Black Papers' with an interview with the Director of the Libyan folklore group.

The serious talk was less frequent in these programmes, modelled in contemporary terms on Radio 4 rather than on Radio 3, than in the early programme, and the charge of triviality which Marmorstein brought in 1966 is understandable, even if hard to maintain. The nearest thing to the older intellectual diet was the long-lived series, *Men and Ideas*, which started with a talk by Nevill Barbour on the British orientalists in 1966 (which was criticised at the time for its conservative approach to the subject). But the change of programming to move away from a Third Programme bias had been a conscious decision made in 1958 on very well-considered grounds.

After 1967 the most stable entertainment element in the programme was the daily fifteen-minute dramatic serial; often there would be two different serialised plays a day. There was a revival of in-house dramatic features in 1987 with the serialised *Spy Who Came in from the Cold* of le Carré: and to mark the 1988 anniversary a production of Hardy's *Mayor of Casterbridge* was planned. Other plays remained mostly within rather narrow time limits, like *Thirty-minute Theatre* (which could again take a serial form, as it did with *Great Expectations*), and the rather elaborate, lengthy play productions of the past became rare. This meant that the Service was no longer an important patron for serious new Arabic drama, which must be accounted a loss. But the judgement that listeners could give the programme only a very limited attention span, was bound to make the full-length play into a rarity. Arabic poetry, on the other hand, continued to make a mark on the programme, and so did other elements of the inexhaustibly rich Arabic tongue: for example, the long-lived programme, *A Saying on a Saying*.

Many serials achieved very substantial success. *A Student's Diary, The Prisoner of Zenda*, and some of the dramatised versions of Dickens's novels were all hits. The short story also remained an element in the programme, but again only in a rather reduced way. Whether this was because it had become much harder to find good new Arabic short stories, is uncertain. But the old policy of using a lot of translations of Western short stories had been abandoned.

Music continued to be one of the main parts of the programme. Having started with a scratch collection of Egyptian popular songs, the Service came to possess one of the finest collections of Arabic recorded music in the world. Over the years it had received the care and attention of some formidable musicologists, of whom Basri was the most important.

Music represented 37 per cent of the output in 1958 and 34 per cent in 1967; in the 1980s the proportion was in the region of 20 per cent. Musical policy presented some quite difficult choices. It was too expensive to buy the latest popular singers as their songs came out, except in the ordinary commercial issues, and it was out of the question to commission new ones. To some extent the BBC could live on its Arabic hump, by going back to great classical songs of singers like Umm Kulthum and Muhammad Abdul Wahab which had been recorded specially for them in the war period or soon after: these went out in programmes like *From London Alone*. A similar technique of using the classical records collection was used for *Today's Singer*, in which Leila Murad, Sirri Tamburji, Sayyid Darwish, Fayda Kamil are names which recur in the 1960s. Programmes of regional music were Basri's speciality from the beginning: there was also a lot of regional music in the very long-lived regional programmes like *Kashkul al-Maghrib*. There was an immense variety of listeners' request programmes of music, from *Listeners' Rendezvous* and *Listeners' Requests* onwards: there were also some rather more specialised programmes like *Musicians' Forum*.

Western music had in the past been largely used in the fadeout and background music. There was, however, a steady influx of letters requesting western musical items, and these were met by the weekly *Western Listeners' Requests* and *Top of the Pops*.

V

The public addressed by the Arabic Service has grown by giant steps during the past thirty years. In 1958 the total population of the Arab countries was in the region of 80 million, excluding the several million Arab speakers in regions like East and West Africa and Iran. The conventional figure for radio ownership given in the BBC, in 1958 was about 2.75 million, a distribution of one to every thirty members of the population, as compared with one to every five members of the European population. The transistor revolution changed this state of affairs speedily. In 1965 the number of receivers was reckoned already at 12.25 million, or 4½ times that of seven years earlier, and by 1967 the figure was already at 15.8 million. In 1974 it was 27.4 million, in 1980 41 million, in 1985 58 million. In less than thirty years the potential radio audience had thus increased by a factor of more than twenty.

Audience research has been pursued in the same painstaking way as before. The results of this research have always confirmed what has occasionally been an embarrassing fact to some BBC officials, that they are pursuing an essentially popular democratic activity. As the 1958 Report said, 'We know from other sources that prime ministers and members of governments, Nasser included, listen to the BBC, and it may be supposed that others in less prominent but still influential positions – senior officials, newspaper editors, army officers – also listen.' But except on very rare occasions the letters do not come from such eminent persons:

The majority of the letters we receive are from people who cannot be judged, by their writing, to be very well educated; many are clerks, shopkeepers and skilled or semi-skilled workers – drivers, mechanics and operatives in the oil fields. At the same time, the correspondence is by no means wholly made up of music requests, and it never fails to give evidence of attentive listening to such items as the poetry programme, the political commentaries, and *Political Question and Answer*; and this sort of listening presupposes an audience of people accustomed to intellectual activity in the course of their work. Professional people, especially teachers, are fairly well represented in the correspondence.

This could hardly be better said, and it is very doubtful if the situation it reports has changed very much since 1958.

By 1980 there were 11.8 million television sets in the Arab world, and by 1985 19.5 million, that is to say as many as there had been radio sets in the area in 1971–2. The relations between the television medium and radio are very hard to define. There is little doubt that the BBC finds listeners in areas of the Arab world where television is least developed, like the Yemen Arab Republic, where four years ago the listeners in the towns were estimated at nearly half the male adult population. But other figures from recent audience research surveys correlate rather strangely. In Egypt, where the television is excellent, 9 per cent of urban adults are said to listen to the BBC, which is a higher percentage than Egyptian listeners could show thirty years ago. In Morocco, where television is neither particularly good nor particularly bad, the urban adult listeners to the BBC stood in 1986 at 15 per cent – this is an impressive figure, since there is no medium-wave BBC transmission to Morocco, and to receive the programme listeners must fiddle in the short-wave bands. It is interesting that

in Tunisia, where domestic television is strong, and over half the programmes are internally produced, the BBC still enjoys an appreciable
share of the radio audience (7.9 per cent of the urban audience in 1986). In
the Gulf, where television is as much a part of the way of life as anywhere
in the Arab world, BBC listening was reported in 1979 at between 19 and
22 per cent of urban adults in three states, and at the same time at 23 per
cent in Saudi Arabia – though in the four Emirates it was rather lower at 9
per cent.

What seems to emerge is that BBC radio cohabits with Arab television
services in somewhat the same way that BBC domestic radio cohabits
with television services in this country. That television is the same immensely powerful medium in many Arab countries that it is in western
ones, is beyond doubt. But the availability of a trusted BBC information
service, and of a programme which attracts loyal listening, means that
people all over the Arab world turn to its Arabic Service, not merely in
times of crisis, but in a comfortable and familiar daily way.

One way to try to guide the listener and to keep him inside a sort of BBC
ring fence is to offer him a programme guide and house magazine. This is
Huna London, which replaced the defunct *Arabic Listener* in 1960, first as a
fortnightly and then as a monthly. It did not try to reproduce the old *Arabic
Listener*, and in any case the kind of learned talks which were the staple of
the old magazine were no longer given in such numbers: but some talks
were nevertheless reprinted. Essentially *Huna London* was a programme
guide, the Arabic *Radio Times*. It was printed first in Beirut, then in Cairo,
and finally after 1982 in London. The print run was initially ten thousand,
but by the early 1980s over seventy-five thousand. There was, finally,
quite an important role for *Huna London* as a market showcase for British
goods and products: it tied in closely with the trade and industry programmes, and carried announcements for British products both in the text
and in advertising material.

VI

It is customary in the BBC to refer to 'the competition' offered by other
broadcasting organisations to the BBC External Services. How that competition is defined amounts to a definition of the aims of the British
Services. If it is primarily that of the other so-called external broadcasters,
of Moscow Radio, Monte Carlo, Voice of America, Deutsche Welle and
so on, then the BBC is asking people to consider it primarily as a propagandist service. But Arabic broadcasting cannot be considered in such a
schematic way, because of the enormous geographical spread of the Arab
linguistic area. This has meant that in many parts of the Arab world there
has been only a rather shadowy distinction between domestic radio services and those directed to foreign Arabic-speaking listeners. Pan-Arab
ideology has also helped to blur the distinction. The Libyan 'Voice of the

Arab Homeland', for example, is said to make no hard-and-fast distinction between external and domestic audiences.[5] The Egyptian 'Voice of the Arabs' has, on the other hand, become primarily a foreign-language service, and now broadcasts in Arabic for only seven hours daily against the BBC's nine.[6] On the other hand, some Arabic broadcasting services transmit programmes in languages other than Arabic, addressed to their own people, for example the Moroccan transmissions in Berber and the Tunisian and Algerian transmissions in French.

The only sensible way to consider the competition seems to be that competition to the BBC comes from any radio station which broadcasts in Arabic. The history of the development of Arab-language radio over the last thirty years is an enormous subject which cannot be more than touched on here. The knowledge that propagandist broadcasting to the Arab world was developing so quickly was the main reason for the expansion of the BBC Arabic Service between 1950 and 1959, as has been related above.

Worries before 1955 concentrated on the development of Arab-language broadcasting from behind the Iron Curtain: worries after 1955 were mainly concerned with Nasserist propaganda from Cairo and elsewhere. In 1958 there were twenty-two non-Arab nations broadcasting to the Middle East, of whom France and Britain broadcast for more programme hours than anyone else – although most French output was at that time destined for North Africa. Moscow broadcast for forty-two hours (half the BBC 1959 output), and at that time occupied an output place between the BBC and the Voice of America. By 1960 Poland was the only Iron Curtain country not to broadcast in Arabic. There was thus a strong cold-war element in the competition to broadcast in the Middle East. But at that time the most feared competitor was not Moscow (to whose radio few Arabs have ever listened) but the Voice of the Arabs, which broadcast roughly as many hours as the BBC Arabic began to use in 1959.

The peculiarly competitive nature of Arab broadcasting arises from the culture widely shared over a big geographical area, but also from a curiosity, perhaps more marked among Arabs than elsewhere, to know what neighbours, friends and enemies are saying. Perhaps scepticism about the veracity of their own home stations is a factor. A 1972 study made in Jordan concluded that almost three-quarters of adult Jordanians listened regularly to foreign radio stations, and that the preferred type of programme was news, followed by music. This particular survey must have comforted the BBC at the time, since it said that over a third of Jordanians listened to the BBC.[7] But what is more important is the out-listening habit: not only did a third of Jordanians listen to the BBC, but another (possibly overlapping) third listened to the Israeli Broadcasting Service.

There is, however, no psychological law which says that an Arab listener will, before tuning in, choose which foreign broadcasting service he prefers. The choice before him at that moment is not between the various broadcasting stations located outside the Arab world which use Arabic, but between all Arabic broadcasting stations which he can at that moment receive on the set. The struggle on the air is one of all against all, and the BBC must contend with the sum of domestic Arab radio competition.

The nature of that competition has changed. From 1967 onwards the Voice of the Arabs spoke with a far more moderate tone, and from 1979 onwards it has been still further restricted by its government being committed to policies which are in conflict with the old Pan–Arab ideal. It may now be accounted a conservative station, and in some respects Egyptian radio has gone back to ideas and methods which are to a large extent shared with the BBC. No other Pan–Arab radio has succeeded to the role and influence of the Nasserite Voice of the Arabs, although Libyan, Syrian and Iraqi broadcasting have each at some points had aspirations in this direction. On the other hand, most important Arab states now possess the technical radio equipment to transmit propagandist programmes capable of being received over a large part of the Arab world. Inter-Arab war over the air waves has not been lacking over the past twenty years, but it has had the fragmentary and confused character of Arab international relations in that time.

In practical terms the keenest competitor of the BBC in the Arab world is the French commercial station Radio Monte Carlo, which has been broadcasting on the medium wave from Cyprus since 1971. Monte Carlo is mainly owned by the French government,[8] and the French government has a stake in another similar commercial radio station operating from Tangier, Médi Un, which is part-owned also by the Moroccan government. The Monte Carlo formula is not unlike the old Sharq al-Adna formula, that is, excellent and up-to-the-minute popular music programmes backed up by frequent news bulletins. The programme has a rather Lebanese flavour, but that does not stop it from having been over the last ten or fifteen years the most widely-heard 'pop' radio programme transmitted from abroad to the Middle East. The Arabic Service response to the Monte Carlo challenge was to sharpen up its news presentation, though without compromising its traditional sobriety and judgement.

Politically there is a certain comfort for the British in the nature of the effective external broadcasting competition to the BBC in the Arab world, which comes mainly from the radios of other EEC countries (Monte Carlo, Médi Un, Deutsche Welle) or from a NATO ally (Voice of America). VOA has always had a following in Arab countries, but its 'orientalist' style and dependence on Middle East specialists, and its proclaimed governmental control, make it less popular with Arab audiences than the BBC. The Israeli broadcasts in Arabic come from within the

Middle East, but from a government unacceptable to most Arabs, with the important exception of Egypt. However, the Israeli news in Arabic is widely listened to, especially because of its reputation for being faster with Middle East events than other services.

To keep an eye on the competition is clearly one of the main duties of the BBC External Services. Measuring how many people listen to whom, and which broadcasts are made at which times, is only the first step. The judgements involved are partly professional and partly political. It is essential that the way indigenous Arab stations handle news and programming, and the ways in which they handle the technical resources of radio and television, should be closely monitored (in both senses) by the BBC. But the political content of broadcasts is also important. To some extent this is a technical responsibility of the BBC monitoring service, and no doubt the eventual political responsibility for assessing the information and propagandist operations of other countries falls on the FCO.

But the BBC has such an important role to play that it cannot be indifferent to the political messages of other people's broadcasts. This was recognised by Sir Ian Jacob when, facing the new situation of the post-war world, he set up a Political Information Section in the office of the Director of Overseas Services, in the autumn of 1946. The Political Information Section was short-lived, but the principle involved was restated by Jacob in 1957, when he said that in order to deal with the problems of local war and cold war, with aggressive nationalism and with racialism, it was essential to consider the background:

We have to consider the state of knowledge of the audience, their access to other information. To know what they are being told from other sources, to know the state of mind of people, some of whom may be living under a grinding tyranny or who have no opportunity whatever for travel outside their countries. In other countries we have to interest audiences who have free access to information and who are living full and varied lives.[9]

Programme, public and political message are thus inextricably bound up, and it is the delicate task of the broadcaster to decide how the changing climate of culture and politics ought to influence what he puts out. The BBC has no editorial policy, no political views of its own. But it does need to have its say about Britain and its place in the world, in a way which is going to find a receptive audience or to establish a dialogue, and that will not be shrugged off as propaganda. A public as geographically huge, as culturally and politically diverse, as that of the Arab world, calls for sensitive and imaginative programming policies. The history of those policies seems to show that they have, so far, been responsive to the needs of their times.

CHAPTER 9

INFORMATION POLICY
IN THE TRANSISTOR EPOCH

I

British policy in the Arab world in the 1960s was navigating in uncharted waters. The 'northern tier' of defensive alliances which had been negotiated in the preceding decade had come badly unstuck with the collapse of the Bagdad Pact, though important agreements continued with non-Arab powers (Turkey, Iran, Pakistan). The Palestine question remained unsolved, as did the problem of securing acceptance of Israeli statehood and borders by her neighbours. Secure access for Britain to Middle East oil, which had been a main motive of British policy in 1956, had not been obtained, and the Canal was again to be blocked during the 1967 war. The epoch of 'decolonisation' was upon the British, and this had consequences in the Arab world as well as in Africa, notably in the growing difficulty in remaining in Aden and the Protectorate, and in the approaching end of the treaties with the Gulf states. The Qaddafi revolution of 1969 was to end the British and US military presence in Libya. The Cyprus affair was also not without its effects on British Middle East policy.

In this period the social and technological transformation of the Middle East area went on apace. Middle East governments acquired the technical capacity to assess and monitor oil company operations, and if necessary to operate such companies themselves. They began to acquire armies and air forces equipped with modern weapons and staffed by people who knew how to use them. They began to appreciate the place which they occupied in the world economy: the children of Middle East leaders were now more likely to attend Harvard Business School or the Massachusetts Institute of Technology than to go to Oxford or Sandhurst. Below these exalted levels Arab society was undergoing seismic changes. Certain areas, like those experiencing the oil revolution in the east of the Arab world, Algeria after independence, and Libya after the fall of the Idrisi dynasty, saw the whole of their societies in change and ferment. The Palestinian diaspora brought elements of social change and ambiguity wherever it went.

This era of shifting social and political landmarks, before the Arab states had set up fresh institutions to canalise and control the new social processes, and before the development of powerful Arabic television services, was perhaps from the point of view of its social influence the heyday of the

BBC Arabic Service. Equipped for the first time with the transmitters to make itself clearly heard, and financed for the first time so that it could run a programme of substantial cultural significance, as well as offering its traditional news and information, it enjoyed wider scope than had been given to any other BBC foreign vernacular service.

In 1968, after the reduction in the preceding year of the daily length of transmission from twelve hours to ten, the Arabic Service still spent every year almost a third as much as the annual expenditure of the English-language World Service, and 11 per cent of the total expenditure of the External Services as a whole.[1] Audience reaction continued to show the liveliness of the response in the Arab world. The number of letters received by the Service in the 1960s from listeners seldom fell below twenty-six thousand a year and went up to forty thousand in 1967; their numbers had more than doubled between 1955 and 1961. The programme expanded in an imaginative and impressive way, which interpreted the social revolution taking place in the Arab world, when it was at its most interesting point.

The BBC has also exerted influence over Arab broadcasting in the Middle East in a rather backdoor way through the training of personnel: this began with the original setting up of Cairo radio in 1934, and has continued in a spasmodic way since the post-war period. Partly because of the short-term nature of the employment which the BBC gave to many Arab nationals in the Arabic Service, it was inevitable that many of them should return to various parts of the Arab broadcasting world with BBC experience. There have also been, at various times, more formal arrangements for seconding and training personnel from Arab radio services in the BBC, especially from Egyptian State Broadcasting and its successors: the main brake on this has been that the BBC have sometimes found it expensive.

Besides financing the operation of the Service, the government showed itself willing to have new transmitters built to carry a stronger signal, especially so that there should be a medium-wave signal which would reach the Arabian peninsula and the Gulf. Bad luck dogged earlier attempts to effect this. Somalia closed the Berbera station in March 1963, and the new station built on Perim Island was destroyed by fire in 1965. Sir Thomas Rapp, a former head of the Middle East Office in Cairo, headed a committee on government information abroad in 1964–5 which stressed the need to increase BBC audibility overseas. The Sultan of Muscat and Oman agreed to the construction of the Eastern Relay Station on Masirah Island, a large 1500 kW medium-wave transmitter which was opened on 1 June 1969, and carried relays of programmes in Arabic, English, Hindi, Urdu and Persian. This transmitter effected a revolution in the coverage of the Arabic Service almost as important as that effected by the handing over to the BBC of the Cyprus transmitters in 1957: for the first time a strong medium-wave signal reached Iraq, the south of the Arabian peninsula, and the Gulf. The power of the Cyprus station was further reinforced by the commissioning of four 100 kW short-wave transmitters between 1963–5, and of a 50 kW transmitter in 1969.[2]

The Middle East continued to be in the centre of British foreign policy preoccupations. The continued importance of radio was strikingly shown in the Arab–Israeli War of 1967, which broke out only three months after the Arabic Service had been cut back to ten hours daily from twelve, among the economy measures of that spring. It immediately became necessary to counter the charge made on Egyptian radio that the British and the United States were militarily involved on the Israeli side. Ahmed Said, in the last days of his power in Voice of the Arabs, had it broadcast that 'With the utmost treachery, baseness and vileness, the USA and behind its tail Britain . . . have stood side by side with racialist, Zionist aggression.'

The war broke out on 5 June. The Arabic Service expanded its output by three hours on the following day and a further 4¼ hours on the day after. There was thus a continuous stream of British broadcasting from 0345 to 2100 GMT, with frequent bulletins and news flashes. The BBC *Annual Report* remarked that:

The flow of objective information did much to nullify the lie about British involvement in the war, a lie which put a further strain on the staff of the Arabic Service, stretched as they were . . . and shattered by the disastrous news from the fighting areas, where many of them had relatives . . . As soon as the immediate crisis was over, the transmission was cut to twelve hours: it reverted to ten hours on 12 July.

The charges of British involvement had been specifically dealt with and denied in a despatch by Ronald Robson from Cairo on 6 June. It is also worth mentioning that a broadcast on 20 June about 'How the British are debating the Middle East Crisis' was given not as it would have been ten years earlier by an Englishman, but by Musa Mazzawi, a Palestinian resident in England.

The *Annual Report* did not mention that during the war Egyptians were virtually obliged to listen to the BBC if they wished to know what was happening. The Ahmed Said regime at Cairo radio over-reached itself in fictitious tallies of Israeli losses and Egyptian gains, and Ahmed Said was disgraced: the Voice of the Arabs never broadcast in the same tone again.

II

For twenty or more years after Suez the makers of British foreign policy were engaged in rather tortured attempts to reassess Britain's role in the world and the ways in which she could best try to assert and defend it. In the information field this led to a long series of Foreign Office and Cabinet committees, whose deliberations often closely concerned the BBC, but which sometimes tended to be viewed in the Corporation as bureaucratic interference from Whitehall which it could well do without. This was an excessively defensive reaction: the relinquishment or part-relinquishment of great-power status, the completion of the decolonisation of British Africa, the British accession to the EEC and the long-term changes in British military and economic ranking were all matters which were bound to have effects on information policy, in which the BBC External Services played an important and expensive role. Even if the External Services were, as Jacob had put it in 1949, 'the voice of the British people and not the voice of the British government', they still could not afford to treat government policy reviews with disdain.

The list of the government committees concerned with information policy is long. The Hill Reports of 1958–9 (Cmnd. 225, Cmnd. 685), the Vosper Report of 1961–2, the Rapp Report of 1964–5, the Beeley Report of 1967, the Duncan Report of 1968–9 (Cmnd. 4107), may be mentioned. The Plowden Report of 1962–3 (Cmnd. 2276, 1964) and the Central Policy Review Staff Report of 1975–7 (1977), both on Overseas Representation in general, were both important in the policy positions they took up concerning the BBC, although many conclusions of the CPRS 1977 Report were rejected.

In these reports certain principles were proposed, some of which have been challenged within or outside Whitehall. The first is that the way British foreign policy is conducted, and the way Britain is publicised, must be appropriate to her changing resources and international status. The Duncan Committee agreed with Plowden that 'there must not be an incongruity between Britain's powers of influence in the politico-military and economic fields, and the size of her propaganda effort. Political propaganda cannot in our view be effective if conducted from an inadequate power base.' This, indeed, was what the propagandists had told the governments in the past (though usually they had spoken to deaf ears) whenever the latter had directed them to make defeats into victories.

Gerard Mansell has challenged Plowden's major premise, and argued that there was 'abundant evidence in the short-wave bands' that the Plowden argument about the relation between the changed 'power base' and propaganda is false.[3] It is true that Britain's influence in the world is a complex matter which is not directly determined by her political, military and economic status, and that she can sometimes win friendship and support for her policies in ways quite unrelated to the number of divisions she can put into the field or to her current balance of trade. But prestige and propaganda are indivisible, and it is hard to deny, as Mansell seems to be denying, that British power as commonly estimated in the world must be taken properly into account when we try to work out a good information policy which will present the country to the world in a favourable but realistic light.

How the policy consequences of a reassessment of British power and British interests ought to be worked out, was even more debatable. The principle laid down by Plowden and developed by Duncan was that information work on behalf of the government should be directed to specified geographical areas and targeted to specific policy goals. Plowden criticised the vagueness of the 'projection of Britain' projects of government departments and of organisations like the British Council and the BBC. This vagueness had been one of the undoubted weaknesses of Sir Stephen Tallents's original concept of the 'Projection of England' in 1932 – indeed, the vagueness enters even into the title of Tallents's original book, with its confusion between 'Britain' and 'England'. It was an imprecision which has continued to plague all subsequent attempts to make specific the positive elements in the 'Projection of Britain', and to make them sound abstract and arid. It has, indeed, been sometimes argued that specific 'projection of Britain' programmes have been less effective on the Arabic Service than others which allow the message to enter the listener's mind in the form of values which are implied rather than stated.

Plowden said that where a 'Projection of Britain' campaign was called for, it should be related to specific areas and to our policy requirements in them:

> For example, a campaign to stimulate the tourist trade may be well worthwhile in certain countries. But such a campaign should aim to do more than simply convey the idea that Britain is a fine country, with a fine past and a promising future.

However, Max Beloff (now Lord Beloff, then Gladstone Professor at Oxford) saw fit to challenge Plowden's hankering after precise information targets. Beloff emphasised in 1965 what the BBC had always emphasised – the continuity and long-term nature of information policy, and the impossibility of suddenly persuading people that you are close friends, when you have been cutting them dead for years. As Beloff observed:

> unless people have a high regard both for the country which is endeavouring to persuade them of the advantages of a certain course of action, and for the credibility and reliability of the institutions through which it purveys information in support of its views, the machinery available will not be able successfully to perform its function when a specific case arises. Successful work in the information field demands a high degree of continuity both as to the regional area of concentration and as to the substantive content of what is offered. It cannot be simply turned on and off at will.[4]

In other words, having been cut dead, he will continue to cut you dead, and deny you the favour you ask.

A concept much-emphasised by the Duncan Committee which had profound policy implications for the External Services was that of distinguishing different concepts of British information to be applied to differing target geographical areas. As far as the BBC was concerned, the Duncan Committee's so-called Area of Concentration (Western Europe and North America) was in the Committee's view to become an area of planned neglect. A general principle advanced by Duncan was that English-language broadcasting was to have precedence over foreign-language broadcasting, on the principle that the 'influential few' in countries abroad whom it is desired to reach, are now virtually all English-speaking. Arabic broadcasting was to be a partial exception to this, 'for the rather different reason that Arabic is the lingua franca in a fairly concentrated area and one which is of considerable importance for British interests, where English is not perhaps used by the influential few to the same extent as in some other areas.' The Committee was, however, less certain that the existing level of broadcasting in Arabic of seventy hours a week, should be maintained indefinitely.

Thus the Committee came back to the old crux of whether propaganda should be directed to the elite or to the masses. It was a question which had been given so many conflicting answers in the past that some informed people no longer felt confident that they could answer it. The Duncan Committee thought they could, and said that it was 'simply not possible, except at prohibitive cost, to provide blanket broadcasting aimed at the masses.' When the immensely experienced Oliver Whitley, the Managing Director of the External Services, was interviewed by the Estimates Committee in 1969, and was discussing the relative importance of broadcasting in English and in foreign languages, he said:

If somebody could decide definitely whether it is more important to broadcast to the elite of the country rather than to the masses of the country, perhaps we might have the beginnings of the answer of the relative importance of vernaculars and English, but that in itself is a most unanswerable question in the long term.

He was further interrogated – 'You do not attempt to answer it yourself pending advice?' – and replied, 'No, and in the meantime we do both.'[5]

The position of the Arabic Service in these debates was rather ambiguous. Since 1957 it had itself become an example of Foreign Office targeting of a chosen geographical area to the disadvantage of other geographical areas. It was not really an example of what was later to become known as the 'universalism' of the BBC, or of the BBC determination to keep up broadcasting to so-called peripheral countries or zones. The Arabic Service was also an example of a Foreign Office decision (which had been influenced, no doubt, by the earlier success of Sharq al-Adna) to back up a programme of mass appeal as opposed to one geared to the idea of influencing the influential few. It was also capable of being 'targeted' at short notice, as it had been during the Six-Day War of 1967, and as it was again in the Yom Kippur War of 1973, when the transmission was again extended, this time only by an extra hour daily, during the war.

The BBC had been at pains to warn the government that the massive expansion of their Arabic Service was not going to be a recipe to 'deal with' the Voice of the Arabs, which was still a disturbing influence to British policies in the late 1960s in, for example, its incitements to violence directed to the population in British-controlled Aden. Sir Hugh Greene added his caveat in 1969:

The power of Cairo Radio as a weapon in Col. Nasser's hands has been much exaggerated by many people. In so far as Cairo Radio achieves anything it is through the exploitation of feelings (pan-Arab, anti-British, anti-French) which are already there. It does not create them. Those who expect British or French or American broadcasts to compete with Cairo Radio are equally mistaken. Our policy is not one of lies and agitation and we should be false to ourselves, and do no good at all, if we descended to Col. Nasser's level. The truth is an unexciting weapon and it often works too slowly for those who, naturally enough, are eager for quick results.[6]

That is all truly said, and this cautious note had been sounded by the Tangye Lean Report in 1958, though less emphatically. One may ask, however, whether the BBC would have got the money to double the size of the Arabic Service in 1958, if it had pointed out to the British government as forcibly as Greene in 1969 how hard it was to have a 'voice in the bazaar'.

In its attitude to the government the BBC shifted occasionally from one foot to another. A year before Hugh Greene had sounded the classic note of caution and balance, Charles Curran (then Director of the External Services and subsequently Greene's successor as Director-General) had emphasised in the *BBC Handbook* the equally permanent element of BBC support for the national interest. Curran was concerned to scotch the recurrent stories that the BBC had 'some affinity with that part of the British press which was once thought to judge every country right but its own.' Denying that the BBC ran the External Services with 'bloodless objectivity', Curran cited in evidence the behaviour of the External Services in the Arab–Israeli war of 1967, in which the commentaries had 'rightly expounded the damage which was suffered by the Arabs [as a result of the closure of the Suez Canal] as well as the inconveniences to the British'.

III

The lines of thought sketched out by the Plowden and Duncan Committees were taken to their logical conclusions in the Review of Overseas Representation carried out by the Central Policy Review Staff in 1975–7. The CPRS followed its predecessors in seeking for a schematic representation of information policy aims which would enable them to be effected by setting up narrowly defined targets. It was part of the utilitarian current which swept through Whitehall in the 1960s and '70s, linked in some respects with the old anti-imperialist spirit which had in the past been the prerogative of radical opposition and not of government. These reports produced some important reforms, but, as often happens with utilitarian schemes, the tendency was to define aims rather too narrowly and dogmatically.

The CPRS Report identified the BBC's two main objectives as being, first, to provide an unbiased source of news and information, and second, to convey information about Britain and its culture. It proposed to reduce very sharply the importance of 'projection of Britain' in broadcasting as in other information work. It also proposed very drastic cuts in the number of languages in which the External Services broadcast, and in the programme hours of the transmissions: the Arabic Service came off relatively well in these proposed reductions, with a cut of only 50 per cent in the hours to be broadcast.

It can be argued that the CPRS took much too restricted a view of the aims of broadcasting. As a later parliamentary review of the CPRS Report pointed out,[7] BBC aims had been defined in a civil service department review of 1974 as being:

to provide comprehensive, unbiased news of domestic and world developments, a British elucidation and interpretation of these developments, and the reflection of the main currents of British thinking on world problems; secondly, to project a picture of British life and institutions, thereby maintaining and developing British standing abroad and a greater awareness of British achievements.

This explains the matter in less elegant prose than that used by the CPRS, but it does more justice to the BBC, and assigns it 'a rather wider objective than the CPRS would wish to see the BBC pursuing.' For example, BBC treatment of the news in commentaries and discussions is itself a projection of the British democratic way of life and thought; this forms a very large part of External Services output, but its significance does not emerge in the CPRS assessment.

The CPRS Report was savaged in a long House of Lords debate, in the course of which Lord Hill remarked on the oddity of a proposed reform which for a saving of 10 per cent in cash would cut the External Services' broadcasting by 40 per cent.[8] The Report was sharply criticised by the relevant parliamentary committee. This committee took especial notice of the figure of 73 per cent listenership to the Arabic Service among the urban population of Saudi Arabia, which the CPRS Report itself had quoted. The eventual verdict of the committee was that it 'would be madness . . . to impose swingeing cuts on the present [External] service precisely at a time when, as the CPRS acknowledge, other countries are stepping up their efforts.' The committee therefore refused to countenance the 'emasculation' of the External Services.

Had all the recommendations of the CPRS been put into effect the Arabic Service would have suffered, even if less severely than many other services. The hours of Arabic broadcasting (already reduced to nine hours daily in 1976) would have been halved, and the discontinuance of the night-time External Services transmissions would have led to the cancelling of the dawn Koranic reading and news, which had been one of the best-known and best-liked features of the Service since early in the war. The CPRS would have thought such a defence sentimental and conservative, but it overlooked the sentimentality and conservatism of most listeners, Arab and otherwise. It was also submitted by the BBC in evidence to the parliamentary committee that the Arabic Service extends over four time zones, and owes much of its success to its availability at all likely listening times: halving its time on the air would simply drive much of a notoriously demanding audience to listen elsewhere.[9]

On the other hand, the CPRS Report, like earlier and later similar reports, advocated giving the External Services transmitters adequate to their needs, and this part of their proposals was listened to. It was no use having splendid and attractive programmes which no one could hear, or which prospective listeners abandoned after frustrating twiddling with the dial. Financial constraints made the implementation of the proposals slow. The Rapp Report (1965) and the Beeley Report (1967) had emphasised the importance of plant, and Duncan and the CPRS confirmed them. But by 1975 only half the Rapp recommendations for transmitters had been implemented, and one of the essential projects still unexecuted by 1980 was that of four 250 kW short-wave transmitters in Cyprus.[10] However, the determination of the FCO to support the BBC in getting a proper range of modern transmitters has survived several upheavals in Whitehall: it is misleading to give the impression that the history of the last decade has been only that of bureaucratic sniping against the External Services. In 1981 the government embarked upon a ten-year audibility programme to improve the transmissions of the External Services, and £75 million had been spent with this object by the spring of 1987.

1979–81 was a period of considerable tension between the Corporation and the government over the drastic financial cuts which the latter required in the operating costs of the External Services. Government assurances about the integrity of the capital expenditure programme did nothing to pacify the BBC about the proposals to abolish several language services. The defence was, in the short term at least, successful. 1982–3 was mentioned in the 1984 *Handbook* as a 'period of stability and reconstruction in which relations with the FCO were friendly and constructive', an emphasis which leads the reader to imagine that there had been times when the relationship was rather less than ideal.

It was not that the BBC had not striven to comply with the new emphasis of government information policy since the 1960s. Programmes which aimed to sell British trade and industry to the Arab world, for example, had occupied a substantial place in the programme since the policy had first been introduced. Trade and industry programmes were broadcast in the Arabic Service several times a week: these programmes immodestly mentioned individual British firms. Contacts between the Arabic Service and British businessmen became close, and running this side of the Service became a new part of the job.

In the early 1980s the BBC External Services were still, with the British Council and the other information services, subject to scrutiny by a government which placed efficiency high among its values, although it was quite willing to examine the question 'efficient for what?' The Arabic Service, as the foreign-language service which transmitted for longer hours than any other, could expect to be in the forefront of that scrutiny. This was not a necessarily hostile scrutiny. The CPRS Report, which had made so many proposals for the Services which the Corporation had found unacceptable, had nevertheless described External broadcasting as 'one of the UK's success stories', and cited the Arabic Service as an example of the areas where the BBC was 'the most popular external broadcaster'. And in any case the External Services were not, and had never been, the mere instrument of government departments (a Non-Departmental Public Body, in Whitehall terms). BBC managerial independence is recognised as well as BBC editorial independence, although the former is unwelcome to some advocates of central control. Behind that independence lies the BBC Charter, and behind that lie Parliament and public opinion.

In 1984 the External Services took one of the coldest of their cold government baths, and for four months submitted to a review (chaired by Alan Perry of the Treasury) in which the FCO, the Efficiency Unit, the BBC External Services and the BBC auditors all participated. This was 'the most thorough and searching of the many enquiries into the External Services since the war.' The aims of the enquiry were very similar to those of the CPRS enquiry of nine years earlier, but this time with more detailed attention paid to efficiency and financial effectiveness: the effect of new technological developments on the future of broadcasting was also considered.

The FCO had become directly responsible for administering the grants-in-aid of the External Services in 1977, and this apparently formal change had, in the context of modern government arrangements, a considerable impact. It is too early to examine the results of this enquiry, but there is no doubt that it represents a continuing pressure from central government to review and in some respects to control the operations of such bodies as the BBC External Services, whose momentum is by no means exhausted. On the BBC side the Report was welcomed, but it was regretted that its emphasis was on methods of achieving a better use of existing resources: 'It held out little hope for those who argued the case that more resources should be devoted to strengthening Britain's international voice at a time when competition in international broadcasting is increasing rapidly.' The

BBC welcomed, however, the recommendation that the grant-in-aid should be determined at the same time and for the same period as the Home Licence fee. In practice this has made financial planning for the External Services a good deal more effective.

The aims of the External Services were said in the 1984 Perry Report to be to provide in the national interest a credible, unbiased, reliable, accurate, balanced and independent news service; and to give a balanced British view of international and national developments and of world problems in general, taking into account British government policy and, in particular, Britain's membership of the European Community, the Commonwealth, and NATO. On the projection of Britain side the Services should give an:

accurate and effective representation of British life, institutions and achievements in the many fields of human activities – political, social, economic, industrial, scientific, literary and artistic, thereby promoting, where appropriate and relevant, British trade, industry, technology and expertise.

This definition, like many earlier ones, may be thought to be couched too much in terms of an abstractly conceived national interest, and to leave little room for the exercise of imagination and sensitivity which is so essential to good radio. The freedom of the BBC to plan its programmes in the way which its experience and competence dictated was protected in the Perry Report by a further 'objective': 'To make programmes of a high professional quality, relevance and interest, to attract and retain audiences, and thus to enhance Britain's standing abroad and form amongst listeners a better understanding of the UK, its values, way of life, policies and politics.' The last clause of this objective overlaps rather puzzlingly with the objective quoted in the paragraph above. But there is no doubt that it permits the free exercise of BBC media professionalism, and that it also allows the BBC to observe the cultural conventions of the people to whom it is broadcasting.

On the question of the priority to be accorded to English-language or vernacular broadcasting services, the FCO is said to have tended recently to favour the vernaculars, a preference which is of some importance to the Arabic Service. On the closely related issue of whether the output should be directed to a popular or to an elite audience, official guidance appears to have remained somewhat ambiguous.

It was said of target audiences to the 1984 Review Committee that they:

are those who are in, or who might one day arrive at, positions in which they could influence the attainment of British objectives. In this context we interpret British objectives both in the narrow sense of sustaining a sound bilateral relationship with the country concerned . . . and in the wider sense of preserving and encouraging democratic institutions and fostering an understanding for and sympathy with the viewpoint of the West. In countries with a well-established democratic tradition it is necessary for the BBC to make its appeal wide. In countries with a smaller and more narrowly based ruling elite it would be appropriate for the BBC to aim at a relatively small number of decision-makers, always bearing in mind that such countries' elites can change rapidly and unexpectedly.

How these carefully balanced words were to influence programme producers for a Service intended for the diverse social and political systems of
Morocco, Egypt, and Iraq (among others), it is not entirely clear.

It is clear that the BBC External Services retain huge popular audiences.
Surveying the Arabic Service in the era of universal indigenous Arabic
television, its then Head, E. R. Bowman, found in July 1985 that letters
from listeners were being received at the rate of about eighty thousand a
year, double the totals of the 1960s, and indicating an audience which
could be measured in millions. Bowman also noticed how the Arabic
Service is listened to outside its normally defined 'target area'. 'There has
always historically been an Arabic listening audience in East Africa and
also on the eastern side of the Gulf,' he continued, 'but of late we have been
impressed by growing correspondence from all the countries of sub-
Saharan Africa. Last year we commissioned an admittedly small survey in
this region which showed that the audience is not as we suspected of
emigré Arabs but predominantly the indigenous people of these countries.' It is the ability to produce new and unexpected offshoots like this
which convinces that the Arabic Service is a genuinely flourishing plant,
and not an imposing old tree whose sap may be running a bit short.

The latest words come from the Arabic Service contribution to the
evidence given by the BBC to the Foreign Affairs Committee on 'Cultural
Diplomacy' in 1987:

The Arab world has come to regard the BBC Arabic Service in certain important senses as an
Arab broadcasting network in its own right. Day in and day out an adult audience conserva-
tively estimated at about ten million listening at least once a week (but many more at times of
crisis) hears a voice which is at once British and Arab – British, because it describes the world
seen from London as comprehensively and impartially as is humanly possible, and Arabic
because for nearly fifty years the Arab-speaking staff of the BBC have been consistently
striving, with notable success, to have their Service perceived as a major Arabic-language
radio station.

APPENDIX

HEADS OF ARABIC SERVICE: 1938–1988

For the first twenty-one years of its life the Arabic Service had no separate Head of Service. It started with a Programme Organiser and a News Editor working to J. Beresford Clark as the person in charge of Empire and foreign-language broadcasting. During and immediately after the war it was brigaded with Turkish and Persian in the Near Eastern Services, whose Programme Organiser was Evelyn Paxton. It then became part of the wider Eastern Service. Gordon Waterfield presided over the creation of the separate Arabic Service at the beginning of 1959.

	First Organiser		First Editors
1938–39	Stewart Perowne	1938 only	A. S. Calvert
		From 1938	Donald Stephenson
1940	Director Near Eastern Services		Sigmar Hillelson
1945	Director Eastern Services		Donald Stephenson
1948	Head Eastern Services		Charles Pennethorne Hughes
1949	Head Eastern Service		Gordon Waterfield
1959	Head Arabic Service		Gordon Waterfield
1964			James ('Tommy') Thomson
1971			Charles McLelland
1976			Hamilton Duckworth
1981			Eric Bowman
1986			James Norris
1988			Bob Jobbins

NOTES

All books cited were published in London unless another place is given.

CHAPTER 1

1 *The Projection of England* (1932) 39–40. See also P. M. Taylor, *The Projection of Britain: British Overseas Publicity and Propaganda 1919–1939* (Cambridge, 1981).

2 BBC Written Archives, Caversham, R34/399, 'The Use of Languages Other Than English in the Empire Service'. See also G. Mansell, *Let Truth be Told: 50 Years of BBC External Broadcasting* (1982); A. Briggs, *The History of Broadcasting in the United Kingdom*, i (1965).

3 C. B. Peper (ed.), *An Historian's Conscience: The Correspondence of Arnold J. Toynbee and Columba Cary-Elwes* (Oxford, 1987), 37, 40.

4 *Hansard*, 331, 5th ser., 16 February 1938.

5 For Leeper (1888–1968), see Taylor, *The Projection of Britain*, 28–43 and passim: other judgements on him are collected in W. R. Louis, *The British Empire in the Middle East: Arab Nationalism, the United States, and Postwar Imperialism* (Oxford, 1984), 83n. See also Sefton Delmer, *Black Boomerang* (1962), 64; R. Vansittart, *The Mist Procession* (1958), 399. The suppression of his communiqué of 26 September 1938, which should have been broadcast in German that night, is referred to in M. Gilbert and R. Gott, *The Appeasers* (1963), 165–6. There is a lot of information (of varying degrees of credibility) about him in *The Diaries of Sir Robert Bruce Lockhart*, ed. K. Young, e.g. i (1973), 352; ii (1980), 56, 63, 76, 82, 116, 207 and so on. And in B. Pimlott (ed.), *The Second World War Diary of Hugh Dalton 1940–5* (1986), xxiii, 271, 282.

6 PRO, FO 395/546.

7 C. A. MacDonald, 'Radio Bari: Italian Wireless Propaganda in the Middle East and British Counter-Measures 1934–38', *Middle Eastern Studies*, xiii (1977), 195–207.

8 A. Adamthwaite, 'The British Government and the Media, 1937–1938', *Journal of Contemporary History*, xviii (1983), 281–97. Adamthwaite's account is better balanced than that of W. J. West in *Truth Betrayed* (1987).

9 Briggs, Taylor and Mansell, works cited above. BBC Written Archives, Caversham, R34/399; E2/245. The Report of the Committee is in PRO, CAB 27/641, ABC (37). J. C. W. Reith, *Into the Wind* (1949) is essential, and there are valuable comments in A. Boyle, *Only the Wind will Listen* (1972).

10 E2/125. Some documents are duplicated in E1/629.

11 E2/125.

12 E2/125.

13 Taylor, *The Projection of Britain*, 58–9.

CHAPTER 2

1 Details in a report by Gordon Waterfield to the Director of External Broadcasting, dated 27 February 1963. See also E2/605; R34/399; PRO, FO 395/557.

2 R. Bullard, *The Camels Must Go: An Autobiography* (1961), 206.

3 FO 395/557; Taylor, 214.

4 FO 395/557. Leeper's comments (below) are in the same file: so is his account of his interview with Graves and Clark (also below). See also Taylor, Mansell.

5 On his position, which he held for fifteen months, see Briggs, 404; Mansell, 51; Taylor, 206–7. Calvert was so little proud of his time at the BBC that he later omitted it from his entry in *Who's Who*.

6 FO 395/558, Warner reporting the following day on a meeting on 13 January.

7 Mansell, 51–2; Briggs, 404. It is often implied that Clark's statement was some kind of challenge to the government, but this is not so: it was contained in a memo from the Service Director to the Arabic Editor. It was quoted as encapsulating 'the principle that was to govern editorial decisions then and in the future' in the BBC submission to the House of Commons Foreign Affairs Committee, 12 May 1987, *4th Report, Session 1986–87: Cultural Diplomacy*, 78.

8 FO 395/558. Taylor, 206–7, does not cite this letter.

9 FO 395/558.

10 E2/261.

11 FO 395/558.

12 Briggs, 404, n.

13 FO 395/560.

14 FO 395/561.

15 Taylor, 206. W. J. West, in *Truth Betrayed* (1987), 100–3, states that 'Within a few months, the BBC foreign-language services were under almost total direct control by the Foreign Office.' The evidence he cites proves nothing of the sort; it shows that the Foreign Office offered detailed briefing to the South American Service but he gives no indication of how the BBC acted upon it.

16 E. Monroe, *Britain's Moment in the Middle East 1914–1956* (1963).

17 *Hansard*, 331, 5th ser., 16 February 1938; *Hansard*, 343, 5th ser., 15 February 1939.

18 Typical is R. L. Lambert, *Propaganda* (1938); see especially 150–3. Complaint about 'the present lackadaisical outlook' in official circles regarding propaganda, with an illustrative story about an unnamed radio commentator, in S. Rogerson, *Propaganda in the Next War* (1938). The stronger view is in A. J. Mackenzie, *Propaganda Boom* (1938), which does not propose any particular scruple. For 'Truth will Out', see A. L. Pemberton, 'Propaganda: Its Theory and Practice', *United Services Institution Journal* (1939). There is a more morally scrupulous and academic view of the subject in F. C. Bartlett, *Political Propaganda* (Cambridge, 1940).

19 R13/113/2, 15 February 1939.

20 E2/39/1, 2 September 1938. Quoted also by Taylor, 213–14.

21 BBC Arch., Arabic Service Expansion 1958.

CHAPTER 3

1 B. Balfour, *Propaganda in War: 1939–1945* (1979); I. McLaine, *Ministry of Morale: Home Front Morale and the Ministry of Information in World War II* (1979); Taylor (1981), 216–19.

2 McLaine, 235; J. Charmly, *Duff Cooper* (1986), 150.

3 I. Colvin, *Vansittart in Office* (1965), 70, quoted by M. M. Stenton, 'British Propaganda and Political Warfare 1940–44: A Study of British Views on How to Address Occupied Europe', MS. PhD thesis, Cambridge, September 1979.

4 Ogilvie's notes on this speech (dated 7 September 1939) are in R34/941; see also Briggs, iii, 170.

5 N. Tönnies, *Der Krieg vor dem Kriege: Englands Propaganda bis zum 3. September 1939* (Essen, 1940), 189–93.

6 E2/605, undated.

7 For equipment see E. Pawley, *BBC Engineering 1922–1972* (1972), 134. For the trouble in recruiting announcer/translators, E2/290, Hillelson to Bowen in the Ministry of Information, 1 February 1940.

8 FO 395/557, 558; India Office, EI 885, 880.

9 E2/289/1.

10 PRO, INF 1/869.

11 For Pick see Briggs, iii, 330–1; see also Lord Birkenhead, *Walter Monckton: The Life of Viscount Monckton of Brenchley* (1969), 185–6, and M. Peterson, *Both Sides of the Curtain* (1950), 236. Peterson's appointment and subsequent disillusion with the MOI in Bruce Lockhart's *Diaries* (1980), 67, 105.3/13 INF 1/874. Note by R. Williams, 1 January 1941.

12 PREM/365/11.

13 INF 1/874. Note by R. Williams, 1 January 1941.

14 E2/289/2; E2/190/1; Briggs, iii, 281–2.

15 R. H. S. Crossman, in *Royal United Services Institution Journal*, xcvii (1952), quoted by Balfour, *Propaganda in War*. For the Near East Intelligence Section Programme Monitoring Report, dated 9 December 1940, see E2/39/2.

16 E2/289/2, letter to Barbour dated 25 July 1940. See also the 'Note on Planning for the Arabic Service' in E2/39/3.

17 See the same 'Note on Planning', and also an undated paper by D. Stephenson rebutting the Rushbrook Williams charges, in the same file.

18 E2/289/2, letter of 9 August 1940 to Barbour.

19 Note by Tallents in the same file; also Wellington's letter dated 22 August 1940.

20 R13/113/2, memo by Tallents dated 13 July 1940. See also Briggs, iii, 282.

21 PRO INF 1/869, Sir Maurice Peterson to the Director-General of MOI (Pick) and the Minister, 10 October 1940: 'while I have secured the services of Sir K. Cornwallis for supervision of the BBC's Arabic programme from the middle of this month, I am having a good deal of difficulty (which I shall, however, overcome) in inducing the BBC to give him the status and degree of control which I require.' For Cornwallis's feelings about his proposed propaganda work, see Bruce Lockhart, *Diaries*, 75.

22 E2/295/1, Wellington's memo of 25 October 1940.

23 INF 1/869; R34/469; Briggs, iii, 282–3. Stephenson's paper on the Arabic Service, in E2/605.

24 For Reith's views, see *Into the Wind* (1944), 437–8. For Ogilvie and Tallents, see E2/295/1, the Director-General's note of 18 November 1940, and that of Tallents dated the following day.

25 PRO, CAB 65/10; CAB 66/14. Briggs's account (iii, 283, 329–33) was written before the relevant public records were opened to inspection.

26 INF 1/893, memo dated 23 November 1940.

27 INF 1/893. See also C. Cruickshank, *The Fourth Arm: Psychological Warfare 1938–1945* (1977).

28 INF 1/869. Memo by Hood dated 3 December 1940; Duff Cooper's letter of 4 December 1940.

29 See *Into the Wind*, 438. INF 1/869, Duff Cooper's memo to Monckton, 31 December, refers to 'the words underlined in red'.

30 *Britain's Moment in the Middle East*, 89–91.

31 For propaganda theory in 1941, see the paper on 'Unity and Diversity' in E2/295/2, dated 13 January 1941, and also Stephenson's memo on 'Arabic News Bulletins: Some Notes on Objects and Method', dated 31 December 1941, in the same file. For Persia and Iraq, see Briggs, iii, 520–7, and the 'Near East Service Report', E2/424/2. Hillelson repeated that 'it is generally believed . . . that the Persian broadcasts of the BBC played a very significant part at the time of the abdication of Reza Shah Pahlavi' in the 1945 *BBC Handbook*.

32 R34/469. 17 July 1941. James MacGregor to Ogilvie: 'It would be a great help and kindness if you could let me have a copy of what you circulate inside the BBC [about the Advisers] so that I may know at least what the understanding of the position is at your end. Between you and me, I despair of discovering what the understanding at this end may be.'

33 E2/295/2, memo of 12 May 1941.

34 E2/295/2. For quarrels about 'indiscretions' in reporting the Libyan campaign in June 1941, see J. Dimbleby, *Richard Dimbleby: A Biography* (1975), 136 ff.

35 E2/255/1. See also Briggs, iii, 524, and FO 898/127.

36 E2/255/1. For the whole question see W. R. Louis, *Imperialism at Bay 1941–1945: The United States and the Decolonization of the British Empire* (1977), especially 130–3.

37 INF 1/875. Bracken telegrams of 31 July and 9 August: Lyttelton of 13 August 'from Lord Curzon', beginning, 'I am sorry, Dear Brendan, that you should have misunderstood my telegram.' See also A. Boyle, *Poor Dear Brendan* (1975).

38 For Monckton's mission, including the reference to a Foreign Broadcasting Section in Cairo and the objections to SOE's broadcasts in Jaffa (11 June 1942), see INF 1/875, 1/876. FO 898/114 also contains relevant material. FO 898/116, which is probably relevant, is embargoed. The earlier Broadcasting Section in Cairo seems to have been run by Col. C. J. M. Thornhill: see FO 898/114.

39 E15/129. Report as Middle East Director, March–June, 1943.

40 E2/400;. Briggs, iii, 526.

41 E2/295/2. Stephenson's interview with Rucker at War Cabinet offices, 18 December 1942; Briggs, loc. cit.

42 E2/39/3, 25 April 1947: 'The formula to which we have been working for several years is on the approximate basis of three-quarters of the available programme funds to be spent at the home source and one quarter at the Cairo source.' For Sharara and programme production, see E1/667/1 and E1/667/2, and for 1943 programmes, see E15/129, Appendix A to Liveing's report.

43 Report by Mr Murray, on the staff of P. C. Vellacott, the Director of Political Warfare, Middle East, 30 November 1942. FO 898/118.

44 FO 898/9, agreement of 8 August 1941; BBC Arch., E2/289/6, report of meeting at MOI, 19 September 1942; FO 898/118, Glenconner to Vellacott, 4 December 1942. The Cairo agreement between SOE and PWE was supposed to come into force on 1 January 1943, but the station does not seem to have been handed over until March 1943: see M. R. D. Foot, *SOE: An Outline History of the Special Operations Executive 1940–46* (1984), 40–1; B. Sweet-Escott, *Baker Street Irregular* (1965), 98. Barbour found Squadron Leader Marsack in charge there, 18–24 May 1943, E15/129.

45 E2/39/3; E2/289/10; E2/400.

46 Sole responsibility for PWE was assumed by the Foreign Secretary on 17 June 1945, PRO, PREM 3/365/11; for the place of Sharq in Arab broadcasting in general, see D. A. Boyd, *Broadcasting in the Arab World: A Survey of Radio and Television in the Middle East* (Philadelphia, 1982), 264–6.

47 E2/295/2.

48 E2/39/2. 18 September 1941.

49 *BBC Handbook 1945.*

50 E2/39/2. See also Briggs, iii, 282, n.

CHAPTER 4

1 E9/25, letters dated 11 May 1939 and 1 June 1939. See also FO 395/557.

2 E2/39/3.

3 For relations with the Arab News Agency see E2/36 and E9/2, especially Cryer's comments on its importance, dated 24 November 1949. There are some despatches in the ANA file under Programmes.

4 Interview with I. K. Sabbagh, 25 September 1987.

5 E2/39/2.

6 E2/38/3.

7 E2/324/4. The French Ambassador had complained to the Foreign Office, letter of 20 September 1951. The programme was sent on cassette to President Bourguiba in 1978 as part of the celebrations of the fortieth anniversary of the Arabic Service.

8 FO 953/1649, January 1956.

9 E2/295/2, 11 March 1949, commenting on Waterfield's report on the Arabic Service. Unfortunately I have not traced this particular report. There are other comments on Waterfield's paper in E2/38/1.

10 E2/38/1.

11 *The Yemen: Imams, Rulers and Revolutions* (1963), 17, 23.

12 Paxton's letter of 1 October 1946 [filed under Programmes].

13 E2/39/3, 12 January 1945.

CHAPTER 5

1 E20/65. Guidance issued by A. J. Pollock, 9 February 1945. Later in the year the Foreign Office were corresponding directly with the Arabic Service on the same issue, E9/25. R.M.A. Hankey had complained of a supposedly inaccurate BBC report on 11 June that 'Beirut was at a standstill and all shops were closed' (Thyne Henderson's letter of 23 August).

2 E2/286/3. Memo sent by Stephenson on 5 September 1946 to 'Pyman, Fitzgerald, and Garran (who takes the Chair at the weekly Persian meeting at the FO).'

3 R34/99, 8 August 1946, reporting a meeting at the Foreign Office attended by Stephenson, Barbour and Mackenzie.

4 Same file, which came to the Director-General on 20 November 1946.

5 R34/395. Radcliffe's final letter, dated 19 December 1944. See also A. Briggs, *The History of Broadcasting in the United Kingdom*, iv (1979), 142.

6 On Marmorstein, see E. C. Hodgkin's obituary note in *Middle Eastern Studies*, xx (1984), 131–2, and T. Hodgkin, *Letters from Palestine 1932–6* (ed. E. C. Hodgkin, 1986), 169. See also Marmorstein's article, 'The fate of Arabdom: a study in comparative nationalism', *International Affairs*, xxv (1949), 475–91.

7 E2/295/2, memo by the Liaison Committee for Broadcasting to the Near East, 18 October 1941.

8 E9/25. Note of FO request dated 23 February 1940. See also R. W. Zweig, *Britain and Palestine during the Second World War* (1986), 62, 66, 67. The *Sakariya* had been intercepted on 13 February.

9 E2/289/3. Hillelson to Rushbrook Williams, 12 May 1941.

10 E2/289/5, Hillelson to the MOI, 9 February 1942, for the report on Haj Amin al-Husseini. E2/289/7, from MOI, 8 October 1942, saying that Jerusalem had just sent a telegram about the BBC attack, stating that it passed unnoticed in Palestine.

11 E2/299, Hillelson and Barbour to A. H. M. Jones in MI2a, 27 September 1943.

12 For the censorship see D. Trevor, *Under the White Paper: Some Aspects of British Administration in Palestine from 1939 to 1947* (Jerusalem, 1948). For the suppression of the Reuters report of 22 September 1945, by Kimche, in Jerusalem and also in London by the Arabic Service (which acted on the advice of the Colonial Office), see Trevor, 148, and E2/155, Eastern Service Committee, 24 September 1945.

13 E2/155, 2 April 1946.

14 *BBC Handbook 1947*. For the Arab Office, see E2/155.

15 E2/286/3, meetings of 14 February 1948 and 28 February 1948, both at the Foreign Office.

16 E1/1137.

17 See W. R. Louis, *The British Empire in the Middle East* (1984), 32–40, and also Louis's contribution in W. R. Louis and R. W. Stookey (eds.), *The End of the Palestine Mandate* (1986).

18 Louis (1984), 538.

19 Louis (1984), 580–1.

20 PRO, FO 953/1208, R. S. Scrivener, 6 April 1951.

21 Mansell, *Let Truth be Told*, 221–4.

22 FO 953/1208, note by J. S. H. Shattock, dated 10 May 1951.

23 FO 953/1208.

24 Submitted to the Select Committee on Estimates, Session 1951/52 and printed in the Ninth Report, no. 287, pp. 127–9.

25 E2/39/3. Stephenson's memo of 8 April 1947.

26 E2/295/2, Paxton to Assistant Head of Eastern Service, 11 March 1949; E2/38/1, 7 April 1949.

27 FO 953/398, Top Secret and Personal from Major E. C. Last to J. V. Riley. For the medium-wave transmitters, see D. A. Boyd, *Broadcasting in the Arab World* (1982), 265.

28 PRO, CO 875/42/4. The list is dated 18 November 1949. A parliamentary reply of 1956 states that the company running Sharq al-Adna 'was established in 1948 under a licence granted by the Governor of Cyprus'. *Hansard*, 5th ser., 560, cols. 749–52.

29 E15/22: appendix, dated 18 March 1950, to a report on Libya.

30 E1/667/3, 10 December 1951, to R. Allen at the Foreign Office.

31 E12/238/8. John Sheringham's tour of Aden, British Somaliland and Eritrea.

32 Wilfred Kirkpatrick kept an interesting Listener's Log in Bagdad from December 1953 to April 1954, which he sent to the BBC [E2/377]. He referred to the 'heavy barrage of insults against Britain' maintained by Cairo radio, and also to the anti-British broadcasts of Major Salah Salem, to which the BBC Arabic Service had specifically replied. But he did also mention (10 March) a Voice of the Arabs news bulletin which was 'very similar to the BBC news', and which surprised him by the fullness of the coverage and the impartiality of the tone and editing.

CHAPTER 6

1 FO 953/1561. For 1954, see the BBC Arabic Service Expansion file.

2 FO 953/1640. J. B. Clark's letter of 9 December 1955.

3 The record of a meeting with the Post Office about the site for a new medium-wave transmitter is in FO 953/1649. Tangye Lean's letter is in FO 953/1646, a file otherwise remarkable only for the number of documents which have been withheld from it.

4 FO 953/1641.

5 FO 953/1074. Dodds-Parker to P. F. Grey. The subject is a letter from Sir Ivone Kirkpatrick to Sir Ian Jacob, which I have not traced.

6 FO 953/1641.

7 FO 953/1640, Grey's minute of 19 June 1956.

8 R34/1580/1. Jacob to Kirkpatrick, 16 May 1956 and 31 May 1956; Kirkpatrick to Jacob, 25 May 1956.

9 FO 953/1641, Dodds-Parker to Kirkpatrick, 10 July 1956. Grey was to be the FO representative on the Committee. For the interview with Selwyn Lloyd which follows, see the same file.

10 FO 953/1641, notes dated 24 July 1956.

11 FO 953/1641, and also Grey's note dated 26 July in FO 953/1643.

12 Interview with Abdel-Kader Hatem, Cairo, 4 July 1987. The date of Poston's trip to Cairo is uncertain, although it certainly took place.

13 FO 953/1643. Note by Grey, dated 26 July 1956, in response to a request by Sir Harold Caccia, the Deputy Undersecretary.

14 FO 953/1642.

15 R34/1580/1.

16 FO 953/1643, note by Kirkpatrick to J. O. Rennie, head of the Information Department, 28 August 1956.

17 R34/1580/1.

18 Same BBC file.

19 FO 953/1643. C. C. B. Stewart's memo of 20 September 1956, seen by Kirkpatrick on 3 October.

20 CAB 128/30.

21 FO 953/1645, Cosmo Stewart's notes for the Lord Privy Seal's Committee on Overseas Broadcasting, dated 17 October, for the meeting due to take place on 18 October.

22 *The Inner Circle* (1959), 156, gives Kirkpatrick's reflections on the wartime BBC. He thought that the original wartime 'gentlemen's agreement' that the BBC would accept official advice while reserving their right to execute it in their own way, had not worked very well. Evidently he thought in 1956 that a similar gentlemen's agreement was unlikely to work any better.

23 CAB 128/30.

24 FO 953/1645.

25 *One Thing at a Time: An Autobiography* (1968), 199. William Clark told him this 'one day towards the end of October'.

26 R34/1580/1.

27 FO 953/1644.

28 A. Briggs, *Governing the BBC* (1979), 209–17.

29 FO 953/1644. The BBC letter is in R34/1580/2, with a letter from Harman Grisewood to Bottomley, dated 2 November, which was used for Bottomley's reply of 9 November.

30 The final history of Sharq al-Adna, and the story of its successor-station, are both very obscure. See H. Thomas, *The Suez Affair* (Harmondsworth, 1970), 144–5. For the Voice of Britain see also *Hansard*, 5th ser., 560, 9 November 1956, cols. 517–27, especially col. 521.

31 R34/1580/2. Report by the Director of External Broadcasting, 27 November 1956.

32 FO 953/1648, Grey's memo of 19 December 1956. See also Mansell, *Let Truth be Told*, 231–2.

33 Briggs, *Governing the BBC*, 216.

34 *Hansard*, 5th ser., 560, cols. 1023–1102, especially cols. 1097–1100.

35 FO 953/1648.

36 R34/1580/1.

37 *Hansard*, 5th ser., 564, col. 102 (written answers), 8 February 1957; ibid. 565, col. 14, 18 February 1957. See also Mansell, 234.

38 Mansell, 233.

CHAPTER 7

1 The best source for Waterfield's philosophy is an address given to a broadcasting conference in Paris in 1953, E15/222. I have also used some material from the Select Committee on Estimates, 9th Report, Session 1951–2, no. 287, pp. 98–9, where there is an interview with Gordon Waterfield.

2 Arabic Service Expansion (RMC location no. 0020/8). On 29 June Treasury approval was given for four Programme Assistants (B-) and two other posts (C/B1).

3 Pawley, *BBC Engineering*, 450–1.

4 FO 953/1644. 12 December 1956, to Cosmo Stewart, Top Secret. 'I have been able to work out a project to radiate at a very much higher power from Cyprus and estimate that with an expenditure of £500,000 spread over two years we can set up a transmitter which will radiate one megawatt.' The recurring cost of this project would be about £100,000. Stewart minuted: 'I do not see how, even with the most enormous dose of bicarbonate of soda, we can get this at present down Sir A. Johnston's stomach. The Treasury are having enough hiccups already about digesting the 100 kW transmitter that you have bought.'

5 Arabic Service Expansion, 2 January 1957.

6 Arabic Service Expansion, Whitehead's memo of 19 September 1957.

7 *Hansard*, 5th ser., 594, cols. 582–3, Dr Hill, 3 November 1958. See also Ormsby-Gore's remarks about answering the allegations against Britain carried on the Voice of the Arabs, 23 April 1958, *Hansard*, 586, col. 930.

8 *Hansard*, 5th ser., 592, cols. 90–91. For the hours of transmission compared with those of other services, see the table in *Hansard*, 717, 212–14 (2 August 1965).

9 Arabic Service Expansion.

10 The figures for radio sets are given in *BBC Report and Accounts, 1965–66* (November 1966, Cmnd. 3122), 63, and thereafter in the Annual Report and Accounts. The 1954 estimate of maximum audience figures is in the Arabic Service Expansion file.

CHAPTER 8

1 E2/39/3, 28 April 1947.

2 Wilfred Kirkpatrick, 'A Listener's Log for the six weeks 6 December 1953 to 16 January 1954', compiled for the Arabic Service.

3 Boyd, *Broadcasting in the Arab World*, 108–9.

4 *Third Report of the Estimates Committee, 1969 (House of Commons Paper, 387)*, 35–9.

5 Boyd, 190–2.

6 *Annual Book Summary of Egyptian Radio and TV Union, 1985–1986*.

7 Boyd, 236–9.

8 Boyd, 273–5.

9 Jacob's letter of 26 September 1946 to E. J. Passant at the FO; Sir Ian Jacob, *The BBC: A National and an International Force: An address to the Eighth Annual Conference of the Institute of Public Relations, 18 May 1957* (1957).

CHAPTER 9

1 *Report of the Review Committee on Overseas Representation 1968–1969* (Duncan Committee) [Cmnd. 4107, 1969], Annex M. 196.

2 Pawley, *BBC Engineering*, 454, 460.

3 *Let Truth be Told*, 255.

4 'The Projection of Britain Abroad', *International Affairs*, xli (1965), 478–89.

5 *Third Report of the Estimates Committee, Session 1968–9*, House of Commons Paper 387 (1969), 40.

6 *The Third Floor Front: A View of Broadcasting in the Sixties* (1969).

7 *Fourth Report from the Expenditure Committee (Defence and External Affairs Sub-committee): The Central Policy Review Staff Review of Overseas Representation*, Session 1977–78, Parl. paper 286–1, lxxix.

8 *Hansard*, 5th. ser., House of Lords, 387, col. 957.

9 *Minutes of Evidence taken before the Expenditure Committee*, 6 December 1977, 286–2, 108.

10 *House of Commons, Foreign Affairs Committee*, Session 1979–80, Supply Estimates 1980–1, HofC 362, xviii, Minutes of Evidence, 25 June 1980, 440–1.

INDEX

Roman numerals refer to the plate section which falls between p. 86 and p. 87.